WHEN INNOCENCE IS NOT ENOUGH

Hidden Evidence and the Failed Promise of the *Brady* Rule

THOMAS L. DYBDAHL

THE
NEW
PRESS

NEW YORK
LONDON

Published in the United States by The New Press, New York, 2023

Distributed by Two Rivers Distribution

ISBN 978-1-62097-704-0 (hc)

ISBN 978-1-62097-778-1 (ebook)

CIP data is available

The New Press publishes books that promote and enrich public discussion and understanding of the issues vital to our democracy and to a more equitable world. These books are made possible by the enthusiasm of our readers; the support of a committed group of donors, large and small; the collaboration of our many partners in the independent media and the not-for-profit sector; booksellers, who often hand-sell New Press books; librarians; and above all by our authors.

www.thenewpress.com

Composition by dix!

This book was set in Garamond Premier Pro

Printed in the United States of America

For Trish and Patrice, who made this book possible,
and for Chris, who lived the story

It seems, in tragedy, that innocence is not enough.
—T.H. White, *The Once and Future King*

CONTENTS

FOREWORD

In the spring of 1982, I agreed to write to a man on Louisiana's death row. It seemed like a small step.

I'd been a nun for twenty-four years. I was dedicated to God. I prayed every day for a better world. But I was just starting to see I needed to put my prayers into action. I had recently moved into the St. Thomas housing project in New Orleans to live and work there.

After we exchanged some letters, Pat Sonnier asked me to be his spiritual adviser. I began visiting him at Angola Prison. He got an execution date. Like most white Americans, I didn't know a lot about the justice system. Suddenly, I was with Pat in a life-and-death situation. And totally unprepared.

As Tim Robbins later said, "The nun was in over her head." Way over.

That's when I met Tom Dybdahl. Tom had come to New Orleans as a Mennonite volunteer. His job was working with all the death row inmates—visiting the men and their families, recruiting lawyers, investigating complaints. Tom was living near Hope House, where I taught. We soon became good friends. We started visiting Angola together. Mostly, we talked.

Without Tom, I might have drowned. He had an amazing ability to make complex legal issues plain. He was the first one to explain to me just how the machinery of death worked. To detail how the system routinely put the poor and powerless—mostly people of color—in prison and on death row. He helped me to walk beside Pat on the dark road to the execution chamber.

Tom is a slow talker. But it's (almost) always worth the wait. Over many conversations, and an occasional Scotch, his words played a key part in fanning the embers of social concern inside me into a blaze. That fire burns still.

Turns out Tom writes even better than he talks.

This book is a history of the *Brady* rule—the legal doctrine that requires prosecutors in a criminal case to disclose favorable information to the defense. It was intended to make sure trials were fair. It hasn't. With clear, painful examples, Tom shows how a rule that was supposed to enhance justice turned into a rule that enables injustice.

Alongside that history, Tom tells the compelling story of the killing of Catherine Fuller. Eight young Black men were convicted of her murder after the prosecutor, concerned about losing the biggest case of his life, withheld evidence that the defendants argued could have proven their innocence.

The Fuller case illuminates why prosecutors break the *Brady* rule: how easy—and enticing—it is to hide favorable evidence, how powerfully that concealment impacts a trial, how difficult it is to uncover violations, and how courts routinely excuse these infractions. It puts a human face on what can seem a dry legal argument.

This blatant disregard for fairness is all too common. Although *Brady* violations are the single most common cause of wrongful convictions, prosecutors have shown little interest in supporting reforms. They like the unfair advantage the status quo gives them. That's where you come in.

In the last section of the book, Tom reports on a way to bypass the resistant criminal system and to achieve the intent of the *Brady* rule through legislation. State laws requiring prosecutors to share all their investigative information with the defense—called open-file discovery—have proven to make the process fairer and more transparent.

After broad, citizen-led efforts, open-file rules have been passed in surprising places like North Carolina and Texas. That needs to happen in many more states, and at the federal level. Once you understand the widespread injustice the *Brady* rule allows, and how its aims might be realized, you can become part of the reform movement.

Read this powerful, beautiful book. It will stir your heart and trouble your mind. It will make you sad, and angry, and hopeful.

But be careful. If one isn't burning already, it may start a fire in you, too.

Sr. Helen Prejean, CSJ
New Orleans, LA
November 2021

INTRODUCTION

The *Brady* rule was supposed to transform the U.S. justice system.

In lofty language, the Supreme Court decreed in 1963 that prosecutors must share favorable evidence with criminal defendants. The rule's premise was that "the United States wins its point whenever justice is done."[1] William O. Douglas, who wrote the *Brady* opinion, hoped it would help remake our adversarial process into a joint search for truth and fairness.

But reality intervened. The opinion itself was poorly reasoned. The rule's claims to precedent were dubious at best. Key terms in the rule were not defined. It clashed with the foundations of the established system. Three of the justices said the rule was merely "advisory."

Those flaws would be *Brady*'s undoing. Over time, its promise not only went unfulfilled, it turned bitter. The rule made a stunning turnaround. The principle intended to promote fairness ended up doing the very opposite.

The effects have been dire. Withholding favorable evidence is now the leading cause of wrongful convictions. Of 2,400 documented exonerations between 1989 and 2019, *Brady* violations helped to convict 44 percent—1,056 innocent people.[2] These infractions also fell most heavily on people of color.

And what were the consequences for the prosecutors responsible for most of these abuses, the ones who put so many innocent defendants in prison? Eleven were disciplined by their employers.

Three were disbarred. Two were fired. And just one prosecutor—one!—went to jail for breaking *Brady*. That's a key reason why the violations continue.

How could this terrible transformation happen?

No matter what the words of a law may be, they mean whatever the courts say they mean. Period. The course of a law can only be understood through stories—the tales of cases with real people in real situations.

This book tells the winding history of the *Brady* rule through the cases that created and defined it. The story is anchored by the odyssey of the Catherine Fuller murder, perhaps the most savage and senseless crime in Washington, DC, history. Together, the narratives illustrate the *Brady* rule's potential, detail its slow demise, describe the human cost of its failure, and point the way to making its promise real.

1

LOVE, DEATH, AND THE
BIRTH OF *BRADY*

John Leo Brady was in love.[1] In early June 1958, he was also in some trouble. His sweetheart, Nancy Boblit McGowan, had just told him she was pregnant with his baby. Nancy was only nineteen and was married to another man. Brady was twenty-five and was broke.

He'd never had an easy life. He grew up poor in southern Maryland. His young parents, scraping their living from a small tobacco farm, couldn't cope with a fussy baby. They gave him to his paternal grandparents and his aunt Celeste, who raised him. From infancy through his late teens, Brady suffered from serious otitis media. His ears regularly oozed a thick, vile-smelling pus. At school, his classmates called him "Stinkears."

Brady gladly dropped out during the eighth grade to work full-time on his uncle's farm. At nineteen, in 1951, he enlisted in the U.S. Air Force and served as a military police officer at bases in Washington State and Greenland. Over the next four years, his otitis stopped, he got married, left the service, earned his high school equivalency, got divorced, and returned home to Maryland.

In March 1958, Brady met Nancy and her brother, Charles Donald Boblit. Their parents were good friends with Aunt Celeste. Donald Boblit was twenty-five, gawky, lonely, and barely literate.

In the pre-feminist jargon of the 1950s, a friend of Nancy's called her "just a dumb good-looking blond." Both Nancy and her husband, Slim, were living with her parents, and the couple hardly spoke to each other. Nancy let everyone know she intended to do whatever she wanted. Brady and the two Boblit siblings soon became close. Nancy fell for Brady's "sulky blond good looks," as a biographer later put it. Before long she was pregnant.

Brady was working at a local tobacco packing company for $1.50 an hour. He had recently bought a used 1947 Ford and was behind on his bills. But he wanted Nancy to know he was committed to her. She had planned a trip to New York to visit family, leaving on Monday, June 23. Brady spent that Sunday with her. They drove around in his car and parked by the Patuxent River.

Sometime in the afternoon he impulsively wrote her a check for $35,000, postdated to July 6. This was a dream sum—a huge number pulled out of the air. If he could make it real, Brady guessed the money would solve all their problems.

Nancy asked no questions. She put the check in her purse. Brady reminded her to wait, saying, "Somehow, in two weeks it'll be in the bank."

He saw only one way to get that kind of cash—stick up a bank. He knew he could get Boblit to help. Over the next few days, the two men hashed out a sort of plan. Nearby big cities like Baltimore and Washington, DC, had too many cops and guards. They settled on the one bank in tiny Stevensville, Maryland, thirty miles away, just over the Chesapeake Bay Bridge. They'd do it on Saturday morning. Folks would have deposited their weekly pay on Friday afternoon.

Even though he'd bought it recently, Brady worried his Ford was too old to be reliable. Especially if they got in a chase. For a successful getaway, they needed a more dependable car.

William Brooks had one.

Brooks, fifty-three, had known Brady for most of his life. He'd been a hired hand on Brady's grandfather's farm. He'd recently stayed with Brady and Aunt Celeste for a week while recovering from surgery. The two men had shared a room and played checkers. Now Brooks had a good job working the late shift at a small plastics factory in Odenton, about twenty miles southwest of Baltimore. He was living in a shack in the woods, not far from the plant. His landlady, Mary Elliott, had a house nearby. She worked at the same factory.

Less than two weeks earlier, Brooks had gotten his first new car: a blue two-tone Ford Fairlane. When Brady dropped by to visit, he'd looked it over—and coveted it. Elliott had driven past and seen the two men together.

Brady and Boblit decided to waylay Brooks as he came home from work after midnight. Boblit would blindfold Brooks, since he would recognize Brady. They would tie him up, then stow him in a vacant house Boblit knew about. When the robbery was done, they'd let him go and give him his car back.

Brady was adamant Brooks not be harmed. "I don't want him hurt, not at all," he said repeatedly. "He was good to me when I was a kid."

Late that Friday night, June 27, the two men put a log across the narrow dirt road that led from the highway to Brooks's home. He would have to move it to get by. They waited in the dark.

Things went awry from the start. When Brooks stopped for the log, Boblit stepped out of the shadows with a double-barrel shotgun. He ordered Brooks to get in the rear seat of his Ford.

Brooks seemed confused and started to get back into the front seat. He kept pleading, "Please don't kill me. Please." He wouldn't shut up.

Boblit hit him in the back of the head with the shotgun, knocking Brooks woozy. He forgot about the blindfold. The men laid Brooks on the back seat of the Fairlane and drove away. Brady, improvising, wanted to find dense woods where they might leave Brooks unnoticed.

Boblit had a different thought. "We got to kill him," he said. "He seen me."

"Put that goddam gun away," Brady replied. "Someone might hear a shot."

When they parked near a stand of trees, Brooks started to wake up. They got him out of the car. He was wobbly. Together, Brady and Boblit walked him into the small forest. He was holding his lunch pail from work. They stopped in a clearing.

Brady walked away a little, trying to think. He knew Brooks had recognized him.

Boblit didn't hesitate. He took off his red plaid shirt. He twisted the sleeves until they were tight. He used it to strangle Brooks, who was too frail to resist. When Brady turned and saw what was happening, he ran back and pushed Boblit away. It was too late.

"He's dead," Brady said, staring at Boblit.

"Let's get out of here, John."

The men carried Brooks's body a little deeper into the woods. Before they left, Brady put a few branches over his face and head. On the way back to the car, he picked up Brooks's lunch box and threw it as far as he could.

Their escape plan was no better than their robbery plot. The two drove to Chestertown. But when dawn came, they decided not to hit the bank.

"I just can't do it," Brady said. "Done enough." They had gotten $255.30 from Brooks's wallet. Brady figured they should head for Washington State, the only other place in the United States where he'd lived.

They made it to Lynchburg, Virginia, about two hundred miles southwest. Already, Boblit was asking to go home. Brady didn't want to fight. They parked Brooks's Fairlane on a downtown street, walked to the bus station, and caught a Trailways. They were in DC by late Saturday afternoon. From there they took a cab up to Glen Burnie, a suburb of Baltimore, where Brady had left his car.

Both men thought nobody would miss Brooks for at least a few days. But Elliott, his landlady, reported him missing when he didn't show up for work at 4:00 p.m. on Saturday. She also told police she'd seen him with Brady, and they might be together.

In the meantime, Brady, dreamer of crazy dreams, had been toying with the idea of going to Cuba and joining Fidel Castro's rebels in the mountains. He had met a few Cubans during his time in the air force. They had talked up their revolution. Brady had even helped them move small shipments of guns intended for Castro. That Sunday morning, he drove down to DC. He stopped by an aunt's place just after noon.

When she told him two officers had been there a little while earlier looking for him, his heart nearly stopped. The police must already be on to him and Boblit. After a short pause, Brady handed his keys to his aunt and pointed to his car. "I'm going out of the country," he said.

From his share of the robbery money, Brady bought a ticket to Cuba on a flight leaving early Monday. He was in Havana before noon. After a good sleep, he walked around the old city, wondering how to contact someone connected to Castro.

At about the same time, Nancy went to the bank in Maryland to cash his check. She hadn't waited two weeks. It wouldn't have mattered. There was no money in Brady's account. She felt humiliated when the teller laughed at her.

But Brady kept thinking about Nancy and her brother. Somehow he convinced himself he was only guilty of a minor crime: stealing Brooks's car. He loved Nancy. Their child was on the way. If he turned himself in, he could say they just hit Brooks and left him by the road and didn't know where he was now. That might get Boblit off the hook. Maybe he could still work things out with Nancy.

That Tuesday afternoon, rather than heading off to the Sierra Maestra mountains to seek out Castro, he walked into the American embassy in Havana. A few hours later he was in a Miami jail cell, talking to two FBI agents. Brady said he knocked Brooks out, and he and Boblit had stolen Brooks's car. He told them where to find it. Sure enough, an agent in Virginia found the Fairlane.

Brady said nothing about any killing.

On Wednesday afternoon, Brady was formally charged with transporting a stolen car in interstate commerce. Bail was set at $25,000. The next morning, he told the agents he was ready to plead guilty. As a first-time offender, he was hoping for a short sentence, maybe even parole.

Two hours later, the FBI men returned. "Your friend Boblit's been picked up," one of them said shortly. "He took us to where the body was."

Brady thought Boblit had been in jail since Sunday, when the police were in DC looking for him. And that he had kept his mouth shut. But Boblit had not been arrested until Wednesday, and only after Brady said his name to the legal counselor in Havana. Three officers had come to Boblit's house late in the afternoon.

In an interrogation room, they started asking Boblit about Brady and the stolen car. They'd hardly begun when he looked at the floor and blurted out: "Well, I might as well tell you. You're going to find out anyway. . . . The man's dead." He didn't even know Brooks's name.

Suddenly he said: "Brady did it. It wasn't me. I didn't do nothing. . . . It was all his idea, and he done it all."[2]

Boblit told the officers Brooks had not been killed near his home but in the woods close to the Patuxent River. He said he could show them where, and he did. Back at the station, in barely legible handwriting, he wrote a brief statement of what had happened.

> [O]n the 27 day to help Jhon B to rob one W M B and to take his body to the river bridge and I sow Jhon B kill hin. I did not no that he was gorin to kill hin. Jhon B say that he was gorin to let him stay a alive just knok W M B out and leve hin.[3]

Boblit signed the document, and two officers wrote their names as witnesses.

Over the next six hours, three detectives questioned Boblit in detail. A transcript of the interview shows he again told them Brady had strangled Brooks. He said he'd tried to stop Brady: "I told him not to do it." He hadn't reported the crime because he was "scared to."

The next day, in Florida, FBI agents told Brady what his friend had said. At first, he wouldn't believe Boblit had put it all on him. The agents pointed out that what Boblit said fit with what Brady himself told them earlier.

Brady gave his own statement, saying Boblit hit Brooks with a shotgun and later strangled him. When he'd said before that he was the one who struck Brooks, he was just trying to protect Boblit. He said when he and Boblit parted, he told Boblit "to go back to his home, that I would take the blame and for him not to admit anything."

That night, the front-page, banner headline in the Annapolis *Evening Capital* was "Police Charge Two with Slaying of Severn Man."[4] The story reported that "an odd, almost senseless series of events" had led to the murder charge. It said that "astute police work was not needed" to solve the case, because the two men "seemed pathetically anxious to be caught."

Brady waived extradition and was taken back to Maryland. He soon learned Nancy and her family blamed him for what had happened. She wanted nothing to do with him. He talked to her just once more, when she came to visit her brother at the Annapolis jail. She stopped by his cell and asked: "Did you kill that man?"

"No."

Nancy began to cry, then turned and left forever. Brady would never speak to their son.

During his first week in custody, Boblit made five statements to the police. In the first four, he put everything on Brady. But after Brady returned to Maryland and said Boblit was the real killer, officers confronted Boblit once again. This time he had a different story.[5]

Q: In your previous statements you have indicated that John
     Leo Brady struck William Brooks in the head with the
     shotgun. . . . We would like to ask you at this time if John
     Leo Brady struck Mr. Brooks with the shotgun, or did you?
A: I did.
Q: [Y]ou indicated in your previous statements that John
     Leo Brady strangled Mr. Brooks with your shirt, is that
     correct?
A: That's what I told you, yes.
Q: Do you wish to change this part of your statement?
A: Yes.
Q: What did occur at the scene of the strangulation?
A: I took and twisted my shirt sleeve and choked him. Then
     we carried him back into the woods.
Q: Charles, why didn't you tell us these things before?
A: I don't know.

At the end, Boblit said the statement was true and correct.

It seems likely this last story was the truth: Boblit was the actual killer. Brady's precise role in the murder would remain in dispute. In his initial statement to Maryland police, Brady allegedly
told them, "We decided we would have to kill him because he had
seen Donald. . . . Donald wanted to shoot him, and I said no, for
him to take and use his shirt."[6]

Asked "exactly how this strangulation was carried out," Brady
said, "Donald put the shirt around his neck, threw him to the
ground and choked him to death."

Q: What did you do while Donald choked Mr. Brooks to
     death?
A: I just stood there.

Brady would later dispute many of the details in the written version of this statement. He would say things were not put down the

way he had said them; that he felt intense pressure. He had believed Nancy was in custody and that if the police didn't like the way he answered their questions, she would pay. He claimed that when the interrogation was typed up, he said he "wouldn't sign it because it wasn't true. Then all of them [the policemen] . . . said 'What about Nancy?'

"When they said that, I said all right. I'll sign it. And so I signed it."

The officers involved denied Brady's version of events. They maintained they put no undue pressure on him and that everything in the document was just as he had said it.

The two men were charged with first-degree felony murder for a killing during the course of a robbery. Each was blaming the other, so the government decided to try them separately. Brady went first. He opted for a jury trial. The state chose to ask for the gas chamber.

Brady had no money for a lawyer. His aunt Celeste, with help from other family members, rounded up $500 and hired a man named George Woelfel, who had once been a fine defense attorney. That time had passed. Now in his sixties, he was often distracted and prone to drowsing during trials.

Brady had confessed to taking part in the crime, so his defense would be an extended plea for mercy. His lawyer's only viable argument was that Brady should be spared a death sentence because he had not actually killed Brooks.

Prior to the trial, Woelfel requested any statements Boblit had made about the robbery. The prosecutor, Osborne Duvall, disclosed the first four confessions. He withheld the fifth.

When this issue later became paramount, Duvall would have a different recollection of what happened. He would say that he had either shown Woelfel all of Boblit's confessions, or none of them. Woelfel would insist he'd seen all of them except the last. The court would accept that Woelfel was unaware of Boblit's self-incriminating statement at the time of the trial.

This would be the biggest piece of luck Brady ever caught.

John Leo Brady's trial began on Monday morning, December 8, 1958. It took only an hour to seat the twelve-man jury. In his opening statement, prosecutor Duvall said Brady was guilty of a murder that "was coldly calculated and premeditated."[7]

In response, Woelfel said Brady "may be guilty of robbery, burglary and other things. But he is not guilty of murder."

Brady took the stand on the morning of December 9. He stuck to the story he had told in Miami: he helped take Brooks's car and money but didn't kill him. There were no other defense witnesses. No one spoke about his background or character or the stresses he faced at the time of the crime.

In his closing, Woelfel asked for mercy. He said Brady was not a killer, only a young man "caught up in a foolish scheme."

Duvall reviewed the evidence for the jury and disagreed. "I see no reason why mercy should be shown to this defendant," he said. "No mercy whatsoever was shown to Brooks."

The jury deliberated for less than three hours. There was only one real question: whether Brady would get life in prison or death. The foreman read the verdict—guilty of first-degree murder. That was it. The entire trial took only two days.

On Friday, December 12, the judge sentenced Brady to die "by the administration of a lethal gas."

Boblit later chose a bench trial, but the result was the same.

In the summer of 1959, as Brady languished on death row at the state penitentiary in Baltimore, a Catholic chaplain helped him get a new lawyer, E. Clinton Bamberger, to work on an appeal. Bamberger was a partner in a local firm but ten years later would become dean of the Columbus School of Law at Catholic University in DC.

Reviewing the transcript of Boblit's trial, Bamberger saw Boblit had claimed his final confession about the crime was "not true." From the context, Bamberger divined that in the statement Boblit must have admitted to the killing. He realized that could be the basis of a successful appeal.

Bamberger was right, but it took two years to prove it. Several execution dates came and went. Brady lost his first appeals in the lower courts. In October 1961, the Maryland Court of Appeals held unanimously that "there was a duty on the State to produce the confession of Boblit that he did the actual strangling."[8] The failure was a violation of Brady's constitutional right to due process of law.

Despite the unanimity, the opinion was lukewarm at best. The Chief Judge wrote:

> We cannot . . . assume what their [the jury's] views would have been as to whether it did or did not matter whether it was Brady's hands or Boblit's hands that twisted the shirt about the victim's neck. . . . Not without some doubt, we conclude that the withholding of this particular confession . . . was prejudicial to the defendant Brady.[9]

The relief granted, however, was limited. Brady was guilty of felony murder for taking part in the robbery. Nothing in Boblit's fifth confession could have reduced Brady's offense below first-degree murder. But the court said Boblit's admission might have changed the jury's mind about Brady's sentence. They might have added "without capital punishment" to his verdict. He was entitled to a new trial on the issue of punishment alone.

Brady and Bamberger were both disappointed and feared a new sentencing trial might end like the first. They decided to appeal, hoping for a reversal of the conviction as well as of the sentence. In October 1962, the U.S. Supreme Court agreed to hear the case.

The Court was led by Chief Justice Earl Warren. He had been governor of California before his appointment by President Eisenhower. On the bench, he used his political skills to great effect. He was always looking for ways to cobble together majorities in support of key decisions.

Warren had an activist, pragmatic view of the law: it should help promote fairness and justice. During his tenure (1953–69) the Court expanded a range of civil and criminal rights and decided several historic cases. These included *Brown v. Board of Education* (1954), ending segregation in public schools; *Loving v. Virginia* (1967), holding that anti-miscegenation laws were unconstitutional; and *Miranda v. Arizona* (1966), requiring that suspects in police custody be expressly advised of their right to keep silent under questioning.

March 18, 1963, was an auspicious day: the justices spent the morning announcing their ruling in *Gideon v. Wainwright.* They held—for the first time—that indigent criminal defendants have a Sixth Amendment right to free legal representation in serious cases.

Brady's attorney and the state of Maryland presented their claims that same afternoon, with questions the next morning. Bamberger was generally pleased with how things went on March 19. He was sorry that Justice William O. Douglas, a strong supporter of individual rights and liberties, was the only justice who didn't ask any questions. As the argument proceeded, Douglas was writing letters and ostentatiously sealing them.[10] When it was over, Bamberger expected to win.

The justices had other ideas. Less than two months later, on May 13, 1963, they affirmed the lower court ruling in a 7–2 vote. The opinion, written by Justice Douglas, said Brady was not entitled to a new trial on his guilt. Under Maryland law, Boblit's last statement would not be admissible at such a proceeding, so it could not help Brady.

This claim was "almost certainly" mistaken, in the words of one legal commentator.[11] During arguments in the case, the state had conceded the opposite—that the undisclosed Boblit statement would have been admissible at a new trial. But the Court had the last word. Brady's conviction stood. Only his sentence remained vacated.

There was no legal need to say more. Douglas, though, was just warming up.

Despite his apparent indifference at the oral argument, Douglas had decided to use Brady's case to advance his own agenda. After a few paragraphs in support of the lower court ruling, he turned to what was really on his mind.

"We now hold," he wrote, in words dear to every defense attorney, "that the suppression by the prosecution of evidence favorable to an accused on request violates due process where the evidence is material either to guilt or to punishment." [12]

The purpose of Douglas's new rule was not to punish erring prosecutors. It was to protect defendants' rights. In soaring language, more common in a church than in a courtroom, he wrote:

> Society wins not only when the guilty are convicted but when criminal trials are fair; our system . . . suffers when any accused is treated unfairly. An inscription on the walls of the Department of Justice states the proposition candidly. . . . "The United States wins its point whenever justice is done its citizens in the courts."

No one had seen this momentous decision coming. Particularly not in a case where the appellant lost and the Court majority had merely upheld a decision by the Maryland Court of Appeals. Further, the issue itself—suppression of favorable evidence by the prosecution—had not been briefed or argued by either side during the proceedings. And although Justice Douglas had begun his key sentence with the phrase "we now hold," this rule was not, in strict legal terms, a "holding." It was unnecessary to the actual decision in the case.

Douglas was probably the only man on the Court who would have tried something like this. He was an FDR appointee and a maverick. He would end up being the longest-serving justice in

Supreme Court history. He sat from 1939 to 1975, writing hundreds of opinions.

By the end of his tenure, Douglas had dissented in almost 40 percent of the Court's cases. In more than half of those, no other justices had joined him. His colleague, Justice Potter Stewart, reportedly said that "Bill Douglas seems positively embarrassed if anyone agrees with him." [13]

Douglas's abrasive personality and eccentric habits made him a polarizing figure. He regularly fought with his colleagues on the Court, even with those who shared many of his views. In a 1947 article for *Fortune* magazine, historian Arthur Schlesinger Jr. summed him up: "Douglas inspires fanatical loyalty in some people and absolute mistrust in others." [14]

The Constitution wasn't a neutral document to Douglas. It was "designed to take the government off the backs of the people." [15] Broadly speaking, he believed "[t]he aim of law in its civilized sense is justice." [16] With the *Brady* rule, he was not merely announcing a new disclosure requirement. He was proposing no less than a "revolutionary shift" in criminal procedure, in the words of Judge Stephanos Bibas, a former law professor on the Third Circuit Court of Appeals. [17]

Douglas had somehow gotten a majority of his colleagues to support him.

The Supreme Court's ruling left John Leo Brady in limbo. He was guilty of murder, but not sentenced. Neither his lawyers nor the prosecutor knew what to do next. The state of Maryland had never had a punishment-only trial and wasn't sure how to conduct one. Brady's lawyers knew a new trial might end once again with a death sentence and negate his partial victory.

They decided time was on their side; that waiting was the best legal strategy. Feelings would cool, police officers and witnesses would move on, memories would fade. For a decade, they did nothing.

Finally, in 1973, Brady's attorneys decided that the state's ability to make its case was now significantly weakened. They asked for a punishment hearing. After legal maneuvering on both sides, the governor granted Brady clemency. He was paroled in 1974.

If the prosecutor had not kept Boblit's last confession from the defense, and if the jurors had known Boblit admitted killing Brooks, Brady would likely have received a life sentence at his trial. Had that happened, once his appeals were denied, he might have spent the rest of his days behind bars. Instead, thanks to the error, after sixteen years he walked free.

The time on death row had been difficult. In a 1965 letter to one of his lawyers, Brady described his feelings.

> For six long, lonely years I have watched the great stars march and wondered if I would be alive to watch them another day. I have died a thousand deaths during the past years. Each day I die a little more. . . . I look out upon the world and see only darkness. I am alone, without love, without friends, without hope. My only companion is fear.[18]

Despite this eloquent expression of anguish, Brady was not without hope. He married a Baltimore nurse he met while on work furlough from prison. After his release, he started taking college classes, majoring in criminal justice. He figured it was the one field where his real-world experience might be helpful. He and his wife had a son and a daughter.

His ex-friend Boblit did not fare so well. Boblit's life was spared in 1972 when the Supreme Court ruled that the death penalty, as imposed at that time, was unconstitutional. In 1992, a few years after being paroled, Boblit was convicted of rape. He died while serving life in a Maryland prison.

When Brady's son was a teenager, Brady told him his life story. Later, the boy found a phone number for his dad's old lawyer and called Bamberger. "I'm John Brady's son," he said. "I just wanted to thank you for saving my father's life." [19]

After twelve years of marriage, Brady and his wife divorced. He moved to Florida. He worked as a truck driver, married again, and became a serious fisherman. By all accounts, Brady was never in trouble again. He lived to be seventy-six and died of natural causes in 2009. He always said he was sorry for his part in the crime. William Brooks had been his friend.

Brady's name lives on, forever attached to the principle announced in his case. But what of the rule itself? Would it—could it—actually transform the justice system and help establish a new era of trust and cooperation between prosecutors and defense lawyers? Or would its promise prove as bogus as the $35,000 check that had helped to set the entire matter in motion?

A full answer to those questions would come slowly. But in 1984, ten years after John Brady's release and just twenty-five miles south of his home base, the saga of a savage murder in our nation's capital would illustrate in painful detail how important this issue was in our legal system and how powerfully—for better or for worse—the *Brady* rule could impact a criminal case.

2

THE WOMAN IN THE ALLEY

A street vendor found the body.

William Freeman set up shop about 8:00 a.m. near the northeast corner of 8th and H Streets NE, in front of a branch of the National Bank of Washington, DC.[1] He and his boss, James Robinson, unloaded their van and spread a variety of goods on a table: jewelry, body oils, hats, toys, sweatshirts.

Though October 1, 1984, was a cool, rainy Monday, Freeman, a lanky nineteen-year-old, figured business would be good. It was the first of the month, the time many people received government welfare or disability checks or veterans' benefits. That part of H Street was a bustling commercial strip. People's Drug, Cutty Cleaners, La Dominga's Bar, and Nat's Records were all in that 800 block. There was always foot traffic. H Street was the main route through the neighborhood and a crossing point for several bus lines.

The area was mainly residential, with blocks of two-story brick rowhouses. Many of the neat yards inside wrought iron fences marked the homes of young people who had recently moved there to work on nearby Capitol Hill. Other tidy lawns belonged to longtime residents who hoped the neighborhood could return to the stability it had enjoyed before the disruption from the riots following Martin Luther King Jr.'s assassination in 1968.

Despite the challenges, the area was still a real community: most people knew their neighbors, looked out for one another's children, and gave a helping hand when they could. The stores on H Street were small and catered to a local clientele.

On the southeast corner of the 8th and H intersection, right across from Freeman's stand, was an area that passed for a park. It was a small expanse of dirt and grass and pavement with concrete benches. The *Washington Post* would later call it a "dismal, trash-littered" spot.[2]

But teenage boys and grown men hung out there year-round. It was the heart of the community, the busiest intersection. They could watch the women at the two nearby bus stops and holler greetings and catcalls. It was a place to socialize and to be seen, to play cards or chess, to share a joint or a sip of cheap wine in a paper bag.

As Freeman began his day, eighteen-year-old Christopher Turner was asleep, barely half a mile away. Chris had lived most of his life with his paternal grandmother, Mildred Turner, in her brick rowhouse on 11th Street NE. The household included his two brothers, Carlos and Charles, and his father, Gary "Buck" Alston. Buck had struggled with drugs and alcohol all his adult life and had been in and out of prison.

Mildred, called "Mimi," was the center of Chris's world. She had a good job in the administrative office of the Peace Corps. One of her goals was to make sure Chris didn't end up like his father. He loved her so much he had promised he would never drink or use drugs. And he hadn't.

Chris's first love was sports, mainly football and basketball. He wasn't tall, but he was trim and athletic. He played on local teams and with the children who came to his job at the Northeast Neighborhood House on 10th Street—which everyone called the Center. His abstinence didn't harm his social life. On weekends he would often go to concerts or dances at one of the nearby clubs with his friends.

The previous June, Chris had graduated from Calvin Coolidge Senior High School in the Takoma section of Northwest DC. His

grandmother had sent him there because she believed it was a better school than Spingarn High or Dunbar High, both of which
were closer. He was planning to enlist in the air force but had
dislocated his shoulder playing basketball and needed to be physically fit before he applied.

Chris had never been in trouble with the law, but he was sometimes in trouble with the opposite sex. He liked girls, and they
liked him. He was brown-skinned, with a broad, handsome face
and a quick smile and was known for his gentle demeanor. Since
his junior year in high school, Chris had dated a girl named
Rachel Fletcher. To her dismay, he sometimes spent time with
other young women as well.

His official title at the Center was Senior Youth Aide. His
main job was tutoring elementary students in reading and math.
He was paid for thirty hours of work each week. But if a student
needed extra help, Chris often stayed late. He started a basketball
program. When some local boys needed a place for their band to
practice, Chris opened the Center to them in the evening.

At the beginning of September, Chris's boss told him the grant
that paid his wages would run out at the end of the month. It
could be renewed. But she thought he was someone special, who
could earn more and develop his talents more fully in a different
job. She urged him to explore other options. He loved his work,
but he knew she was right.

With some hesitation, Chris agreed to call it quits on Friday,
September 28. He would regret that decision every day for the rest
of his life.

During the weekend of September 29 and 30, Chris stayed with
his good friend, Kelvin Smith. Among Smith's many female ad-
mirers, he was known as "Hollywood," for the movie-star way he
carried himself. He was also eighteen, with wavy, close-cut hair
and a football player's build of broad shoulders and a thick neck.

Hollywood had dropped out of high school in the ninth grade

and sold the drug PCP to make pocket money. In the last year he had been arrested on charges ranging from disorderly conduct to burglary. None of the cases had stuck, though, and he hadn't spent any time in jail. Chris sometimes tried to talk to him about getting a real job and planning for his future, but Hollywood just shrugged and said life right now was good.

The two teens had been close since middle school. Chris was almost a member of the household on 4th Street NE, where Hollywood lived with his mother, grandmother, and sister, LaTonya. Chris often slept over when the two were out late. This weekend he was staying at Hollywood's house because the gas at his grandmother's home had been shut off. The kerosene space heater they were using didn't warm his bedroom at the back of the house.

On Sunday they shot hoops and watched football. Chris didn't have to get up the next morning for work, so the two went out that night then played *Donkey Kong* on Atari until 3:00 or 4:00 a.m. Chris always won.

Chris remembers getting up about 2:30 p.m. on Monday. He watched soap operas with LaTonya. When he got hungry, he ate a bowl of cereal.

Hollywood was feeling a bit sick and didn't get up until 4:00 p.m. He spent the next few hours on the phone, talking with various girls. On one of the calls, around 7:00 p.m., he heard surprising news: someone had been killed down on H Street.

Hollywood came out of the bedroom, still in his blue pajamas. He told his grandmother, Carrie Anderson, what he had learned. She said she hadn't seen any story about it on TV yet.

When Hollywood talked to Chris, they decided to get dressed and go over to the scene. The neighborhood wasn't the safest or the most peaceful in town, but violent crime—especially murder— was rare. And it was their home.

Hollywood told his grandmother they were going down "to see who it is." She was having none of it. "Boy, you better keep your behind home," Anderson said, "because you know they are going to try to put you in there."[3]

Chris and Hollywood stayed inside. They watched Pittsburgh beat Cincinnati on *Monday Night Football*.

The police would put them in there anyway.

Three blocks from Freeman's stand, around 4:30 on that drizzly afternoon, Catherine Fuller left her house at 923 K Street NE.[4] Her destination was Family Liquors, ten minutes away in the 700 block of H Street.

At 4:15 p.m., Catherine climbed the stairs to bring an early dinner to her husband, David, who was known as "Junior." She told him her leg was hurting, and she had no cash. He gave her $50. He watched her fold the bills and place them in her little brown coin purse. A few minutes later, he heard her talking on the downstairs phone, and then nothing.

Catherine was a small woman: 4 foot 11 inches tall, weighing 99 pounds. She was born on Christmas Day, 1934, in the Georgetown section of Washington, and was the oldest of three sisters. Junior, despite his name, was jumbo. He stood 6 foot 3 and weighed about 350 pounds. He had worked for the General Services Administration in DC for seventeen years, but at fifty-three was now on disability from a back injury. He spent much of his time lying down and rarely went out.

Catherine had met Junior at a party in 1955. She had been married before and already had three children. She and Junior began dating, and soon they were a couple. They married in 1969, and together had three additional children: Laura, who was now eighteen, David III, now seventeen, and William, twelve.

One neighbor called Catherine a "smiling good Samaritan" who would do anything she could to help others.[5] But life was turbulent in the brick rowhouse where the Fullers lived with their children.[6] Both Junior and Catherine were heavy drinkers. People who knew them said they sometimes saw her with bruises on her face from fights with her husband.

For some weeks, Catherine's good friend, Hattie Raspberry, had been thinking something was wrong.[7] Catherine was going to the liquor store for a bottle two or three times a day, far more than usual. She often asked Raspberry to keep an eye on her children when she went. Raspberry wanted to ask her friend about the situation, but she never probed.

Catherine had previously worked at the food service department of Sibley Hospital in Northwest Washington, DC. In recent years, she had been employed by General Maintenance, working nights as a janitor at the World Bank downtown. Her normal hours were weekday evenings from 6:00 to 11:30. That night she didn't show up for work and she didn't call in sick.

Though Junior was mostly housebound, Catherine and her older son, David, were well known in the neighborhood. They had lived on K Street for thirteen years. David was a student at nearby Dunbar High School. He knew most of the local boys from school and from playing sports. He was also in a band with several of his friends.

Catherine was a familiar sight as well, often stopping to chat with neighbors on her way to work or to the store, or just out to pass the time. She didn't patronize bars, but she had what she called "drinking buddies"—friends she knew well enough to sometimes share a bottle with.[8]

James and Maggie Pendergrast, who lived on 9th Street NE, were two such buddies. Most afternoons, except in the cold months, they sat on their screened front porch and watched neighborhood life go by.[9] Catherine regularly passed their place, coming and going from work or shopping or visiting.

The Pendergrasts were sitting outside as Catherine walked by that Monday afternoon.

"Where you going?" Mr. Pendergrast asked.

"Liquor store."

They chatted a few minutes, then Catherine went on her way. The Pendergrasts saw her walk south on 9th, cross the street, and disappear into the alley. She was heading west toward 8th Street.

Near the corner of 8th and H Streets, Freeman had covered his stock with sheets of clear plastic, since it was raining on and off. During slow times he and Robinson sat in their van, hopping out whenever a potential customer slowed or stopped.

At about 2:00 p.m., Freeman had to urinate. He left the van, walked a short distance north on 8th Street, and turned right into the alley behind H Street, heading toward 9th. The alley was narrow, just eleven feet wide, with cracks and potholes, weeds along the sides, and scattered trash. People often walked through this alley as a shortcut to avoid the traffic on H Street. It was common for locals to use drugs or to drink here, out of the public eye.

Halfway down, a branch of the alley ran north toward I Street, backing the rowhouses on both 8th and 9th. At the junction was a dilapidated garage with double wooden doors and a barred window. Freeman looked in through the broken glass and saw that the concrete floor was littered with debris. He pulled one of the doors open, slipped inside to relieve himself, and went back to work.

Just before 6:00 p.m., he needed to urinate again. Freeman went back into the same alley, back down to the same garage. This time he didn't go inside. He stopped by the entrance.

Freeman started to unzip his pants and looked down. He saw something red on the ground, trickling from inside the garage. He stepped through the partly open right door to investigate. A figure lay on the floor behind the closed left door. It was so small he thought it was a girl. He couldn't tell whether the person was sleeping or drunk or dead.

"Get up," he said. "Get up." [10]

There was no reply, no movement. Freeman didn't touch the body. He went into the alley and found a little stick. He poked the body on the shoulder with it. No reaction.

Freeman ran back to the sidewalk stand, which he said took just a few seconds. Robinson was sitting in the van with a woman friend, Jackie Tylie.

"There's a girl in the alley," Freeman said, breathing hard. "She's dead."

The first broadcast on a police radio channel—"unconscious person" in the area of 8th and H Streets NE—was at 6:10 p.m.[11] Officer Stephanie Ball, alone in a marked car, responded. Freeman and Tylie were waiting at the garage.

As Ball drove into the alley from 8th Street, she saw "two black males running towards me from 9th Street." When the men saw her car, "they turned and ran the other way." Officer Ball never got a good look at them. She parked her squad car diagonally so its headlights would shine into the dark garage.

"Why did those men run?" she asked Freeman.

He shrugged. "I don't know."

Ball stepped inside the garage. The woman lay on the floor on her right side, naked from the waist down.[12] Her head was toward the open door. Her blue sweater and white bra were pulled up to her armpits, exposing her breasts. She had several pink curlers in her hair. Her back was parallel to the closed left door, and her feet almost touched the side wall. Her body was covered with dust and bits of glass. Her white underpants, pantyhose, and a pair of blue jeans were on the floor nearby. All the clothing was dry.

Blood had flowed from the woman's mouth and nose, down the right side of her face, and onto the cement floor. Blood was also coming from her rectum. It trailed down her right thigh and along the floor to a pool just above her head. A thin thread had made its way under the garage door to the alley outside, where Freeman had seen it.

Ball checked the body for vital signs. Not finding any, she called for a homicide unit to come to 8th and H Streets NE.

Detective Patrick McGinnis was having dinner with another officer at Scholl's Cafeteria downtown when he heard the call.[13] He didn't want to go. It was a cool, wet evening, and he was enjoying his meal. But no one else responded. He paid his check and left for the scene.

McGinnis was in his late thirties, a fifteen-year veteran of the DC Metropolitan Police. After a brief stint on street patrol, McGinnis had spent eleven years working as a mobile crime technician, processing serious crime scenes. He was hardworking and intense, with great faith in his own instincts. More than a few of his colleagues considered him arrogant.

In October of 1984, McGinnis had been a homicide detective for two years. He always wore a suit on the job and felt more at ease in the office than on the street. He had only been at the crime scene for a few minutes when his partner, Detective Ruben Sanchez-Serrano, showed up.[14] Sanchez had been a detective for twelve years, assigned to homicide for the last two.

Sanchez was born in Puerto Rico, but he'd grown up in Michigan. He had done well in DC, working in drugs and sex crimes before coming to homicide. His aggressive questioning of suspects in this case would earn him a new nickname from the prosecutor: "Puerto Rican polygraph."

They had been together only a few months, but the two detectives felt they made a good team. They were just a year apart in age. McGinnis was analytical and skilled at putting a case together. Sanchez was more relaxed and could get people to talk to him. At that time, DC detectives worked citywide, rather than being assigned to one district as they are now. Neither of them had worked much in this neighborhood, so neither was familiar with its local dynamics.

After examining the small garage, the detectives walked to the 9th Street end of the alley. A crowd had gathered outside the secured area. McGinnis spoke to about ten of them. He said he and his partner were investigating the death of a woman and needed help. The two detectives passed out business cards with their names and phone numbers.

Several people asked the detectives about the age of the victim, but no one had any information to share.

At 6:50 p.m., two crime scene technicians came to the alley.[15] They took photos and collected the evidence: jeans, pantyhose, underwear, a brown leather change purse, and a pair of wine-colored boots.

Soon after 7:00 p.m., assistant medical examiner Michael Bray, MD, arrived. He did a visual exam of the body.[16] From the blood flow on the woman's cheek and thigh, he determined she had bled in that position and that the body had not been moved since the time of death. He pronounced her dead at 7:30. Based on her body temperature—90 degrees Fahrenheit—and an outside air temperature in the upper 50s, Bray believed that her time of death was about 5:30 p.m.

Before leaving the scene, McGinnis took a last look around. At the 9th Street end of the alley, where a crowd had been, small pieces of paper were scattered over the wet pavement, as if a parade had gone by. He bent to pick one up. It was his card, torn in half.

At the homicide office in DC police headquarters, McGinnis interviewed the two sidewalk vendors. Robinson confirmed that Freeman had gone into the alley to "take a leak" and returned with news of a dead "girl."[17]

"Did you hear any sounds like screams or yelling or gunshots?" McGinnis asked him.

"No."

Freeman told McGinnis he was "right there by the shed door" when he looked down and "saw something red."[18] After seeing the body inside, he tapped it "with a little stick and I told it to wake up and that was it." He didn't think he had ever seen the victim before.

Most of Freeman's statement was about the two "dudes" in the alley when the first police car came. He told McGinnis he had never seen them before that day. But "they kepted [sic] walking back and forth by our stand" and were "walking up and down H Street all day today." When he and Tylie were in the alley waiting for the officers, the "two dudes came up the alley from 9th Street," then stopped "at the corner by the garage."

Freeman said the two young men "stood there for about five minutes . . . just looking around." They seemed focused on the garage. When the police car came in the alley, "one dude said to the other dude, 'Don't run.' " Then they both ran north up the side alley toward I Street. One of them "had something in his coat because it was puffed up." Both were Black males.

Aside from these two young men, Freeman said he had not seen anyone when he went into the alley. Nor had he noticed any groups of young people crossing the street from the park and moving past his stand. And he never heard any shouts or screams or sounds of struggle from the alley.

TV crews were on the scene by 7:30 p.m. Their first reports were on the air by 10:00 p.m. But no one had any real details.

In the meantime, rumors were spreading through the neighborhood. People said someone had been raped and killed in the alley. Those who claimed they saw the body said it was naked from the waist down, which fed the rape stories. Because the victim was small, both Freeman and Robinson described her as a "girl." That was also the early word on the street.

By the time McGinnis left work that night, he was angry.[19] The investigation was just beginning, but he saw the torn cards on the ground as a sign that he would get no respect—or help—from the neighborhood. Based on the actions of a few bystanders, he was already framing the case as us versus them. He was already indicting a whole community.

He was also upset by the "carnival" atmosphere; the young crowd treating the killing like a curiosity, not a crime.[20] The image stuck in his mind was of bright red blood running from a small floodlit body, mixing with the pools of rainwater in the alley.

The first tip came in at 2:45 a.m. on Tuesday.[21] Hosea Dyson, the detective on duty, took the call. The man on the line would not give his name.

"I know about seven or eight guys that hang in the alley where the body was," the caller said. "They call themselves the 8th and H Crew, and they live in the area near there." The man claimed he had overheard three members of this crew, "Monk Harris, Levy, and Ernie Yarborough," talking about "pulling females into the alley to rape."

Dyson tried to get more details—the caller's name, where he got his information—but the man hung up. The detective reported the call and wrote a summary. The caller had said nothing about the murder, nothing to suggest he had firsthand information about it.

The lead was slim at best. But as officers came to work that morning, the call was what they had. And it fit with a hunch that had begun to nag at McGinnis the previous night: That some of the young people in the watching crowd knew what had gone down. That when they asked the age of the victim, they already knew who it was. That some of them might have been involved.

It's a curious jump, to assume that asking questions about the victim's age suggests some involvement in the crime. But McGinnis was dealing with a vicious murder, and he had no evidence of who might have done it. The case was in dire need of some direction.[22] In the absence of any real clues, he chose to rely on his hunch.

Police hit the streets, aggressively canvassing the neighborhood. They were looking for the three young men the caller had named and any members of this so-called 8th and H Crew.

Over the next year, everyone in the city would hear about the 8th and H Crew. Police claimed it was a criminal group that terrorized the community. But anyone in the neighborhood could have told the detectives they were mistaken. It wasn't a gang. It was what Chris and Hollywood and other guys from the area called themselves at go-go concerts.

Go-go was DC's indigenous music, and it drew crowds to various local clubs every weekend.[23] People danced and listened to popular bands play for hours, blending one song into another, nonstop. Go-go music is driven by a pronounced syncopated beat, maintained by drums and bass. Chuck Brown, a DC native considered the founder and godfather of go-go, mixed Afro-Caribbean rhythms and instruments to create songs that kept dancers moving.

One of the rituals of go-go is a lead vocalist who uses call and response in the performance. At that time, audience members commonly identified themselves as "crews"—a name for groups from various places around the city. At concerts, the singer directed calls to these local crews, which gave go-goers an opportunity to respond. A vocalist might yell, "Is Barry Farm Crew in da house?," referring to residents of a Southeast DC housing project. People from that neighborhood would respond on beat, "Barry Farm Crew is in da house!"

The Washington Coliseum at 3rd and M Streets NE, just half a mile from 8th and H, was one of the most popular go-go venues in DC. Anyone who went to concerts there would have heard the lead singer call, "Is 8th and H Crew in da house?" Chris and his friends would holler back, "8th and H Crew is in da house!"

In the fall of 1984, young people all around the district were singing and dancing to Brown's latest hit, "We Need Some Money."[24]

I'm gonna lay it right on the line,
That dollar bill is a friend of mine.
We need the money
Talking about money, yo.

The prosecutor would later argue that in these widely popular lyrics he had found the motive for Catherine Fuller's robbery and murder.

At about 10:00 that Tuesday morning, Dr. Bray started his autopsy of the victim.[25] Detective Sanchez was present.

There were extensive injuries to Fuller's torso, all on the right side. On her back, from below the shoulder blade to just above the hip bone, most of the skin had been scraped off. The medical examiner called it a "pattern injury," from being dragged a considerable distance over a rough surface. The wound contained "a large amount of debris, sand, bits of broken glass."

In Fuller's midsection, the second, third, fourth, and fifth ribs on the right side were all broken. The broken ends had been pushed into the right chest cavity. Underneath the ribs, the liver was basically "shattered," with "such force that you'd think she had fallen from a building or been struck by a car." Bray would testify that it was "one cluster of injury." It could have been produced by a "single forceful impact" of something like a shoe.

A toxicology test later showed a blood-alcohol level of .20.[26] Bray's estimate was that, given her height and weight, Fuller's alcohol level "would require five drinks, probably give or take one drink either way," during the hour prior to death.

The body had no damage to the vaginal area. But beginning at the anus, Bray found the most vicious injury of all. The rectal opening had tears that extended out about half an inch from the anus. Internally, there was a rip in the wall of the rectum. The line of trauma continued up through the free space in the body to the left side of the uterus. There was another hole in the broad ligament of the uterus similar to the hole in the wall of the rectum. "She had been impaled," Bray said later.[27] "I never saw anything like that."

Dr. Bray concluded that the cause of death was blunt force trauma and the manner of death was homicide.

Earlier that Tuesday, Catherine's husband, Junior, had called one of Catherine's younger sisters, Barbara Wade. He and Wade were not close. They seldom spoke by phone.

Junior got right to the point. "Catherine hasn't been home.[28] I haven't seen her since 4 or 4:30 yesterday afternoon."

"Had Catherine been drinking?" Wade asked.

Junior said Catherine was sober when she left home.

He told Wade he had heard on the news that a young woman was found dead in a garage near 8th and H Streets NE.

"Don't even think like that," Wade said.

Then, to her surprise, Junior started crying on the phone. "I hope it ain't her."

"Call the police and report her missing," Wade told him. And at Junior's insistence, she agreed to go and ask about the body they had found.

At the morgue, Wade spoke with staff members. She told them, "Catherine . . . didn't weigh more than 99 pounds. She wore a size 4½ shoe." Soon both Sanchez and Bray came out and introduced themselves. Sanchez held out a photograph that showed half of a woman's face. They had covered the other half so it would not show her beaten, bruised side.

It was Catherine.

After identifying the body, Wade went to the homicide office and gave a written statement. She summarized her phone conversation with Junior that morning. When that was done, Sanchez asked her point blank: "Do you suspect David [Junior] Fuller?"

She thought for a moment. "He waited until this morning," Wade said, "and he started crying and sobbing on the phone. This is not normal for this man. . . . I have never seen this man cry before when she was sick."

Sanchez didn't probe further. And Wade said no more.

A second phone tip had come in at 11:17 a.m. from a caller who identified himself as Michael Lee Jackson.[29] He told the operator he knew who had raped and killed the girl and would give up this information if the price was right. He hung up when the operator tried to get more details.

The name sounded like it might be fake. But officers started running down any Michael Lee Jackson in their records. Around 8:15 that night, they found the man who had called. He agreed to an interview.

Jackson had oversold his story. In person at the homicide department, he said that he and three friends had walked through the alley behind H Street late Monday afternoon on their way to Family Liquors. As they passed the garage where the body was later found, they heard "one single groan." They "remarked" about the sound but didn't stop. That was it.

This information didn't seem like much. Yet it would come to play a significant role in the case.

On Tuesday afternoon, McGinnis went to the crime scene again. Now that he knew about the rectal assault, he wanted to find the object that had been used. An evidence tech recovered more items, including a piece of metal pipe and Fuller's raincoat and umbrella.

The last two items, a navy blue umbrella with white polka dots and a light blue raincoat, were in a small alcove near the 9th Street end of the alley, a good distance from the garage. The raincoat was dry and neatly folded. In contrast, the umbrella spokes were all bent. Inside the umbrella was an empty half-pint bottle of Velicoff Vodka and a liquor tax stamp that had been torn from the bottle when it was opened.

Having confirmed Catherine Fuller's identity, police released her name. Word quickly spread that she was the victim. The locals were shocked and sad and angry. They didn't yet know many facts about the brutal crime. They had no idea the murder would mark their neighborhood forever. But Fuller was one of them.

When Chris learned that Fuller had been killed, he was stunned. Fuller's son David often came to the Center. His go-go band sometimes practiced there. Chris had spent time sitting on the Fuller's porch with David and his friends. He had seen Catherine come and go. A few times he had seen her out on the street, asking for spare change to get a drink.

The same was true for most of the young men living near 8th and H Streets. They knew Fuller, if not by name, at least by face. They knew David from going to school and to concerts and playing basketball and just hanging out. They were all part of the same neighborhood.

In their report, police did not disclose the awful facts about Fuller's injuries they had learned from the autopsy. She had been violated in a manner so vicious—and rare—that keeping specifics from the public could help solve the crime. Only the real killer would know the dark details.

On October 3, police found Levy Rouse—the Levy mentioned in the anonymous phone tip. He had come to DC Superior Court for a hearing on a pending theft case.

Levy was nineteen, a regular in the park at 8th and H, and no stranger to the police.

At the court building, Levy had run into Detective Johnnie Green. He recognized Green from the neighborhood and asked about the murder. Green, in turn, began questioning Levy. Levy offered a few details. Green asked him to come next door to police headquarters for an interview when he was done with court.

At 4:20 p.m. Detective Sanchez took a one-page statement from Levy.[30] He said he was at his girlfriend's house the previous evening when a friend came by to tell him a woman had been robbed and killed. The friend also claimed police had found fingerprints in the alley.

Sanchez never asked Levy if he had any connection to the murder.

That evening, officers learned that Fuller's wedding ring had been sold on the street the night of her murder.[31] Ronald "Touché"

Murphy had bought it for $5 from a thirty-something man he met outside Family Liquors. He'd given it to his girlfriend, Jackie Watts, who lived nearby. When the two learned about the killing, and the theft of Fuller's rings, they wondered if there was a connection.

Jackie showed the ring to Junior Fuller. He confirmed it as Catherine's. So Touché, Jackie, and Jackie's sister, Vivian, who had been with Touché that night, all went down to the homicide office. They gave written, signed statements about buying the ring.

Touché also told the police he had been to Family Liquors earlier on the evening of October 1, between 5:30 p.m. and 5:45 p.m.[32] That time, he was with Jackie and two or three other friends, including Michael Jackson—the second tipster—and a man named Willie Luchie. They took a shortcut through the alley where Fuller's body was later found.

Touché said he didn't hear or see anything unusual on the walk. But as they passed the garage at the junction of the side alley, Jackie said she heard something like a moan. Luchie and Jackson had looked back; they had heard the sound as well. But since both garage doors were closed, no one went to check inside.

Later that night, the lead crime scene examiner called McGinnis. He had tested the items from the garage for blood and feces. The results were negative.[33] None of the evidence they had found so far provided any clues about who the killer or killers might be.

As the hours after the murder became days, pressure on the detectives began to build. The ugly details of the assault had not leaked out. But McGinnis wanted a quick solution, for the victim's sake as well as his own.

Both detectives knew the conventional wisdom. The first forty-eight hours of an investigation are critical. If a case is not solved in that time, chances of a resolution drop. Despite several searches of the crime scene, they'd found no useful physical evidence, such as fingerprints or hair or a traceable murder weapon, that might help them find answers.

After these two crucial days, McGinnis and Sanchez had four possible crime scenarios. Fuller might have been killed by (1) her abusive, alcoholic husband, Junior; (2) the two young men who ran from the garage when the police arrived; (3) members of an alleged gang called the 8th and H Crew; or (4) the man who had sold Fuller's wedding ring only hours after her killing.

Despite lacking any direct evidence of the crime, the detectives had some useful details about the circumstances. They knew—from Fuller's history and the empty vodka bottle in her umbrella—she had been drinking heavily just prior to her death. They knew her raincoat and umbrella had been found 150 feet from her body. They knew the 800 block of H Street was a busy shopping area. At 5:30 p.m. traffic past the alley would have been busy.

Though the investigation was just two days old, they needed to make a decision. They didn't have the money or manpower to pursue every possibility. How should they proceed, given their limited knowledge and personnel support?

Junior quickly dropped off the hot list of suspects. With his size and physical condition, it was highly unlikely he was the murderer. If he had killed Catherine at home, one of the children would have seen or heard it. His limited mobility made it nearly impossible for him to have followed his wife to the alley and killed her there.

Two of the other scenarios had direct links to the scene. The young men who ran when the police arrived were by the garage close to the time of the killing, acting suspiciously. The man who sold Fuller's ring had her property within a few hours of the murder. The detectives had detailed descriptions of all three of these people. And witnesses who had seen them up close.

The remaining option was the first tip. The caller said "seven or

eight guys" who were part of the 8th and H Crew had been talking about pulling women into the alley to rape. Fuller did have
multiple injuries, which could have been caused by a group attack.

The tipster had also given police the names of three potential
suspects from the area. One—Levy Rouse—had already talked to
them. Although he had asserted his innocence, his answers had
made police think he might be holding back information about
the crime.

Further, this anonymous lead was heavily bolstered by a small
but serious mistake. Sanchez had conflated the two phone tips
into one. In his notebook on October 2, and later to a reporter, he
described a single caller who "said he knew who killed the woman
and raped her . . . said it was seven to eight guys who hung in the
alley."[34]

This composite tip sounds very solid. But the first caller had
said nothing about any killing. And the investigation into the second caller—Michael Jackson—had shown he had no direct information about the murder. Despite being totally wrong, Sanchez's
summation of the tip weighed substantially in their calculus.

One other thing pulled McGinnis and Sanchez toward this
scenario. Since the first night in the alley, with the discarded call-
back cards and the curious crowds, both men had nursed a distrust of the people living around 8th and H Streets. They felt sure
the locals knew more than they were saying. That maybe they were
closing ranks to protect their own.[35]

These factors, taken together, led the detectives to conclude
that the initial phone tip was their best lead. Starting from that
call, they came up with a theory. Some young members of the 8th
and H Crew saw Fuller walking alone. They forced her into the
alley behind H Street. When she resisted their robbery attempts,
they went crazy. They dragged her into an empty garage, ripped
off her clothes, and rammed a pipe up her rectum. Then they took
her jewelry and money and left her to die.

To both men, this narrative offered a possible explanation for how such a horrific crime could have happened.[36] "They [gang members] had to demonstrate something to show their solidarity," Sanchez would say later. "When it started, it was like sharks on a feeding frenzy." McGinnis echoed that view, saying that once the attack began, others joined in, "perhaps to show manhood, perhaps to demonstrate allegiance."

Just two days after the murder, their theory gave them a powerful, riveting crime story. The focus of the investigation became the 8th and H Crew. That would never change. But this narrative was no more than a calculated guess, based on some incomplete—and erroneous—information, filtered through their instincts and experience and prejudices. A *guess.*

McGinnis and Sanchez also had to know they'd embraced an incendiary theory. In a city with a long history of racial divisions, in a neighborhood still scarred by the damage after Martin Luther King Jr.'s assassination in April 1968, pinning a senseless, brutal crime on a rampaging gang of young Blacks—despite scant evidence—carried heavy overtones.

Their story was sure to stir white fears of dark, dangerous youth stalking the streets, preying on vulnerable innocents. Their descriptions of the accused as "sharks" only fed those feelings. They seemed fine with letting such pronouncements fuel the public's desire for a quick and severe resolution. But their words, and their claims, did nothing to promote a thorough, unbiased investigation into what had actually happened.

This quick embrace of a specific theory is not unusual. Even in high-profile cases, police seldom have the time or means to consider every hypothesis, to pursue every clue. There is powerful pressure to grab the best lead and run with it, to find a quick resolution.

Early adoption of one particular scenario also has significant benefits. It gives officers on the case a clear focus for their investigation. It helps them prioritize their time and finite resources and maximize their efforts.

But there can be a serious downside as well. It makes solving the case synonymous with proving their theory. That leads to confirmation bias. Or as it is more popularly called, tunnel vision. Law professor Daniel S. Medwed describes how it works.

> Once police embrace a particular theory of a case, the detectives may view all subsequent evidence through the lens of this expectation. This can produce distorted images. . . . One of the most horrifying aspects of tunnel vision is that those deepest in its throes may be least aware of its existence.[37]

When officers commit to one story of the crime, they desperately want it to be true. That desire leads them to see everything—physical evidence, other possible leads, potential new clues or suspects—in the light of their belief. They embrace what confirms their theory and ignore or reject what casts doubt on it.

Tunnel vision can lead police to speedy solutions. It can also lead them far astray.

3

SETTING *BRADY'S* BORDERS

From the beginning, the U.S. justice system was adversarial.
Prosecutors and defense lawyers were intended to be vigorous partisans. The premise was that if each side argued its point of view and forcefully pushed its claims, a neutral jury could figure out what the truth was. Neither party had a duty to find or share evidence that might be helpful to the other.

In this context, pretrial discovery—the legal term for disclosing information—was minimal. A common belief, even among judges, was that if a defendant knew the details of the case against him prior to a trial, he might subvert the process by manipulating facts, or creating evidence, or harming or intimidating witnesses. Only toward the mid-twentieth century did that view begin to shift.

With *Brady*, Justice Douglas meant to discard the old model. He saw the rule as the cornerstone of a new era, a way to shift the criminal process from partisan combat to an inquisitorial, innocence-focused system. He imagined a mutual search for facts. The prosecutor would share any relevant information with the defense. The two sides would work together to uncover the truth. A joint effort would protect the rights of an accused while ensuring justice was done.

It was a fine theory, typical of Douglas. Charles Reich, a law clerk for Douglas's colleague Hugo Black and later a professor and bestselling author, called him "a genius and a visionary. He had the ability to take you up to the top of the mountain and show you the entire vista of future issues."[1] That's what he was trying to do with the *Brady* rule.

But Douglas wasn't slightly ahead of his time in dreaming of a new, harmonious era. He was light-years ahead. Between the idea and the reality fell a great gap. In the legal world, *Brady* faced several formidable roadblocks.

While it had some tenuous antecedents, the real source of the *Brady* rule was Douglas's fertile mind.

Prior to his opinion, there had been no serious efforts, from either prosecutors or defense lawyers, to remake the system. The defense bar welcomed the fact that the government now had an ethical and a constitutional duty to disclose helpful information. But neither side had been agitating for a radical shift in the judicial process. Neither side rushed to embrace a new regime.

Further, Douglas had never been a criminal litigator. He was naive about the power of the long-established system. He knew how it worked. What he didn't know firsthand was how entrenched it was. He could not put himself into the mind of a prosecutor or a defense lawyer.

With few exceptions, each side had a deep mistrust of the other. Most defense attorneys didn't want to work jointly with their government counterparts. The reverse was true as well. And the process Douglas envisioned put a heavy burden on conscientious prosecutors. They were to zealously prosecute cases. At the same time, they were to help the defense by sharing favorable evidence.

This conflict would dog *Brady* from the start.

Finally, no one, including the justices who had voted for the rule, was quite sure what it meant. There were two big question marks. First, exactly what was included in "evidence favorable to an accused"? How broad—or narrow—was that category? And second, how should "material" be defined, as in "material either to guilt or to punishment"? In the years ahead, as *Brady* grew from infancy through adolescence, those issues would be argued at length.

Answers would take time. Typically, the high court reviews

lower-court decisions that are in conflict on a legal question and defines the law on that particular matter. In such cases, the issues have already been argued extensively. The justices can study the reasoning in the opposing briefs and opinions. They can see how previous rulings played out in real situations. When they issue an opinion, they have a good idea of the likely impact.

In contrast, *Brady* was a new rule of law. It had not been litigated in any courts, or even disputed in briefs or oral arguments. Douglas knew what he hoped it might do. Yet it began life as an empty vessel. No one could predict how the rule would be implemented or enforced. The meaning and scope of even the simplest law can be understood only through experience, in actual decisions made by judges and juries. *Brady* was far from simple.

Over the next two decades, three cases—and their particular facts—would be pivotal in defining the *Brady* rule and presaging its future.

In June 1966, Robert Taliento, a bank teller at Manufacturers Hanover Trust in New York City, was charged with cashing fake money orders.[2]

Under questioning by the FBI, Taliento admitted he'd been part of a scheme with an accomplice named John Giglio. He gave Giglio a signature card from one of the bank's clients. Giglio forged the client's name on money orders totaling $2,300. Taliento processed them through the bank.

To avoid going to jail, Taliento made a deal with the assistant U.S. attorney on the case. If Taliento would be a witness against Giglio, the prosecutor would let him walk. Taliento went on to testify in the grand jury, and Giglio was indicted.

Two years later, Giglio went to trial with a new assistant U.S. attorney. Prosecutor 1 apparently did not tell Prosecutor 2 about the bargain he had made. Taliento kept mum as well. Under cross-examination by Giglio's attorney, Taliento flat out lied on the stand.

Q:　Did anybody tell you at any time that, if you implicated somebody else in this case, that you yourself would not be prosecuted?

A:　Nobody told me I wouldn't be prosecuted.

In his summation of the case to the jurors, Prosecutor 2—knowingly or ignorantly—said simply: "[Taliento] received no promises that he would not be indicted."

Based on Taliento's testimony, Giglio was found guilty and sentenced to five years in prison. While his appeal was pending, Giglio's lawyer learned about Taliento's deal with Prosecutor 1. He moved for a new trial. The Supreme Court took the case to decide whether the government's behavior required a reversal of Giglio's conviction.

A unanimous Court ruled that the prosecution's failure to disclose this evidence violated Giglio's due process rights under *Brady*. The justices held that—whether the nondisclosure was intentional or negligent—knowledge of the deal was in the government's possession. Taliento had been an essential witness in the case. If Giglio's lawyer had known about his bargain, he could have used that information to impeach Taliento's credibility. They ordered a new trial.

The *Giglio* ruling was a significant expansion of *Brady*. It established that "evidence favorable to an accused" was not just facts directly related to guilt or innocence. The category also included information that could be used to impeach a witness—such as a plea deal, or in this case, the non-prosecution agreement.

Giglio was the first in a series of decisions that brought other kinds of information under *Brady*'s umbrella. Since the *Giglio* ruling, the Court has held that *Brady* includes favorable evidence whether or not it is admissible at trial, information on witness bias, any eyewitness description of the perpetrator that differs from the defendant's appearance, any facts related to a witness's dishonesty or criminality, and evidence about a law enforcement officer's misconduct or abuse of authority.

The Court also ruled that, for *Brady* purposes, any evidence known to the police is deemed to be in the government's possession. A prosecutor has the duty to seek out such information and disclose it to the defense.

This broadening of the category of favorable information was an important step forward for defendants' rights. It seemed to suggest the rule was trending up.

But the Court had yet to tackle the thorniest *Brady* issue. What, precisely, was "material" evidence?

On a drizzly Friday, September 24, 1971, James Sewell met his estranged wife for lunch at a Washington, DC, restaurant.[3] They had talked of reconciliation. They were planning to go to New York City together that evening. But during the meal, they argued. By its end, they decided to go their separate ways. For Sewell, that choice would be fateful.

Mrs. Sewell said later her husband left her at about 2:45 p.m. with $360 in his pocket. Seeking new companionship, Sewell met a sex worker named Linda Agurs. Around 4:30 p.m., the two went to a nearby motel, where Agurs had previously been a guest. They checked in as husband and wife. During that process, a motel employee noticed Sewell was wearing a bowie knife in a sheath.

Barely fifteen minutes later, the desk clerk and two other workers heard a woman's screams coming from the couple's room. When they forced the door open, they saw Agurs and Sewell on the bed, struggling over the bowie knife. The employees separated them and called an ambulance for Sewell, who was bleeding heavily. In the meantime, Agurs left the motel.

Sewell had serious stab wounds to his chest and abdomen, which proved fatal. He also had cuts and slashes on his hands and arms. The medical examiner later testified these were defensive injuries.

Agurs turned herself in the next day. She was subsequently charged with Sewell's murder.

At the trial, the prosecution's theory was that Linda Agurs had brought James Sewell to the motel to ply her trade. They had sex, but Agurs was not happy with what Sewell paid her. After he went down the hall to use the bathroom, she helped herself to the rest of his cash. When Sewell came back and tried to retrieve his money, she picked up his knife and stabbed him.

To support its case, the government introduced evidence that Agurs had been to the motel with other men. When the room door was forced open, she was holding the knife pointed at Sewell's chest. No money was found in his wallet or his pockets. A nurse who examined Agurs the following day reported no cuts or wounds on her body.

Agurs did not testify. Her lawyer argued she had acted in self-defense. He pointed out that Sewell had been carrying the knife, he had a second knife in his pocket, and Agurs was the one screaming for help. A motel worker testified Sewell was on top of Agurs during the struggle.

The jurors rejected Linda Agurs's claim. They convicted her of second-degree murder. She was sentenced to five to twenty years in prison.

A *Brady* issue lurked behind these facts. At the time of the trial, Agurs's attorney did not know that James Sewell had a criminal record. A few weeks later, he learned that Sewell had two prior convictions for carrying a dangerous weapon. In both cases the weapon was a knife.

Agurs filed a motion for a new trial. Her lawyer argued that if the jury had known of Sewell's violent past, they would have been more likely to believe Agurs had acted in self-defense.

The trial judge denied the motion. He noted that the jurors already knew Sewell had carried a bowie knife and another knife.

In his view, learning about Sewell's convictions would have had no effect on their verdict.

The U.S. Court of Appeals for the DC Circuit reversed this judgment, ruling the withheld evidence was material. In their view, Sewell's convictions for knife-related offenses would have been "undeniable evidence" of his assaultive habits and would have supported Agurs's defense.[4]

The Supreme Court disagreed and overturned the appellate court's decision in a 7–2 vote. *Brady* was now thirteen years old. Only three justices remained from 1963. The majority opinion, written by John Paul Stevens, showed that most of the current members saw *Brady* in quite a different light from how their old colleague Douglas had seen it.

For the first time, the Court expressly held that *Brady* included favorable information even if the defense had not specifically requested such evidence. But Stevens rejected the idea that *Brady* disclosure was a discovery right, meant to give defendants broader access to information in the government's hands. "We are not," wrote Stevens, "considering the scope of discovery. . . . We are dealing with the defendant's right to a fair trial."[5]

In that context, he wrote, "The mere possibility that an item of undisclosed information might have helped the defense, or might have affected the outcome of the trial, does not establish 'materiality' in the constitutional sense." Stevens spelled out three standards for materiality, based on the seriousness of the prosecution's misdeeds. The Court's default premise was that evidence is material and nondisclosure is a constitutional error, only if "the omitted evidence creates a reasonable doubt that did not otherwise exist."

Reviewing Linda Agurs's case under this new regime, the Supreme Court found that the government's failure to disclose Sewell's crimes did not deprive her of a fair trial. They reinstated her conviction.

Thurgood Marshall, who in 1967 had become the Court's first Black justice, wrote a strong dissent.[6] Unlike Stevens or Douglas, Marshall had extensive experience defending criminal cases. He saw clearly the impact *Agurs* would have in the courtroom. In his first paragraph, he called the Court's new definition of materiality so narrow "as to deprive it of all meaningful content."

To Marshall, the majority's yardstick was contrary to the Court's stated concern for fairness. "This rule," he argued, "is completely at odds with the overriding interest in assuring that evidence tending to show innocence is brought to the jury's attention." The new criteria would allow prosecutors to withhold any information they deemed nonmaterial and would reinforce "the[ir] natural tendency . . . to overlook evidence favorable to the defense."

Marshall proposed a broader definition of materiality. A defendant should only have to show "there was a significant chance that the withheld evidence, developed by skilled counsel, would have induced a reasonable doubt in the minds of enough jurors to avoid a conviction."

The only justice to join his opinion was fellow liberal William Brennan.

If the *Agurs* majority had intended to establish a clear test for what the *Brady* rule meant by material evidence, they failed. The new, graduated standards managed to be both complicated and imprecise. Their application to actual cases would prove to be confusing and capricious.

Still, it was nine years before the Court took another crack at this knotty issue.

Hughes Anderson Bagley Jr. was a petty criminal with a high-society name.

In October 1977, he was indicted in federal court in Washington State on gun and drug charges.[7] Two of his acquaintances—James O'Connor and Donald Mitchell, both security guards for the Milwaukee Railroad—were the government's key witnesses.

The guards said they had visited Bagley twice at his home. When O'Connor complained of being very anxious, Bagley sold him some Valium. In total, he paid Bagley $8 for the pills. O'Connor and Mitchell had worn hidden recorders at the meetings. But the tape quality was so poor the recordings could not be used in court to corroborate their claims.

Before the trial, Bagley's lawyer filed a motion asking about "any deals, promises, or inducements made to witnesses in exchange for their testimony." The government turned over sworn affidavits of O'Connor and Mitchell that detailed their interactions with Bagley. Both ended by declaring, "I made this statement freely and voluntarily without any threats or rewards or promises of reward having been made to me in return for it."

Bagley opted for a bench trial. O'Connor and Mitchell testified. The prosecutor did not disclose the existence of any deals or promises. After hearing the evidence, the judge acquitted Bagley of the gun charges but found him guilty on several drug counts. He was sentenced to six months in prison, followed by five years of parole.

Three years later, Bagley learned his ex-friends had lied under oath. Using the Freedom of Information Act (FOIA), he got copies of the contracts that O'Connor and Mitchell had signed with the Bureau of Alcohol, Tobacco, Firearms and Explosives (ATF). They stated ATF would pay them "a sum commensurate with services and information rendered." Prior to the trial, both men were paid expense money. After Bagley's convictions, each received an additional $300.

Bagley filed a motion to overturn his convictions. His main argument was that the government's nondisclosure had violated *Brady*; he could have used the contracts to impeach the testimony of both O'Connor and Mitchell.

Bagley's claim followed a long, twisting legal path. After considering the motion, the federal district judge—the same one who had convicted Bagley—denied any relief. He noted that he was in a "unique position" to decide what effect disclosure would have had on his ruling. Even if he had known of the contracts with the prosecution's witnesses, he said, it "would have had no effect at all" on his finding that Bagley was guilty of the drug charges.

Bagley appealed. The U.S. Court of Appeals for the Ninth Circuit overturned the judgment. A three-judge panel ruled the nondisclosure had denied Bagley information to effectively cross-examine O'Connor and Mitchell and "require[d] an automatic reversal." [8]

The government appealed to the Supreme Court, which vacated the ruling by the Ninth Circuit panel.[9] In a divided 5–3 decision, with two written dissents, the Court laid out in significant detail a new standard for assessing the materiality of a *Brady* claim. Then the justices sent the case back to the appeals court to decide whether—under the guidelines they had just announced—Bagley's conviction should stand.

The Ninth Circuit again ruled that it should not. Nearly nine years after his trial, Bagley's conviction was again vacated, and the matter was closed.

In *Bagley*, the Court did two important things.

First, it put to rest forever the hope that the *Brady* rule might reshape the current adversarial legal system. Early in his opinion, Justice Harry Blackmun bluntly stated the majority view of the role the rule should play, which the Court had foreshadowed in *Agurs*. "Its purpose," he wrote, "is not to displace the adversary system as the primary means by which truth is uncovered." [10]

Rather, said Blackmun, the rule's intent was "to ensure that a miscarriage of justice does not occur." In practical terms, this meant that a "prosecutor was not required to deliver his entire file" to the defense. His only duty is "to disclose evidence favorable to the accused that, if suppressed, would deprive the defendant of a fair trial."

So much for Douglas's dream.

Second, *Bagley* defined a single standard of materiality intended
to apply in every case, to every *Brady* claim. Evidence was material
if there was a "reasonable probability" that disclosure would have
resulted in a different outcome at the trial.

That definition, vague and slippery as it was, would have remarkable staying power. It would also set the future course of
Brady.

Justice Stevens, who had authored the *Agurs* opinion, wrote a
dissent only for himself.[11] He believed this new standard would
"stretch the concept of 'materiality' beyond any recognizable
scope . . . transforming it into a result-focused standard" with
"an independent weight in favor of affirming convictions despite
evidentiary suppression." He foresaw that this revised definition
would make it significantly harder for defendants to win *Brady*
claims.

Justice Marshall shared that fear times ten. He wrote a lengthy
and unsparing dissent that amplified the concerns he had expressed in *Agurs*, concerns he believed had proven all too real and
would only be made worse by *Bagley*.[12]

In Marshall's view, the new *Bagley* standard betrayed "the inter-
ests this Court sought to protect in its decision in *Brady*." "[T]he
state's primary concern," he wrote, is "justice, not convictions."
Sharing favorable evidence furthers that goal; limiting disclosure
thwarts it. Drawing on his years as a trial lawyer, he noted that
even a small piece of helpful information can create just the doubt
that leads a jury to acquit.

While the *Brady* opinion had not defined "material," Marshall
pointed out that Justice Douglas had cited two earlier cases that
"state the correct constitutional rule." In both of those cases the
term "material" meant something much broader than the majority's definition here. He saw that as "strong evidence" that Douglas
used the word "in its evidentiary sense" to simply mean germane
to the points at issue.

"There is nothing in *Brady*," he wrote, "to suggest that the

Court intended anything other than a rule that favorable evidence need only relate to a proposition at issue in the case in order to merit disclosure." He—along with most commentators—believed Douglas was not proposing some new standard of review; that he meant "material" to be synonymous with "relevant."

As he had in *Agurs*, Justice Marshall proposed a broader, simpler standard "based in significant part on the reality of criminal practice." The government "must divulge all evidence that reasonably appears favorable to the defendant, erring on the side of disclosure." That standard would clarify a prosecutor's duty and "integrate the *Brady* right into the harsh, daily" grind of the courtroom.

Marshall's dissent was an extended argument for a "return to the original theory and promise of *Brady*," from which the Court had strayed. Unlike Douglas, he could get only one colleague— Brennan—to agree.

If the aim of the *Bagley* court was to narrow the scope of the *Brady* rule and ensure it did not evolve into a discovery right, the opinion hit the mark. The materiality bar was now set at high. If the justices also hoped to clarify what "material" meant, it would prove to be a serious miss. As Marshall observed, their new standard "virtually defies definition."

The conflicting rulings in both *Agurs* and *Bagley* should have put the Court on notice that, despite valiant efforts, the definitions of materiality they had announced were confounding. In both cases, multiple courts had heard the same evidence and had come to opposite conclusions on materiality. Their standard bred confusion rather than consistency.

But neither Justice Marshall's warnings nor his pleas moved the majority.

In that summer of 1985, as the justices argued over *Bagley*, the investigation into Catherine Fuller's murder was in high gear. No one knew it yet, but the *Brady* rule would play a leading role in that epic drama.

4

PRISONERS OF THEIR HUNCH

Around 4:00 p.m. on October 4, 1984, McGinnis and another detective picked up sixteen-year-old Clifton Yarborough at his girlfriend's house on 10th Street NE, a few blocks from the Fuller crime scene.[1] His older brother, Ernie, was already in the squad car.

Cliff, as he was known, was a special education student at Eastern High School. He was also an exceptional basketball player. On his family's mantel were several trophies he had won at the local Boys Club.

Cliff and his family had lived for years in the 8th and H neighborhood. They all knew the Fullers, whose house was nearby. Some Sundays, Catherine's younger son, William, went to church with the Yarboroughs.

Most afternoons and evenings Cliff was either playing basketball or doing homework with his girlfriend. This day he was in front of her house, chasing her little cousin, when McGinnis pulled up and called to him.[2]

"Your mom told us to come up here and get you," McGinnis said, though he hadn't talked to Cliff's mother. "You have to come with us."

"For what?"

"We just want to talk to you and ask a few questions."

"Okay," Cliff said. "Let me go inside and grab my jacket." He went in the house and put on his coat. When he came back out, McGinnis's attitude had changed.

"Did you get on that goddam phone?" the detective yelled.

"No," he said. And when McGinnis asked again, Cliff repeated his denial.

Cliff had a verbal IQ of 66, in the bottom 1 percent.[3] He couldn't read books. But to get by, he had learned to read people. He was skilled at figuring out what they wanted. He often pretended to comprehend, answering yes even if he was confused and uncertain. At that early point, he said later, he knew things were going to be bad.

At homicide, McGinnis—whom Cliff called "Detective Pat"—put him in a room and handcuffed him to a chair. The detectives spoke briefly with Ernie and released him. When they began to question Cliff, he said he knew nothing about Fuller's killing. He told them that after school on October 1 he had just walked to his girlfriend's house.

McGinnis and Sanchez insist they didn't know at the time that Cliff was learning disabled. They did know he was young, inexperienced, and vulnerable. They figured he would be easy to crack.[4] Despite his denials, as day turned to night, they began to press him.

"They put fear in me," Cliff would say.

Police records show that starting at 6:41 p.m., almost three hours after Cliff was picked up, Sanchez began to type what became an eight-page statement. It was in a question-and-answer format, using details allegedly given by Cliff. It ended at 8:30 p.m.

The statement was a mix of things Cliff said he saw and several pieces of secondhand information. His story of the killing is cryptic. It reads in full:

I was standing on 8th and H Street, me and some of my friends and one of them said that that lady has some money, big money. So they say let's go get paid. The lady turned at 8th and H and crossed the street, so they went behind her. And I came across

8th Street [*sic*; should be H Street] the other way. And the lady
started screaming. Then she stopped and I walk[ed] home.[5]

According to the statement, the next day Cliff spoke to his
friend Monk Harris about the crime. Monk supposedly said,
"Only me and Burt [another teenager and mutual friend from the
neighborhood] went back there. Levy came halfway, like he was
afraid to get paid." Cliff asks him, "How much?" Monk answers,
"She didn't have nothing."

He said he never saw the lady after she was in the alley. He just
heard her scream.

Cliff recalls that evening very differently.[6] He says he told the
detectives again and again he didn't know anything about what
had happened in the alley. Then, Detective Pat "started talking
about a guy named Alphonso Harris [Monk]. . . . I said I seen him
go to his girl's house." When they asked about other people from
the neighborhood, he answered their questions. He insists he said
nothing at all about the killing.

After the interrogation, Cliff says they left him alone for a long
time, locked in the room. Eventually, Detective Pat came back
with a written document. He started reading him things about
the park and the alley from it. He told Cliff to sign every page at
the bottom.

Cliff later explained that "they promised I could go home if I
signed. I thought my mother was downstairs." Over and over, by
every answer, he put his initials. At the bottom of each page, he
carefully wrote his name.

Just before 10:00 p.m., they released Cliff and drove him home.
Before dropping him off, Sanchez gave him a warning.

"If we find out you're lying, we're coming back to get you and
you'll never go home."

In a general sense, Cliff's statement supported the detectives' theory. McGinnis later said he was now absolutely sure the crime had

been a gang attack.[7] But there were several serious issues with the particulars of what Cliff said. And what he left out.

The biggest red flag was that he said nothing about the sodomy. Cliff failed the basic knowledge test. The most striking fact of the crime, the central detail held back from the public, was missing from his story. If he—or Monk, for that matter—had actually seen the attack or heard an eyewitness describe it, neither of them would have completely omitted that atrocity.

Cliff's relationship to Fuller and her family was another issue. The detectives began their interrogation by asking him about "the lady in the alley." In reply, he never referred to Fuller by name. He always calls her "the lady." If these were really Cliff's words, at some point he would surely have said that he knew Catherine Fuller and her children well.

The statement also had factual errors. Cliff told McGinnis and Sanchez the lady wore a "dark-colored" coat. Fuller's raincoat was light blue. He said nothing was taken from her. She was robbed of jewelry and money. He said two of the attackers had knives. There was never credible evidence that anyone had a weapon.

Only at the end do the detectives ask Cliff if he can read and write. "I can write," he said, "but I can't read real good." When they asked if he wanted Sanchez "to read your statement for you?," he answered, "Yes."

The detectives had broken Cliff. They had grilled a scared, barely literate teen at length, without a lawyer or an adult present, threatened him with murder charges, and gotten him to talk. But what they did next showed how little faith they had in the truth of what he supposedly said.

Based on his words, they could have arrested Cliff for aiding and abetting a murder. They didn't. They could have picked up Monk's friend Burt, since Cliff put him at the center of the crime. They didn't. They just went after Monk, who was already at the top of their suspect list.

Back at homicide, McGinnis typed up an affidavit for an arrest warrant for Alphonso Lamar Harris, aka Monk, for first-degree felony murder.[8] The supporting information came from Cliff's statement. Relying on the affidavit, the emergency judge signed an arrest warrant at 12:15 a.m. It was now October 5.

Armed with the warrant, detectives immediately went to 14th Place NE, where Monk lived with his mother and several of his siblings. He was arrested without incident at 12:35 a.m., taken directly to homicide, and booked at 1:00 a.m.[9]

McGinnis and Sanchez were ready for him. They believed their hunch was panning out.

Monk Harris was twenty-two and had loose connections to the area of 8th and H. His former girlfriend lived three blocks away. Sometimes he hung out there or fixed people's cars on neighborhood streets. Earlier in the year he'd had a job at AAMCO Transmissions but quit to work for himself.

Monk was a smart aleck. He thought the police were always after him, particularly a detective named Donald Gossage. Starting when Monk was sixteen, Gossage had harassed him repeatedly, trying to get information. Finally, after Gossage came into his yard one day, Monk shot him in the buttocks with a pellet gun, earning himself a juvenile charge.

At homicide, Monk was advised of his *Miranda* rights to silence and to have an attorney represent him. He signed a written waiver of those rights at 1:38 a.m. Then he made a statement about the day of the murder.

The detectives' hopes for a quick solution soon evaporated. Monk denied any part in the crime and detailed an alibi for the afternoon and evening of October 1.[10] He said he was at a friend's house near 9th and I Streets NE from about 1:00 to 4:00 p.m. After that, he visited his on-and-off girlfriend until 5:15 or 5:30 p.m. A friend gave him a ride home. That evening his sister-in-law called to say someone had been killed at 8th and H.

Later that morning, Sanchez summed up Monk's statement on

his arrest report: "The defendant stated that he was not there, did nothing, he only knows what people told him about a lady being killed and raped. Also, that the police were looking for him and two of his friends."[11]

Police quickly interviewed Monk's girlfriend and his mother. With minor variations, both corroborated his story of what he had done on that eventful Monday. Down the road, his swift arrest would prove fortuitous for him.

On the afternoon of October 5, Monk made his first court appearance, known as a presentment, in DC Superior Court. A lawyer from the Public Defender Service (PDS) was appointed to represent him.[12] The only evidence was the arrest warrant affidavit. After reviewing it, the magistrate judge found probable cause to believe Monk had committed murder. He was held without bond at the DC Jail pending a formal detention hearing.

To many, a public defender is synonymous with mediocre, assembly-line legal representation. But not in the nation's capital. PDS was and is widely considered to be the best defender office in the country. Because of its reputation, relatively small size, excellent training program, and good pay, PDS attracted high-quality lawyers, including many from top law schools.

Once Monk was charged with murder, Michele Roberts was assigned to his case as lead counsel. She was a graduate of Wesleyan University, with a law degree from the University of California, Berkeley. She was only twenty-seven, but it would be an understatement to call her a rising star. In two years, she would be trial chief at PDS.

She would later join a major law firm. By 2002, in a city full of attorneys, *Washingtonian* magazine called her "the finest pure trial lawyer in Washington—magic with juries, loved by judges, feared by opposing counsel."[13] And in 2014 she became the head of the National Basketball Players Association.

Representing Monk would be Roberts's greatest challenge.

———

The next day, on October 6, the *Washington Post* ran its first in-depth story about the murder on the front page of the Metro section. Headlined " 'Her Bills Are Paid,' Husband Says," it described Junior sitting in a "small, cluttered dining room" finishing up his dead wife's business.[14] "I have to try to hold out for the kids," he said. He described his wife as quiet but feisty.

Fuller's neighbors said they, too, would miss her. One told the newspaper, "If you asked her to do something, she would do it. I have slow blood and the doctor says I have to walk a little bit each day. Whenever I asked her, she would walk with me."

The *Post* said Fuller was "taking a short cut to a nearby store . . . when she was assaulted and killed." The crime itself got a single sentence: "Fuller's body was found in a litter-strewn alley, apparently beaten to death with a blunt instrument in a manner that shocked hardened police investigators."

There was no mention of the sodomy.

With Monk's arrest, McGinnis and Sanchez had found the three young men named in the anonymous tip. One was locked up. Yet aside from Cliff's dubious statement, they had nothing to corroborate their gang theory. Officers began to cast a wider net, pulling in any young man they found with connections to 8th and H.

First, they went looking for Chris's brother, Charles "Fella" Turner, and Tim Catlett, who both lived near the park. On the afternoon of October 9, McGinnis and Sanchez found Tim on the street and brought him in.[15]

He was nineteen, with the unfortunate nickname "Snotrag." He had been in foster care since the age of two and was on bad terms with his mother.

Through his teens, Snotrag was frequently in trouble. Just three weeks before the Fuller killing, he had been released from prison on an armed robbery charge and was on probation. He was living with a neighbor, Catherine Fuller's friend Mary Overton. Overton had a grown son, Russell, and a soft spot for neglected boys.

At homicide, the detectives questioned Snotrag about what they called the "persons referred to as the 8th and H Street Crew" and about the murder. After "a lengthy period of questioning," Snotrag gave a written statement. He said the only thing he knew about the lady in the alley was that "she was killed." [16]

Fella turned himself in on a car theft case the next day, October 10. As soon as McGinnis and Sanchez heard about it, they brought him to homicide for questioning.

Fella, who was twenty, had been arrested eight times in the previous two years, but all three of his convictions were for misdemeanors. Before he dropped out of school in the tenth grade, he had won several basketball trophies. Now, a typical day might be spent caring for his grandmother or hanging out with friends and smoking weed.

Starting at 6:45 p.m., Fella gave a three-page written statement.[17] He told McGinnis that all he knew was "the lady was murdered." He said he was home at the time of the crime.

Near the end of the interview, McGinnis asked: "Who killed that lady in the alley?"

"I don't know," Fella replied. "I'm serious, man. I don't know."

On October 24, DC city council member Nadine Winter was assaulted and robbed near her home. She was grabbed from behind and knocked to the ground. Her purse was snatched. She told the *Washington Post* her assailant "punched me in the face and kept beating and beating me." [18]

The attack happened in an alley behind the 1100 block of K Street NE—half a mile from the corner of 8th and H.

The next morning, in the 600 block of 12th Street NE, a woman named Marilyn Ludwig was beaten and robbed by two young men. They hit her in the face, broke her nose, and took the plastic Safeway bag she was carrying.

The incident took place four blocks from 8th and H.

Ludwig immediately reported the attack. She also gave a brief description of the two assailants. Police on the way to the scene spotted two young men who matched her information. They arrested both after a short foot chase. One of them, an eighteen-year-old named James McMillian,[19] gave a short statement admitting the crime. He was soon linked to the assault on Winter the day before as well.

James was living at 825 8th Street NE with a woman named Mary Phelps-Hickman.[20] Her yard backed onto the alley where Fuller's body was found, just a few steps north of the garage. His room was at the rear of the house.

James was born in North Carolina and committed to a detention facility when he was nine. Phelps-Hickman, a friend of his mother, became his foster parent. Eventually she brought him to Washington, DC, and she legally adopted him in 1984. By then, James had a substantial juvenile record and a disturbing trait: a vicious streak directed at women.

Police charged James with the two violent robberies. That should have made him a prime suspect in Fuller's murder as well, based on his living situation, his criminal history, and his background. But he was an outsider. He hadn't grown up in the community. While a few of Phelps-Hickman's neighbors knew him, most of the 8th and H guys did not.

James didn't fit with the detectives' gang theory, so they didn't pay him much notice.

That same week, on October 26, police arrested a forty-one-year-old woman for disorderly conduct.[21] She gave her name as Annie Brown. She was taken to the Fifth District headquarters for further investigation.

At the district she was advised of her rights and questioned briefly. She soon admitted her real name was Ammie Davis. After reviewing her case, officers told her she was free to go. But instead of leaving the station, she asked to speak to the person in charge, so was taken to the office of Lieutenant Frank Loney, the supervisor on duty.[22]

Davis told Loney she wasn't sure whether she wanted to give him any information. After a pause, she asked: "What would happen if I gave you something on a homicide?"

Loney, a twenty-year veteran, said, "I'd listen. It apparently has been on your mind."

After a significant pause, she started talking.

"The motherfucker just got out of jail the same day and killed her for just a few dollars. He got out of jail on Monday and he killed her on Monday." Davis told him the murder had happened on October 1, "in the alley off H Street."

"Did he use a gun, knife, or what?"

"He beat the fuck out of her," she said.

Davis told Loney that she and her girlfriend were in an alley "shooting stuff" [heroin] when it happened. "I wasn't with him, but I saw him grab her by the back of the neck and pull her into the alley. My girlfriend saw it too."

"What's the man's name?"

After a period of silence, Davis said, "I don't want to talk about it." There was another long pause. Suddenly she spoke it out loud: "James Blue."

"Who?"

"James Blue did it."

After admitting she was afraid of Blue, Davis would say no more.

When she left, Loney wrote a report of her account and passed it to homicide. He assumed that someone from that unit would contact and interview her. Months later, when he heard the Fuller case had been "solved," he assumed Blue had been one of those charged.[23]

As October turned to November, McGinnis and Sanchez had a murder getting older, a trail growing fainter. Monk's arrest had yielded nothing. After a month of nonstop activity and dozens of interviews, they still had no solid evidence to support their theory. Mostly they heard the same recycled facts, speculations, and rumors that had circulated from the start.

Both detectives would later maintain their efforts had been hampered by the community's deliberate silence. In their scenario, the crime was a raucous rush-hour attack, in a busy neighborhood, with dozens of teenagers involved. It should have attracted wide attention. Lots of people—residents or shoppers or passersby—should have seen or heard *something*.

"Someone had to know about this," McGinnis told a *Post* reporter.[24] "Because of the neighborhood as I knew it—the bus stop, the park, the commercial establishments. Someone had to see the lady go back in the alley. But no one was offering information. . . . It took so long because there were so many people and so little cooperation."

Sanchez shared that view. "Nobody came to us," he said.[25] "Nobody volunteered anything. . . . How could 25 people be in the alley and nobody saw anything?" He told the *Post*, "I thought people would rally around us and come out of the woodwork, but they never did."

The two men had a ready explanation for why the locals were stiffing them: fear of the 8th and H Crew. "As the investigation continued," Sanchez said, "we found out there was . . . a large gang that terrorized not only the neighborhood, but individual people. . . . It was beyond belief that these people [gang members] had that much control over the community."

For the detectives, the case had become the two of them against a whole community. "I didn't want that lady's death to go in vain," Sanchez said. "If the people did not care, the only people who cared were us."

That bleak assessment rose from their singular focus on the gang theory and their utter failure to recognize local sentiment. They insisted on seeing the 8th and H area as a closed Black community defiantly withholding information—and wanted criminals—from police outsiders. But the locals had never been indifferent to Fuller's killing. They'd lost a friend and neighbor. The case reflected badly on them and on where they lived. They wanted whoever had done it to be caught.

Mary Overton was one of many neighbors who had been friendly with Fuller. "Everybody was so sorry about her murder," Overton said.[26] "She was like the rest of us, doing her best to get by." She added that "[i]f anyone in the neighborhood had seen anything, or knew who did it, we would have been knocking down the doors of the police station to tell them."

Sanchez's claim that the 8th and H Crew "terrorized" people into silence, while comforting to the detectives, was flat wrong. They weren't a gang. They were just some local guys who went to go-go concerts. Their neighbors weren't afraid of them; these neighbors had babysat them, gone to school and church with them, talked to them on the streets, seen them grow up.[27]

A year later, even the government would concede in court that "at no time do we intend to prove this [group of defendants] was a gang."[28] By then the damage was done. The gang theory—despite having no basis in fact—was immutably fixed in the public mind.

The community had not been quiet, either. William Freeman, the vendor who found the body, talked to police that night. So did Jackie Tylie, the woman who called 911. Both later looked at police photos to identify anyone who'd been in the area of the crime on October 1. The three people involved with buying Fuller's ring came forward as soon as they learned it was hers.

In addition, not one of the possible suspects the police had brought in had asserted his *Miranda* rights to silence. All of them—Cliff, Levy, Fella, and Snotrag—made statements about

October 1 and about the crime. Even Monk, who'd been charged with the murder, spoke to the detectives. So did his ex-girlfriend and his mother.

When the detectives said "nobody came to us," what they really meant was nobody came to them *with information supporting their theory.* Freeman had not seen or heard any kind of group activity in the alley. Nor had anyone living in the houses on 8th and 9th Streets, nor any passersby. And the man who had sold the ring was too old to be part of any 8th and H Crew.

This would have been a good time for the detectives to take a step back, to rethink their investigation. Fuller had been sodomized in the corner of a small, closed garage. How could twenty-five people have even seen it, let alone taken part? Maybe their theory was wrong. Maybe no one had any information about a gang attack because there hadn't been one.

But self-doubt was not part of McGinnis's makeup. His reputation for arrogance came from his confidence in himself and in his instincts. In the past, both he and Sanchez had been successful by trusting their judgment and working relentlessly. They were not going to change just because things weren't going well at the moment.

Writing about the challenges of highly publicized murder cases, novelist and former prosecutor Scott Turow said that "[u]nder enormous pressure to solve these cases, police often become prisoners of their own initial hunches."[29] That's precisely what had happened to McGinnis and Sanchez. Despite the dearth of supporting evidence, despite repeated signs they had gone wrong, they felt sure they were right about what had happened in that alley.

In their minds, if the investigation had hit a wall, it wasn't because their thinking or their theory was flawed. It was because they were getting no help from the community. To crack the case, they would have to ramp up the pressure.

To spur their efforts, in late October McGinnis and Sanchez asked their superiors to put Detective Donald Gossage on the team. Unlike them, Gossage had frequently worked in the 8th and H neighborhood. He knew most of the potential suspects. He'd even been shot in the buttocks by one of them.

In early November, the request was approved.

Gossage had been a policeman for twelve years. His specialty was developing local contacts. He was a regular at the area Boys and Girls Clubs as well as at the go-go shows. The young people called him "Inspector Gadget" because of his amazing memory for names. Gossage would drive teens and preteens around in his car, treating them to fast food while pumping them for information.

Gossage called McGinnis a couple of weeks after the murder to say he knew Monk. McGinnis told him that so far it was "a weak case. Probable cause, that's it." [30] In mid-November, when Gossage was first briefed about the crime, he was told things were at a "dead end." His mission was to change that. This was the biggest case he'd ever worked. He was determined to seize his chance.

Shortly after Gossage joined the investigation, the U.S. Attorney's Office assigned Jerry Goren to the Fuller case full-time. The killing had become a high-profile matter. For as long as it took, prosecuting this crime would be Goren's only job.

Goren was young, smart, and personable—a fast-rising lawyer who had only begun trying homicide cases earlier that year. Despite his limited experience, Goren's easygoing professional manner made him popular with his colleagues, with court personnel, and even with defense attorneys. From the moment he became the lead prosecutor, his aim was to end with a victory.

The Fuller case would be the last trial of his short legal career.

On Saturday, December 8, Chris and some friends went to a midnight showing of *Beverly Hills Cop*, starring Eddie Murphy. He planned to meet his girlfriend afterward. But when he phoned her, she was angry he'd gone out so late. She hung up on him and he went home.

Just after 7:00 a.m. on Sunday, he woke to the sound of his brother Carlos yelling, "Chris, the police are here." They burst into his bedroom with guns drawn. His grandmother had opened the front door so the officers wouldn't break it down. When he was led outside, Chris saw several marked cars and more police. A helicopter was circling overhead. He had no idea what was going on.

Chris was put into a squad car, but he wasn't taken to homicide. Someone high up in the department—McGinnis says he doesn't know who, and he didn't like the idea—had decided to stage a perp walk. Detectives drove Chris to the corner of 8th and H Streets NE. Before a crowd of reporters and TV cameras, Chris was led from the car, past the street signs, to a waiting police van. Only then did he realize this likely was linked to Catherine Fuller's murder.

He was not alone. Three others—Snotrag, Cliff, and Russell "Bobo" Overton—were arrested about the same time and took the same walk. Levy and Hollywood were supposed to be part of the group as well. But Levy was at his girlfriend's when the police went to his grandmother's house. Later that morning he saw the arrests on TV and learned he was wanted.

Levy went home to get a ride downtown. The police were waiting. When they walked him into homicide, all the officers started clapping. "We got him," they said. "Here he is."[31]

Hollywood was taking a girl home when the police came to his house. They missed him by a few minutes. When he returned, his grandmother told him detectives were looking for him. He surrendered the next morning.

Chris was acquainted with Cliff and Snotrag. He'd played basketball with Cliff and gone to school with two of his brothers. He often saw Snotrag around the neighborhood; they sometimes talked or hung out together. He recognized Bobo from seeing him occasionally in the park, drinking beer and smoking weed.

Bobo was twenty-five, 6 foot 7 inches tall, and a familiar figure around 8th and H because of his size and because he was a park regular. Chris knew his name only because Bobo sometimes spent time with associates of his father, Duke. Bobo's mother, Mary Overton, was a friend and sometime drinking buddy of Fuller's.

Bobo had the longest criminal record of those arrested, with prior convictions for robbery and armed robbery. He was several years older than any of the others and moved in different circles. The only one Bobo knew was Snotrag, because Mary had let him live at her house. Both Bobo and Snotrag were arrested at the Overton home on 9th Street NE, barely a block from the crime scene.

None of the four knew what was going on until they got to homicide. Officers there told them they would be charged with Fuller's murder and gave them *Miranda* warnings. They all agreed to waive their rights and to talk without a lawyer. Each of them denied participating in the crime or having any firsthand knowledge of who might have done it.

The media loved the show. All the local TV stations covered the arrests. The headline on the front page of the *Post*'s Metro section the next day was "Police Arrest 5 in Gang Killing of NE Mother." [32] The article said nine people were now in custody and more arrests were "quite possible."

The *Washington Times* went with "Four More Arrested in DC Sex Murder." [33] The body of the story called the killing a "murder-sodomy." It marked the first time either newspaper had reported that detail and used that term.

The police seized the chance to describe the crime and push their narrative. The *Post* quoted Deputy Chief Alfonso Gibson saying this was "one of the most brutal murders that ever took place in Washington." He added that "as far as we know, it involved the largest number of people arrested for a single murder."

McGinnis told the same paper that robbery was the initial motive for the attack. All of those arrested, he said, belonged to the
"same street gang." He repeated his previous plea: "[N]eighbors
won't be afraid to come forward with some information. I can't
believe that a woman got murdered at dusk and nobody saw it or
knows anything about it."

Once again, there would be no evidence to support his gang
theory.

On December 10, Chris and the others had their first appearance
in DC Superior Court.

Everything seemed unreal. He kept thinking someone would
jump up and say it was a terrible mistake, that he could go home
now. Instead, based on the warrant affidavits, the commissioner
found probable cause to believe they had committed murder.

All five were held without bond, pending a detention hearing
the next Monday.

Chris had never been arrested before. He wasn't sure he could
survive seven hours at the jail, let alone seven days. And he didn't
know what had brought the police to his door that terrible Sunday morning in the first place.

It had started with Detective Gossage. Shortly before
Thanksgiving—he wasn't sure of the exact date—Gossage went
to a go-go show at the Washington Coliseum.[34] A knife fight
erupted. Among the people stopped afterward was sixteen-year-
old Carrie Eleby.

She denied having any part in the melee. But Gossage claimed
that out of the blue Carrie said, "the person who did this is the
same person that killed the lady at 8th and H." At the homicide
office several days later, Carrie told Gossage that while riding
home from Cherries, a local disco, a boy named Calvin Alston
told her he had snatched Fuller's pocketbook and had run away
with her money.[35]

This was the kind of break the detectives had been chasing for two months, served up nicely by Gossage. He later summarized Carrie's importance: "There was no clue whatsoever. Without Carrie there would have been no case. There were no leads."

It didn't matter that Carrie was a deeply troubled teen. Or that in the past year she'd been truant from school, arrested for assault, and started using PCP. What counted to McGinnis and Sanchez was that she had given them all they needed to request an arrest warrant for Calvin.

They got one the next day.

Calvin Lee Alston was nineteen. He'd quit school the previous year and was working part-time doing house painting and repairs.

On the evening of November 29, he was watching TV at his mother's house near the corner of 3rd and M Streets NE.[36] Just after 7:00 p.m., a contingent of police came in several squad cars—along with a helicopter—to arrest him. When his mother opened the door, at least six officers ran inside with guns out.

By the time they left, the house was a mess. Calvin was in cuffs and distraught.

Sanchez thought Calvin was soft, that he "acted feminine."[37] Once they had Calvin in the interrogation box, both Sanchez and McGinnis felt sure they could break him. As soon as Calvin signed his *Miranda* waiver, they started in.[38] They told him they knew he was part of the murder. They knew he had confessed to Carrie.

Calvin said they were wrong. He couldn't have told Carrie anything about the crime because he wasn't there. He had an alibi. He was painting a house the day Fuller was killed. If he could talk to his boss or his customers, he could prove it.

Whatever Calvin said, the detectives said it was a lie. They were sure he was involved. His alibi was bogus. They had witnesses who put him in the alley. When he was convicted, he would go to jail for life. As the minutes passed, Calvin felt more fearful, more hopeless.

Then, in what would become his standard interrogation ploy, McGinnis took out a piece of paper. He drew a large pie and filled in a single piece.[39] He said the pie represented the killing. Calvin had two options. He could continue to deny any role and get the whole pie. He would be found guilty of murder and spend decades in prison. Or he could admit his part and help them solve the crime and get only one small piece of the pie. He could plead to a lesser offense and be out in a few short years. His fate was up to him.

As Calvin sat there, lost and unsure, the detectives threw him what felt like a lifeline. They said he didn't seem like a killer. Maybe he was just watching and didn't do anything to the lady. But if he didn't tell them about it, they would have to believe the worst.

Calvin cracked.

The coercive interrogation tactics the detectives used—false promises of leniency, isolation, deception about evidence—are common. They are also very effective at eliciting confessions, true and untrue, from young people.

The younger a suspect is, the more likely he is to falsely confess. A study led by Samuel Gross, director of the National Registry of Exonerations, examined 340 exonerations between 1989 and 2003.[40] Overall, 15 percent involved false confessions. But for juveniles, the figure was 42 percent. Other studies have shown similar results.

The reasons behind these figures are not hard to understand. Young people are nearly always less experienced, more impulsive, and more vulnerable than mature adults. They are easier to intimidate, easier to lead. They are often unaware of legal niceties. They may not know, for example, that admitting to just being a lookout can make them guilty of murder as an aider and abettor. They may not realize the long-term implications of what they say. They just want to stop their ordeal.

A growing awareness of this issue has begun to spark changes. In early 2022, Illinois became the first state to ban the use of deception and false facts in juvenile interrogations. Oregon quickly followed.[41] As of March 2022, a bill was pending in New York State that would ban these tactics in all interrogations. A major catalyst behind the legislation was the experience of the Central Park Five, all of whom had falsely confessed as juveniles.

Calvin had no such protections. Seeing no other way out, based on McGinnis's notes, he proceeded to say he had seen the crime.[42] He'd been a lookout at the 8th Street end of the alley.

He said "the lady" was walking up 8th when Levy, Bobo, Monk, Hollywood, and Cliff pushed her into the alley. Levy hit her on the back of the head with a "two-by-four-like stick," and she fell. They grabbed her arms and feet and carried her up to "the little cut in the alley." Cliff "picked up the money" and ran off toward 9th Street.

For the two detectives, Calvin's words were a rush. An eyewitness—a participant—had confirmed their theory that the crime was a gang attack. He had implicated more of the young men they believed were part of the 8th and H Crew.

But it was just a start. They had no video record. They believed twenty or twenty-five people were involved. They wanted more names, more specifics. They needed Calvin to be an active participant. They said that if he didn't give them more, they couldn't help him.

Over the next ninety minutes or so, according to Calvin, they went over the crime repeatedly. McGinnis gave him "an outline on what he thought took place."[43] When the detectives finally started recording, he had a new story.[44] This one had far more details and twice as many participants. It also more closely tracked the official narrative the detectives had created.

Calvin's recording began with a group of guys in the park at 8th and H, planning a robbery. When they saw Fuller, they all crossed H Street. They forced her into the alley from 8th Street and knocked her down. Levy and Monk carried her into what Calvin called "an old shack." Hollywood, Snotrag, Bobo, and Chris all started hitting and kicking the lady.

Inside the shack, Calvin said, they took her clothes off. Someone threw her bra. Levy had "like a round pole." He said, "I'm going to shove this up in her." When he did, Monk had one ankle and Bobo had the other. They were holding her legs wide open.

Everyone began leaving when Levy and Monk said, "Let's go." Hollywood had her two rings, Levy had her two chains, and Cliff had her money.

When the tape ended, the detectives were ecstatic. They had everything they wanted, including Calvin. He had confirmed their narrative. He had implicated the three suspects named by the anonymous caller, plus nine others. It was all on video.

Before turning off the machine, Sanchez asked Calvin if he felt better now.

"Much better," he said. Because, "I didn't have nothing to do with it and I don't want it all to fall down on me as they saying I did it."[45]

Calvin had just admitted he was involved in a horrific murder, but because of his limited understanding and the detectives' skill, he didn't know it. He'd said what they wanted him to say. He thought he would go home.

It would be years before Calvin went home.

To this day, the detectives deny any impropriety in questioning Calvin.[46] They did go over his story again and again. They did say he could go to jail for life. But they didn't threaten him. They didn't suggest the lookout scenario or give him any other information.

But Calvin's statements undermine those claims. In his first story, he fails the simple test Cliff had failed earlier. He completely leaves out the sodomy. If he'd been involved, he would have known about that vile act from the start. He fills this gap only after ninety minutes of talk with the detectives. On video, Calvin describes the sodomy three times. He even offers the dimensions of the pole Levy supposedly used.

He's also wrong about things he would have known if he'd been there. He says Levy hit Fuller "as hard as he could" in the back of her head. But her autopsy showed no injury to that area. He says someone "threw her bra." But it was still on her torso. He says Levy used a four- to five-inch pole. But Fuller was penetrated to a depth of at least eleven inches.

The detectives say Calvin's story changed because he was slow to admit the whole truth. Calvin has a simpler explanation. He says he only knew about the sodomy—and a lot of other facts—because the detectives told him, directly or otherwise. Later, under oath, he described how things went when Sanchez asked him how he could see what happened inside the garage.[47]

Q: Had you said anything . . . about a garage before Detective Sanchez said that?

A: No, sir.

Q: And did he say specifically what happened that you couldn't see in the garage?

A: That a pole was stuck in her.

Q: Had you said anything to any of the detectives about a pole being stuck in her when you gave the lookout statement.

A: No, sir.

Calvin would recant within days. Other problems with his story would soon surface. But McGinnis and Sanchez weren't looking that far down the road. Over the next two weeks, they arrested ten young men based on what Calvin had said.

Fella was the first. He was already at the DC Jail on a car theft case. On December 5, he was brought to court and formally charged with Fuller's murder.

He denied any involvement when Sanchez questioned him. Fella said he'd been around 8th and H the morning of the killing, then at home until later that evening. When Sanchez asked if there was anything he wanted to say about the crime, he wasted no words.

"I did not do it," he said. "I did not rob her, and I did not kill her."[48]

He added, prophetically: "I feel as if the police are making a big mistake, one that could cost me my life."

Cliff was one of the three arrested with Chris on December 9.

The detectives knew how vulnerable Cliff was from his interrogation on October 4. Back then, they'd only had the outline of a narrative and a few suspects. Now they had a detailed crime scenario and a long list of possible suspects. Cliff's first statement was no longer useful.

At homicide, officers kept him handcuffed in a locked interrogation room for about forty minutes.[49] Since he was the youngest and weakest, McGinnis figured he would "roll before the older ones."

While Cliff was waiting, McGinnis burst in and said, "Clifton, you lied to me."[50] He quickly left and slammed the door. He said he wanted Cliff to understand "it was a different day." He wasn't just a witness now. He was facing a murder charge.

Once the interrogation began, McGinnis and Sanchez played good cop/bad cop.[51] Cliff said Sanchez yelled and pounded on the table, calling him a liar. When McGinnis pushed Sanchez out of the room, he banged on the door and shouted, "Let me in, let me in." Back inside, he ripped off his shirt and acted like he was going to attack Cliff. Later, Cliff would say they had shoved him into the wall and a cabinet and had put his head in a toilet bowl.[52]

Their tactics worked. Cliff's confession followed the same pattern as Calvin's. At first he repeatedly denied any involvement in Fuller's murder. As the morning passed, the detectives upped the pressure and wore him down. Nearly five hours after his arrest, Cliff began a video statement.[53] He said he'd seen the assault from the 9th Street end of the alley.

Cliff said Fuller was forced into the alley from 8th Street. Monk and Levy were the instigators. Monk "grabbed her in a bear hug" and "threw her down hard." The others hit and kicked her. In the alley near the garage, a neighborhood boy named Derrick stuck a pole in her. So did Levy. Cliff didn't know if it went in her vagina or her rectum. He named thirteen young men who supposedly took part.

On his hour-long video, Cliff looks subdued and often tentative. He speaks softly. But he seems to understand the questions and answers directly. He says he saw the crime and identifies pictures of the alleged participants he knows from the neighborhood.

There's no flow to the story, though. It's mostly a flat series of assertions.

"Monk ripped her blouse off her."

"Snotrag hit her and dragged her."

"Derrick stomped her."

"Levy stuck a pole in her."

The detectives admit they pressured Cliff, but they deny feeding him any details.

A former DC detective who works as an expert in false confessions, James Trainum, disputes that claim. After seeing Cliff's tape, he said it was a prime example of what police call a "recap video"—a summary rehearsed repeatedly off camera and recorded after careful preparation.[54] That's why the story is told in such a cold, cryptic way.

Cliff's narrative, like Calvin's, has some major problems. In his October 4 statement, Cliff said nothing about the sodomy. Now he adds it but gets the facts wrong. He says both Derrick and Levy stuck a pole into the lady. The autopsy showed a single wound track. He says the woman was in the alley when that happened. The blood evidence showed Fuller had been sodomized inside the garage. And from his vantage point at the 9th Street end of the alley, Cliff could not have seen that.

Cliff says Levy was the worst villain. Earlier he'd said Levy was just a timid observer who didn't have "the heart" to come near Fuller. He tells a detailed story about everyone leaving the garage and going up to I Street, where Snotrag disperses the stolen money from a bunch of bills. In his first statement, Monk tells Cliff the woman "didn't have nothing." Cliff originally fingered five assailants; now he names thirteen.

In broad strokes, Calvin and Cliff seem to be telling the same story. But aside from making Levy the most despicable, the roles they give other participants don't match. They disagree on who led the attack and who was the lookout. They disagree on where and how Fuller was violated. They disagree on the roles each of them played, on where the proceeds were divided, and on who got Fuller's money and jewelry.

Later statements from both men help explain these many contradictions. Calvin said when he talked about the details of the crime: "I was scared, and I said anything that came to my mind at the time." Cliff said his video had "some statements that someone else made and then asked for me to say it and I just said it because I thought it would get me out." He never spoke to the police again.

December 17, 1984, would be a bad day for Chris. After a week in jail, he came back to court for a preliminary hearing.

At his first appearance the previous Monday, he had been given a court-appointed lawyer named Robert A. DeBerardinis Jr. DeBerardinis, who was in his early thirties, had been a member of the DC bar for only four years. This was his first murder case.

DeBerardinis asked the court for a bail bond for Chris. But after the prosecution presented its evidence—a description of the crime and a summary of Calvin's video—the judge found probable cause for murder charges. He ordered Chris held without bond. The government now had nine months to indict him.

Chris was stunned. He was facing a long stretch behind bars with no chance of getting out. He wanted to die. What pained him most was the feeling he had let down all the people who believed in him. And since coming to jail, he'd learned he had two sons on the way with two of his sometime girlfriends.

As the days passed, though, he started getting letters from friends in the neighborhood. They said they were sure he wasn't involved. They told him to keep his head up, to keep fighting. That lifted his spirits.

But his good feelings were soon wiped away by what was happening to his beloved grandmother. Mimi always seemed so strong. Now he learned she had lung cancer and was failing fast. She came to see him once. It broke Chris's heart to see how frail she was. He blamed himself for adding to her burdens. In two months, Mimi would be dead.

It didn't take long for Chris and the others to figure out Calvin was behind their murder charges. Their warrants had been issued shortly after his arrest.

Despite his confession, Calvin didn't ask to be separated from any of the other suspects at the DC Jail. For a while he was in a cell next to Chris, on the same tier with several of the others. A few of them talked about beating him for snitching on them—the street term for incriminating someone to earn leniency.

Chris advised restraint. "We shouldn't do anything," he told the others. "If we go after him, we'll look guilty. What we need him to do is tell the truth."

They left Calvin alone.

When Calvin talked to Chris, he wouldn't go into detail about his video statement. But he told Chris that "the detectives got me to say a lot of things." "Man, I'm sorry," he said repeatedly. "I know I messed up your life."

Away from the stress of the interrogation box, Calvin and Cliff began to realize the implications of their actions. Both had believed that if they gave in to the detectives, if they put themselves on the scene as witnesses, they could go home. They hadn't thought about what came next. Sitting in jail, they understood they'd admitted being involved in a murder.

Cliff would not cooperate further. Calvin had one meeting with the prosecutor, then resisted any more contacts. He wrote to the judge who presided over his hearing, saying, "the police no [sic] . . . they forced me to say something that I didn't see or do which was the lie."[55] In letters to family and friends he insisted he'd had nothing to do with the crime.

He set about trying to verify his alibi. Calvin's recollection was that on the Monday of the killing he was doing some painting for a Mrs. Page. He knew her family. He wrote to see if they recalled him working that day until late afternoon. He talked about what he would do "when I come home from this incident that I didn't have anything to do with."[56]

He ended by saying: "So please come to court and help me clear my name."

McGinnis and Sanchez started looking for Derrick Bennett at the end of December 1984.[57] Cliff put him at the center of the attack in his December video. On December 29, Sanchez got a warrant for Derrick's arrest.[58]

Derrick was just eighteen. A relative newcomer to the area, he knew most of the local young men only by sight.

Derrick had no fixed address, and it took some time for the police to find him. On the afternoon of February 6, they arrested him in an alley in Southeast DC.[59] He was taken to homicide, advised of his *Miranda* rights, and told he would be charged with Fuller's murder.

Derrick waived his rights and agreed to talk without a lawyer. He said he had nothing to do with the crime. All he knew was what he had heard on the street or seen on TV.

His interrogation followed the now-familiar progression. McGinnis and Sanchez said they knew he'd been involved in the killing. He said that wasn't true. They made threats and promises. He could keep lying, keep denying, and spend the rest of his life in jail. Or he could admit his part in the murder and get only a small piece of the blame.

About five hours after his arrest, Derrick began a recorded statement.[60] He said he was in the alley when Fuller was killed and implicated most of their suspects. But he insisted he never touched the lady or her money or her jewelry. He just watched because he was "curious." When he saw the "pole shit," he left and went to his girlfriend's house.

As with the other statements, there would be issues with many of Derrick's details. He claimed his memory of the day of the killing was good but said the weather was sunny. It had been rainy all day. He didn't recall anyone singing in the park. He said that day "was just real quiet." He said Levy shoved the pole in the lady's vagina. He implicated two girls and said that "it looked like . . . around 50 people back there."[61] Chris and Hollywood had been only spectators.

For now, though, the detectives had another video that endorsed their narrative. When it was done, Sanchez said, "I think we're pretty well satisfied. I think you gave a pretty good statement. Thank you very much."

"Wish I was going home," Derrick said.

McGinnis responded: "I kinda wish you were too, my man."

The next day Derrick went to court to be formally charged with murder. He did go home, despite the government's opposition.[62] He had a part-time job and no prior record and was released with a few curfew restrictions.

His release turned into a blessing for the prosecution. Two months later, on April 5, Derrick was arrested for selling $50 worth of crack cocaine to an undercover officer.[63] He was stopped with the marked money and identified by the buyer.

Derrick again waived his rights and spoke to the detectives. This time he was truly scared. He said later he knew he would be found guilty on the drug charge because: "I was caught red-handed."[64] He was facing up to thirty years on that offense alone. Goren, the prosecutor, was now involved. The questioning was "more intense."

According to Derrick, they said: "We got you." They told him they had witnesses who said he helped kill Catherine Fuller. If he didn't cooperate, he would go to jail for the rest of his life. He says they also threatened to prosecute his mother for credit card fraud.

"I was so young and inexperienced," Derrick said later. And "I was scared and intimidated" by their words. To avoid the possibility of a life sentence, and to keep his mother out of prison, he agreed to say he was part of the attack and to testify against the other suspects.

During the next week, Derrick said, he met with the police and the prosecutor "over and over" to get ready for the grand jury. He knew about the crime from the news media and from neighborhood talk. But "most of what I said . . . came from Goren and the detectives."

They "painted a picture for me about what had happened. All I had to do was agree."[65]

Derrick's grand jury testimony about the killing was very different from his video statement two months earlier. Now he put himself into the crime.[66]

His admission about his actions in the alley was brief and perfunctory.

Q: What did you do?
A: I participated. . . . Everybody was kicking and hitting her.

Q: Did you do that?

A: Yeah.

Previously, Derrick had said Chris, Hollywood, Snotrag, and Monk were there, but as mere bystanders. He told the grand jurors all four were active participants. Before he was done, Derrick implicated nearly everyone they had accused—and some new suspects as well.

After hearing Derrick, the grand jurors struggled to understand his story. A few of them realized what the detectives and the prosecutor relentlessly ignored: the government's narrative made little sense. It provided no reason for the utter brutality of the attack.

One of the jurors asked Derrick if any of the accused knew Fuller. He answered—correctly—"Well, from what I was told, they all knew the lady." [67]

The juror followed up:

Q: But they never said that this lady had ever done anything to any of them that would make them want to do this to the lady?

A: I'm quite sure the lady didn't do nothing. I'm quite sure she never did nothing to them.

Q: How would this lady happened [*sic*] to have been picked to be the one?

A: I don't know.

In an effort to comprehend, another juror noted the point of the crime had been to "get paid." He asked Derrick why, "in your mind," the attack continued after they could have taken Fuller's purse.

"In my mind," Derrick answered, "I don't know."

He could describe a group assault and say he was involved. But despite his way with words, he could not explain the official story or his role in it. Why would thirty or fifty young men rob and violate and kill a tiny older woman they knew? Why would he jump in and help?

Derrick didn't know.

In Derrick's story, one of the fifty or so people present was a young man named Steve. He said Steve was in the park, joined the attack, and hit Fuller. He also held her legs open in the garage while Levy shoved a pole in her vagina. He identified a photo of Steven L. Webb as the person he was talking about.

Steve, nineteen, was light-skinned, soft-spoken, short, and a bit stocky. He lived with his parents on Emerald Street NE, about a mile from 8th and H. He knew the area; his girlfriend lived nearby.

Because of his association with the neighborhood, police subpoenaed him to the U.S. Attorney's Office on January 24. They questioned him about the murder and showed him some pictures. He insisted he knew nothing at all about the killing. But after Derrick fingered him on February 11, he was arrested at his sister's house.[68]

At homicide, Steve agreed—like all the other suspects—to talk without a lawyer. His version of events did not match any of the other stories or the official narrative. He put Fuller in a bar, said she was attacked on H Street, and claimed she was pulled into the alley because of the ruckus she made. No one else had these details in their stories.

After saying he would make a recorded statement, Steve reversed himself. He told the detectives he wasn't present for any part of the crime. "I'm not going to do the videotape," he said, "because what I just told you all was a bunch of lies."[69]

Derrick had also claimed a girl named Lisa Ruffin got one of Fuller's rings. She was just seventeen, with an eighth-grade education and a spotty employment record. When Goren interviewed her at the U.S. Attorney's Office in early April, she said she knew nothing about the murder and wasn't there. She kept denying any part in the crime before a grand jury later that month.

After weeks with no more information about Lisa, McGinnis still crafted an arrest warrant affidavit based on Derrick's testimony.[70] It put Lisa in the park and in the alley that day and said she took some of Fuller's jewelry. For good measure, McGinnis added that when Levy put a "pole-like object into the victim's rectum," Lisa said, "Fuck that bitch up."

The police arrested Lisa in July. A post-arrest report for court services noted she'd had emotional or nerve problems.

Lisa's biggest struggle was with drug use, particularly PCP. She was under the influence so often her nickname was "Lunchin' Lisa"—slang for a person who is slow or out of it from being high. The Fuller case was her first adult matter.

Whatever her mental or physical state, under questioning Lisa continued to deny any knowledge of the murder or any involvement in it. But based on McGinnis's affidavit, she was held without bond.

Twelve young people from the 8th and H neighborhood were now charged with Fuller's murder. A trial was scheduled for the fall.

Defense lawyers are like poker players. Whatever their skill or experience, they must play the cards they're dealt. In this case, they had a tough hand.

Each of the defendants was assigned an attorney at his or her initial court appearance. Monk, the first one arrested, was represented by two public defenders. Most of the others were given lawyers who took appointments for an hourly rate. Around the DC courthouse they were known as CJA attorneys, for the Criminal Justice Act that established this system for indigent defense.

CJA lawyers ranged from very good to atrocious. They would sign up for certain days to "pick up" new cases and be assigned clients based on whoever was brought to court that day. For defendants with little means, like the accused in this case, it was potluck. They had no say in the matter.

Chris's lawyer, Robert DeBerardinis, was a typical CJA attorney. He was competent, but not much more. Early on, when he didn't respond to phone calls, Chris wrote the judge asking for a new lawyer. DeBerardinis showed up at the jail and promised to keep in better touch. Chris agreed to keep him on.

"I knew my lawyer wasn't very good," he said later. "But I hoped he was good enough."

From the start, the lawyers for the defendants faced two major problems. The first was the narrative of the killing that McGinnis and Sanchez had spun, with a big assist from the media. The second was the defense they chose.

In a criminal trial, whoever has the better story usually wins. Famed defense lawyer Johnnie Cochran explained it this way: "Evidence doesn't win the day. . . . We're here to tell a story. Our job is to tell that story better than the other side tells theirs."[71]

The government had a superb story in this case. A tiny woman, shopping for her family, is grabbed by a gang of thugs. They force her into an alley, beat and kick her, strip her of money and jewelry, and drag her into a filthy garage. They rip off her jeans and underwear. Two hold her legs open as another rams a pipe up her anus. They leave her to die on a cold cement floor.

A murder narrative could hardly be more dramatic than that. Once you hear it, you can't forget it. It's nearly impossible to imagine any other scenario.

What did the defendants have to combat such a compelling story? What alternate version of events could they offer? "It wasn't me. I wasn't there. I didn't do it. I don't know who did." In plain words, not much.

Alibi is a defense, but it's not necessarily a story. In the months after the crime, the public heard just one version of events: a mesmerizing account of a brutal gang killing. Compliments of the detectives and the prosecutor and the media, they heard it over and over and over.

That narrative overwhelmed any actual evidence. Before the case came to trial, before a single piece of real evidence had been presented in court, this story had become the accepted truth. The only question in the public's mind was who exactly had been involved.

Everyone knows what an alibi is. But alibi defenses are uncommon in criminal cases. And rarely successful.

Teenagers, especially if they aren't in school or working regular jobs, lead spontaneous lives. Proving their exact whereabouts at any given time can be difficult, especially weeks or months later. Documentation is rare. And in 1984 there were no cell phones or social media to help recall the events of a particular day.

In addition, the friends and family members most people spend their time with have the best reasons to be extra "helpful." They may be willing to stretch their memories—or the truth—to offer supportive testimony. Jurors are usually skeptical of their claims. They often won't believe them without specific details or other corroborating evidence.

There were other problems with an alibi defense in this particular case. Aside from Monk, all the defendants were arrested at least two months after the killing. Several were charged even later. By then, their recollections about that day were limited at best.

Most of them also lived close to 8th and H Streets NE; several lived less than a block from the scene. Their lives revolved around that neighborhood. Virtually every day they were there: at home or at the arcade or at a friend's place or at the park. It would have taken only ten or fifteen minutes to be involved. None of them could account for every moment of that fateful Monday.

Finally, any alibi has another limitation, which proved particularly damaging here. When lawyers say "my client was somewhere else," there's no reason to challenge the prosecution's story of how the crime happened. The only evidence that matters is identification testimony—whether a witness puts one's client on the scene. Other information is not relevant.

Years later, with barely concealed satisfaction, Goren summed up the problem: "Not a single defense lawyer really challenged the theory of the case. And I think that doomed them. They all agreed that something happened in the alley, but it wasn't my guy. . . . Once you say, 'I wasn't there,' you can't argue about what happened."[72]

When he knew he would be in jail for months, at least, Chris started working on his alibi. He told his lawyer everything he could remember about the Monday of the murder. He gave him the names of Hollywood's family members. It was already ten weeks after the killing. He wanted to get his defense lined up.

DeBerardinis could have talked to these witnesses right away. He could have explained why their specific recollections were so important. He could have helped them think back to the events of October 1 and firm up their memories before more time passed. He could have started preparing them for encounters with the police and possible trial testimony. He didn't.

He was busy. The case was only beginning. DeBerardinis didn't know how things would go. He thought the government had a strong case. He figured down the line Chris would probably plead guilty. If that happened, any trial preparation he'd done would be wasted time.

DeBerardinis's behavior was the norm. Combined with the circumstances of the crime, that approach would make it nearly impossible for the defendants to establish credible alibis.

Soon after Chris's arrest, the government floated a very favorable plea offer. He had no record and a good reputation. He could plead guilty to two relatively minor charges—accessory before and after the fact—and get two to six years. With good behavior, he would serve the minimum.

"The prosecution isn't really after you," DeBerardinis told Chris when he brought up the deal. "They don't think you had a big part in the murder. Plead to something small, and you'll be home soon."

But when DeBerardinis urged him to accept the bargain, Chris went off. "Under no circumstances do I want a deal," he yelled. "I'm not pleading to anything no matter what they come up with."

And he wouldn't. Not then, not ever.

Chris's resolute refusal to even ponder a plea is still a vexing subject. Whatever the government thought Chris had done in that alley, their offer was a concrete way of saying two years in prison was enough punishment—*if he said he did it.* Given what was at stake, why wouldn't he at least consider that option?

He should have been thinking about his future, about his family. But he was only nineteen. He was facing a possible life sentence. He had a lawyer he didn't trust. All he could focus on was that he'd had nothing to do with this killing.

Chris wasn't yet savvy enough to see the distinction between the fact that he wasn't in that alley and the possibility a jury might still convict him. He hadn't done anything wrong. He believed the real story would come out at the trial. That his innocence would be enough to save him.

"My whole thing," Chris explained afterward, "was that I wouldn't deviate from the truth." That attitude would cost him dearly.

Along with the difficulties of an alibi defense, the attorneys for the accused had another serious handicap. Under DC law, prosecutors don't have to disclose the names of witnesses or reveal anything about their likely testimony. The defense lawyers didn't know what evidence Goren had.

They knew he was smart and skillful and that the police had

talked to hundreds of people. They assumed the prosecution had a long list of eyewitnesses ready to testify about the guilt of their clients.

Goren stoked that presumption. He needed to do that to make them reluctant to challenge his narrative.

At a pretrial hearing, Snotrag's lawyer asked the court to compel the prosecution to provide more information about their case. "I don't know what the government has," he told the judge. He said he'd learned from the newspaper that "the government has 30 eyewitnesses." [73]

In response, Goren did not correct that serious misapprehension. He simply told the court, "I have disclosed . . . to all of the attorneys . . . everything that I considered to be in the nature of *Brady*." He added that "[i]f there is anything that I do consider to be questionable, I would present that to the court for an *in camera* [in private] review." [74]

Goren's answer illustrates one of *Brady*'s central flaws. If he chose to hide facts that could help the accused, if he chose to break his promise to the judge, the defense would likely never know. These matters were solely in his hands. That's a key reason why prosecutors often feel free to break the rule and why so many violations stay hidden.

Despite Goren's posturing, as the trial neared, he'd grown increasingly worried about his case.

He had arrested the largest number of suspects for a single homicide in DC history. The media was relentlessly promoting the prosecution's theory. The constant publicity had made the official narrative the only story of the crime. It also put more pressure on him. He needed to deliver.

Since the day of the killing, McGinnis and Sanchez had worked doggedly, with an aggressive modus operandi. They would subpoena anyone—even young teens—with a link to 8th and H. They would order their target to come in for questioning under threat of arrest. They would often bring someone in repeatedly to try to get what they wanted. They said by the end they had interrogated more than four hundred possible witnesses.

Even with these heavy-handed tactics, the investigation was foundering. The confessions of Calvin and Cliff and Derrick—their most malleable teenage suspects—were all sketchy. Neither Calvin nor Cliff were cooperating further. Derrick had agreed to testify, but he first denied knowing anything. He had a sweet plea deal. None of the others were talking at all.

Goren didn't have a single independent witness who had seen or heard anything related to a gang attack in the alley. No physical evidence connected any of the accused to the crime: no weapons, no proceeds, no fingerprints, no blood, no hair, no DNA. Of the thirty or forty or fifty young people who were supposedly involved in the crime, or at least present, not one had apparently confessed to a family member or associate or girlfriend.

Years later, Goren told the *Post*: "We had very, very little for much of the time we were investigating . . . we were really struggling to find the evidence we needed to make the case."[75]

Goren was shrewd. He oozed confidence to the media. He wanted the defendants to think he had a strong case with numerous witnesses. But in private, he and the detectives were scrambling to shore up their investigation. He'd never tried such a high-profile case, and he was determined to win.

In this charged context, Goren faced a critical decision: whether or not to make some major *Brady* disclosures to the defense.

In August, Goren learned for the first time that just weeks after the murder, Ammie Davis told officers she saw James Blue attack Fuller in the alley and "beat the fuck out of her." Inexplicably, it had taken nine months for the report of her interview with a police lieutenant to reach him.[76] When it did, the trial was less than two months away.

Davis's information was too hot to ignore. Goren asked the

detectives to find her. He met with Davis twice. After hearing her story, without talking to the judge, Goren decided on his own that she was not truthful.

He would subsequently admit he had evaluated everything Davis said in the light of the official narrative.[77] It was a sham exercise from the beginning. A large group had committed the crime. Davis had to be wrong. Even when James Blue shot and killed Davis just days after she met with Goren, he didn't change his views of her credibility.

On the evening of the murder, Willie Luchie and his associates had walked through the alley where Fuller was found. They had told police that between 5:30 and 5:45 p.m., as they passed the closed garage doors, three of them heard a moan. They were headed to the liquor store. They looked back, paused, then went on.[78]

That bit of evidence meant Fuller was still conscious and likely being assaulted at that moment. The garage was small, confined. Only a few assailants, at most, could have been inside. If Luchie and his friends were telling the truth, the government's theory—that a rampaging group of twenty or thirty Black youth had done the crime—was fiction. They would lose the racial gang narrative that, despite minimal evidence, had resonated widely in a nervous community.

The most significant piece of *Brady* evidence involved the two men who fled from the garage when the police arrived. William Freeman, the street vendor at 8th and H, and Jackie Tylie, the woman who called 911, had both seen the two runners in the alley. Both had seen one of them holding something under his coat.[79]

In early 1985, the detectives showed their picture collection to Freeman and Tylie. Both of them picked out photos of James McMillian and his sidekick, Gerald Merkerson, as the two men by the garage.[80] Freeman also saw them walking in the 800 block of H Street earlier that day. Another teen told police she saw McMillian in the alley around the time of the crime.

Officers knew by now that despite his youth, McMillian had a history of serious violence. His house backed onto the alley only a few steps from where Fuller's body was. In the weeks after the murder, he'd committed two attacks on women in the area. With the identifications, his suspicious actions at the scene, and the supporting evidence, McMillian made a prime suspect.

But Goren wasn't much interested in McMillian. He was a loner, who'd lived in the 8th and H area only briefly. He didn't spend time in the park. He didn't go to school or to go-go concerts with guys from the neighborhood. He didn't fit the gang theory. And Goren would later say—wrongly—he believed McMillian and Merkerson had only been at the garage more than an hour after Fuller's murder.[81]

The prosecutor knew he had an obligation to disclose favorable evidence. He'd promised in open court he would comply with the *Brady* rule. He'd even added he would consult with the judge if he had any questions.

Goren also understood these three pieces of information directly contradicted the official narrative. Handing this evidence to the accused would give them a ready-made defense, a story far stronger than their flimsy alibis. His case was already thin. Sharing this information could mean losing the biggest trial of his career.

Duty pushed Goren toward disclosure. But his desire to win, to convict the people he believed had killed Catherine Fuller, pulled him toward silence. If he withheld this evidence, he knew it would likely stay hidden. Maybe forever.

That's what he did.

Goren's decision might seem surprising. The whole point of the *Brady* rule had been to require disclosure of favorable information. Prosecutors sworn to uphold the law should have had concerns about failing to follow it. But barely two months earlier, the *Bagley* court had narrowed the rule and signaled they would take a relaxed approach to any enforcement.

Over the next fifteen years, two key *Brady* cases would make those trends even more pronounced.

5

THE BATTLE FOR *BRADY'S* HEART

Nothing good ever happened to Larry Youngblood.[1]
He grew up poor. A childhood car accident left him with
a permanent limp from a foot injury. He had a badly disfigured
left eye and wore dark glasses in public to hide it. At twenty he
was convicted for a robbery. Over the next decade, while living in
Tucson, Arizona, he wrestled with a drug addiction.

Those were minor bumps compared with December 9, 1983.
He was arrested that day and charged with a vile crime.

Six weeks earlier, on a mild Saturday evening, ten-year-old
David Leon had gone to a gospel music concert with his mother.
Her church—the Door—rented space in the Southgate Shopping
Center downtown. There was a carnival in the parking lot that
night.

During the service, when the congregation stood to pray, David's
mother realized he wasn't in his seat next to her. She guessed
where he had likely gone and went straight to the carnival. She
circled the site several times. No David.

He had come to the carnival and met a Black man with a bad
eye. The man offered him $5 if he'd help transport a tent. David
was hesitant. But the money could pay for some fun rides. The
man was persistent. David followed him briefly. But when David
refused to get in the car, the man jumped out, threw him into the
back seat, held him down by his hair, and drove away. The radio
was playing country music.

Outside town, the man stopped near a ravine. He fondled

David. Then he took David to a barely furnished house and sodomized him repeatedly. He tied David up while he went outside and started his car with jumper cables. Before taking David back to the church, he sodomized him again. He threatened to kill David if he told anyone what had happened. The whole incident lasted about an hour and a half.

The pastor's wife called David's mother. His mother took him to Kino Community Hospital, where a doctor examined him. His physical injuries were minimal, but he was badly shaken. His clothes were torn and inside out. The doctor did a rape kit, swabbing David's mouth and rectum. He also collected samples of David's blood, saliva, and hair.

Next, David told detectives what happened. He worked with an artist to make a composite sketch of the man who assaulted him. An officer took photographs to document his injuries and kept his clothes as possible evidence.

Based on what David said, police would call him "a very observant youngster."

David gave officers details about his assailant and about the car he drove. The man was middle-aged, medium height and weight, with "greasy" gray hair and no facial scars. He had an "almost completely white" right eye and wore loafers.

The car was a medium-sized two-door white sedan. The passenger door didn't open. It had a trashy interior with blankets on the seats and a noisy muffler. The car ran with an ordinary ignition key but needed jumper cables to start it. The radio worked fine.

A week after the attack, a detective came to David's school with a photo lineup. It had six pictures of Black men with one eye blotted out. She told him they had arrested the man who raped him. That wasn't true. But police had developed a prime suspect: Larry Youngblood. He was a Black man with a bad eye who lived in Tucson.

David held the photos close to his face when he first looked at them. He had serious astigmatism and had left his glasses in his fifth-grade classroom. He got his glasses and looked at the pictures again. He picked number three: Larry Youngblood. He was "pretty sure" that was the guy. Later, though, he ID'd a different man from the array as his possible assailant.

Based on David's identification, police arrested Youngblood on December 9. Shortly before Christmas, Youngblood was brought to court for a preliminary hearing. David was sitting on a bench with a detective when Youngblood came out of a nearby elevator. He was handcuffed and wearing jail clothes. When David saw him, he asked the detective: "Is that him?"

Youngblood was charged with child molestation, sexual assault, and kidnapping. He insisted he was innocent. He said he'd been asleep at his girlfriend's house at the time of the crime.

The doctor who collected David's samples and swabs—the rape kit—did not examine any of the items. He turned the kit over to police, who placed it in a secure refrigerator. David's clothing was also stored at the station. It was not refrigerated or frozen.

Ten days after the crime, a police criminologist examined the rape kit. On a smear slide from the rectal swab, he detected semen, which meant a sexual assault had occurred. He put the kit back without doing any other analyses on any items. He did not test David's clothing.

After Youngblood's arrest, police seized his four-door 1964 white Chrysler Imperial from the home of Alice Whigham, his erstwhile girlfriend. It was in her backyard, inside a chained gate. They towed the car to the station. Officers took pictures, dusted it for fingerprints, and examined it for hair and clothing fibers. They found nothing linking the car to David.

Unfortunately, Youngblood had not transferred the title to his name when he bought the car, and police disposed of it without giving notice to him or to his lawyer.

Although parts of David's descriptions matched Youngblood and his car, there were many discrepancies. Youngblood was only thirty. He had dry black hair, a sizable scar on his forehead, and a bad *left* eye. He wore laced shoes. He walked with a noticeable limp. David had been satisfied with the police sketch, but it did not look like Youngblood, as he later admitted.

Officers never tested Youngblood's car to see if it—or the radio—was operable. Witnesses subsequently said (1) the car was not running at the time of the crime because of electrical problems; (2) Youngblood had put his car battery into his girlfriend's car; (3) the car started with a screwdriver, not a key; (4) when it ran it was quiet; (5) all four doors opened; and (6) the radio had not worked since he owned the car.

Whigham would later testify that the night of the assault she'd been at her mother's house getting ready for her sister's birthday. She got home just as the ten o'clock news was coming on TV. Youngblood was asleep on her sofa. Her house was a thirty- to forty-five-minute drive from where David had been kidnapped about 9:30 p.m.

But some weeks after the crime, officers had woken Whigham at 4:00 a.m. to ask where Youngblood was "around Halloween." She said he hadn't been with her that night, though he was living in her home at the time. When she learned the date of the assault, October 29, she called police several times to say he had been home then. Her calls were never returned.

Larry Youngblood had no history of pedophilia. His family said he hated country music.

Youngblood went to trial in December 1984. His defense was that David had wrongly identified him as the perpetrator. His lawyer pointed out all the disparities between David's descriptions of his assailant and his car and the actual appearance of Youngblood and his car. Youngblood also offered his alibi.

The police criminologist testified for the state. He said he had done a blood group test on the rectal swab two months earlier. He got nothing.

After hearing the evidence, the jury failed to reach a verdict. They deadlocked 6–6.

In January 1985, the criminologist examined David's clothing for the first time. It was now fifteen months since the assault. None of the items had been refrigerated. He found a semen stain on David's underwear and another on his T-shirt. He tried blood group tests on the stains, but the samples were too deteriorated to provide any results.

At Youngblood's retrial, experts for both sides testified that if the clothing had been examined soon after it was collected, or if it had been properly stored, the semen samples could have yielded blood type results. If the type from the samples didn't match Youngblood's type, he would be exonerated. The judge instructed the jurors that if they found the police had lost or destroyed evidence, they could infer those actions were "against the State's interest."

The second trial took just four days. After deliberating ninety-five minutes, the jury convicted Youngblood on all the charges. The judge imposed concurrent sentences of ten and a half years for each count.

Youngblood steadfastly maintained his innocence. He told the presentence investigator that "any Black man with a bad eye would have been found guilty."

Following his convictions, Youngblood's lawyer asked the Arizona Court of Appeals to dismiss the case against him. His primary claim, based on *Brady*, was that the state had violated his due process rights by failing to preserve crucial evidence.

It was not a textbook *Brady* claim. The specific words of the rule said a defendant was entitled to "evidence favorable to the defense." The evidence at issue here *might* have been favorable. But it was unavailable because the car had been destroyed and because David's clothing hadn't been properly stored.

Youngblood argued that these actions by the police denied him access to helpful, material evidence as surely as if it had been deliberately hidden. *Brady*'s intent was to ensure that justice was done. How could a trial be fair if, due to police malfeasance, a defendant could not obtain and test evidence that could conclusively prove his innocence?

This understanding of *Brady* would require a modest—but logical—expansion of the rule: to say it included a duty to preserve *potentially* favorable evidence.

The state responded that *Brady* didn't apply to this situation. No material information had been withheld. The unavailable evidence might or might not have been helpful to Youngblood. No one could say for sure. The police may have made some inadvertent mistakes, but they never acted in bad faith.

The appellate court agreed with Youngblood.[2] In October 1986, relying on *Brady*, a unanimous three-judge panel held that "dismissal is necessary to avoid an unfair trial." "When . . . the police permit the destruction of evidence that could eliminate a defendant as the perpetrator," they said, "such loss is material to the defense and is a denial of due process."

To support their reasoning, the panel quoted a California rape case saying that "an analysis of the semen sample . . . might have completely exonerated the defendant."[3] In such a situation, police "must take reasonable measures to adequately preserve this evidence."

The judges emphasized that, as in *Brady*, their ruling was not a punishment for the state. Nor was it a presumption of bad faith. It was simply an affirmation of the right to a fair trial.

The panel explained that because they were dismissing the case for failure to preserve the clothing, they did not address the state's "destruction" of Youngblood's car. But in their view "[t]he exculpatory nature of the evidence in the car is clear: It would have corroborated several witnesses' statements and greatly strengthened Youngblood's defense of misidentification."

In March 1987, that decision was upheld when the Arizona Supreme Court declined to review the case.

But Youngblood wasn't home free.

The State appealed, and the U.S. Supreme Court agreed to hear the case. *Arizona v. Youngblood* was argued on October 11, 1988. At issue was whether due process "requires the State to preserve evidentiary material that might be useful to a criminal defendant."

During Arizona's presentation, most of the justices' questions dealt with factual issues: what evidence had or had not been tested, how and when certain testing decisions were made, any test results.[4] The state did not argue that the case should turn on whether the police had acted with or without bad faith.

In grilling Youngblood's lawyer, however, both Chief Justice William Rehnquist and Justice Sandra Day O'Connor focused their queries on the absence of any bad faith. Rehnquist showed where his inclinations lay by asking: "Is the Constitution going to tell prosecutors how they ought to investigate cases?"

These questions were a portent. Seven weeks later, in a 6–3 ruling, the justices reversed the Arizona court decision.[5]

The Court held that "unless a criminal defendant can show bad faith on the part of the police, failure to preserve potentially useful evidence does not constitute a denial of due process of law." Rehnquist, a staunch conservative who had been elevated to chief two years earlier by Ronald Reagan, wrote the majority opinion.

Rehnquist took care to distinguish the facts in Larry Youngblood's case from those in John Brady's case. Boblit's confession had been *clearly* favorable to Brady. Any tests on the degraded semen stains were only *possibly* favorable to Youngblood.

"We think the Due Process Clause requires a different result," he wrote, when the state fails to safeguard evidence that at most "could have been subjected to tests, the results of which might have exonerated the defendant." His characterization of the evidence—it "could" be tested, it "might" be favorable—reflected a belief it was unlikely such evidence would actually help Youngblood.

The chief concern of the majority was not to protect the rights of criminal defendants. It was to avoid putting an undue burden on police. Rehnquist did not believe the "fundamental fairness" requirement of due process imposed "an . . . absolute duty to retain and to preserve all material that might be of conceivable evidentiary significance in a particular prosecution."

Youngblood made bad faith the bright-line test for a constitutional infraction. The opinion argued that requiring an accused to prove bad faith in order to win relief would put "reasonable bounds" on the state's duty to retain evidence. As an example of bad faith, the opinion posited that failing to preserve evidence in a case where "the police themselves . . . indicate that the [unavailable] evidence could form a basis for exonerating the defendant."

Under that yardstick, the court was saying, in essence, that officers themselves could decide the value of a piece of evidence. They would be acting in bad faith only if they deliberately destroyed something they believed could prove a defendant's innocence.

The majority saw the actions—or nonactions—by the police in Youngblood's case as "at worst . . . negligent." No bad faith, no due process violation. The opinion ended by saying "the police do not have a constitutional duty to perform any particular tests."

Justice John Paul Stevens concurred in the judgment only.[6] He was unwilling to join the majority and embrace the Court's new rule. He believed there would be cases in which a defendant could not prove bad faith but the unavailable evidence would be "so critical to the defense as to make a criminal trial fundamentally unfair."

Stevens, a discerning jurist who would drift leftward during his long tenure on the Court, was swayed by the fact that none of the jurors seemed troubled by the state's misconduct. To him, their quick votes to convict Youngblood implied that the unavailable evidence was not material. They must have believed "the other evidence at trial was so overwhelming that it was highly improbable that the lost evidence was exculpatory."

Justice Harry Blackmun wrote a compelling dissent, joined by Justices Marshall and Brennan.[7] "The Constitution requires that criminal defendants be provided with a fair trial," he wrote in his opening line, "not merely a 'good faith' try at a fair trial." "Police ineptitude" had denied Youngblood the chance to present a full defense and had "significantly prejudiced" his case. He deserved a new trial.

Unlike the majority, the dissenters did not target the state of mind of the police. Their focus, as in *Brady*, was on fairness to a defendant and on the import of the unavailable evidence. The claim that bad faith is necessary for a violation of the Due Process Clause "cannot be correct," Blackmun said. "Regardless of intent, police action that results in a defendant's receiving an unfair trial constitutes a deprivation of due process."

The dissent also suggested that the majority's new bright-line rule of bad faith was not all that bright. "The standard 'may well create more questions than it answers,' " Blackmun noted. How would a court decide bad faith? Did it require "actual malice, or would recklessness, or the deliberate failure to establish standards for maintaining and preserving evidence, be sufficient?"

Rather than a bad-faith requirement, the minority offered a different test. "Police must preserve physical evidence of a type that they reasonably should know has the potential, if tested, . . . to exculpate a defendant charged with the crime." They proposed a four-step inquiry to help courts implement that standard.

Applying their test to *Youngblood*, the dissent would have affirmed the decision of the Arizona court. Had the semen on David's clothing been conserved, there was "a genuine possibility" that "results of the testing would exonerate Youngblood." The only evidence implicating him was a ten-year-old boy's tentative, mistake-ridden identification. And police had not only mishandled the clothing evidence, they had also destroyed the evidentiary value of his car by handing it over to a wrecking company.

The minority saw *Youngblood* as a simple case. The prosecution's failure to preserve material evidence had "deprived respondent of a fair trial." The charges had to be dismissed.

Their view did not prevail. But unlike in the great majority of cases, the Supreme Court would not have the last word on Larry Youngblood.

The panel from the Arizona Court of Appeals, and the Supreme Court dissenters, had grounded their opinions on the idea that *potentially* exculpatory evidence should come under *Brady*'s umbrella. It was not a radical notion. Fifteen years earlier, in 1971, the Court of Appeals for DC, the nation's second-most prominent and prestigious court, had endorsed that very concept.

In *U.S. v. Bryant*, federal agents in Washington, DC, somehow lost the tape of a conversation about illegal drug sales.[8] An undercover agent who'd been at the meeting testified for the prosecution at Bryant's trial. He had only limited recall of the discussions. The defense wanted to impeach him with the recording, but it was unavailable. Bryant was convicted.

After discussing *Brady*'s requirements, the U.S. Court of Appeals for the DC Circuit held that

> [t]he duty of disclosure attaches in some form once the Government has first gathered and taken possession of the evidence in question. . . . Hence we hold that before a request for discovery has been made, the duty of disclosure is operative as a duty of *preservation* [emphasis added]. Only if evidence is carefully preserved during the early stages of investigation will disclosure be possible later.

The Supreme Court of California, the highest court in the most populous state, had reached the same conclusion. A 1974 decision, citing *Bryant*, noted "[t]his Court also has recognized the same duty of preservation of evidence required to be disclosed under the due process requirements of *Brady*." [9]

The reasoning of both courts was straightforward. *Brady*'s duty of disclosure would be significantly weakened without an initial duty of preservation. If potentially favorable evidence was lost or destroyed, it could not be divulged or tested. Further, police or prosecutors could avoid disclosure by disposing of evidence before a prosecution began or before the defense asked for it. Defendants could routinely be denied access to evidence that might exonerate them.

But for the *Youngblood* majority, the priority was to minimize any duties imposed on the police. They did not believe the dire consequences predicted by the dissenters would materialize. If the state's good faith ineptitude kept a defendant from obtaining evidence that might prove his innocence, so be it.

Larry Youngblood's case then went back to the Arizona courts, with instructions to resolve it in a manner "not inconsistent with this opinion." Thirteen months later, the Court of Appeals surprised most watchers by reversing his convictions again. [10]

This time the court could not rely on *Brady* for their decision. The Supreme Court had slammed that door shut. Instead, the three-judge panel ruled that Youngblood's due process rights under the Arizona Constitution, as interpreted by state cases, had been violated.

The federal requirements of due process, as dictated by the Supreme Court, apply to the states through the Fourteenth Amendment. But those standards are a floor, not a ceiling. State courts cannot restrict them, but they can expand them. That was precisely what the Arizona court did.

The opinion echoed the views of the *Youngblood* dissenters. "The evidence destroyed by the state," the judges said, "is gone forever. He can no longer get a fair trial on these charges. This is not a case of harmless error, where the evidence against the accused was otherwise overwhelming." Accordingly, the case "requires dismissal."

The Arizona Supreme Court did not agree.[11] Adopting some of the language of the U.S. Supreme Court, in January of 1993, a divided court reinstated Youngblood's convictions. The majority asserted Youngblood had not been denied due process because "there is no evidence to suggest bad faith on the part of the police. Nor has there been any showing of prejudice in fact."

But then there was.

As his case bounced around the courts, Larry Youngblood had been in and out of prison. After he was found guilty in early 1984, he'd begun his sentence. Nearly three years later, he was released when the Arizona Court of Appeals dismissed his convictions. Though the U.S. Supreme Court reversed that ruling in 1988, he remained free while his case was being reconsidered.

He went back inside when the Arizona Supreme Court reinstated his convictions in early 1993. After serving almost eight years in total, he was paroled in 1998. The next year he was in prison again. He hadn't done another crime. His sometime girlfriend had put him out of her house, and he violated parole by failing to notify the state of his change of address.

Youngblood's trial lawyer, Carol Wittels, had always believed in his innocence. After his last re-arrest, she asked her attorney husband, Scott McNamara, to help represent him. Knowing that DNA technology had improved dramatically since the early 1980s, in 2000 they petitioned for testing on the small quantity of semen that had not been spoiled back in 1983.

The state consented to a test—with conditions. Youngblood would have to promise the Tucson City Attorney, the Tucson Police Department, and the Arizona Department of Corrections he would not sue for damages based on the test results. Despite their confident claims of his guilt, the authorities were taking no chances. Absent any options, Youngblood signed a release.

The results of a new, more sophisticated test showed Larry Youngblood could not have been the source of the semen from David's clothes. On August 9, 2000, prosecutors told the court Youngblood was factually innocent, and he was released. The case was finally done.

In its motion to set aside Youngblood's convictions, the prosecution insisted it had done nothing wrong. "The State sought the . . . conviction of the defendant on these charges on the best evidence available at the time." They did not mention that police mistakes had made the most crucial evidence unavailable.

The DNA profile recovered from the semen on David's clothes was put into a national database of convicted offenders. The next year, police matched it to a man named Walter Calvin Cruise. He was serving time in Texas for a cocaine-related conviction.

Cruise was Black, with a misshapen blind left eye. He had two convictions for child sex abuse in Houston, both prior to the rape of David Leon. He'd also been arrested in Tucson for similar charges. There was no doubt he was the right man.

In August 2002, Cruise was brought to Arizona from his Texas prison. He pled guilty to the sexual assault of David Leon. He was sentenced to twenty-four years in prison. He told the court he had no idea another man had been convicted for a crime he'd committed.

Youngblood did not come to court to see Cruise's sentencing, despite an invitation from his lawyer. He told a *New York Times* reporter, "I am angry. . . . For 17 years, I knew I was innocent. . . . They took the best years of my life." [12]

Youngblood spent his last years in Tucson, homeless and panhandling on the streets. Not quite seven years after his exoneration, in July 2007, he died of a drug overdose.

He was not the only victim of the police's mishandling of the evidence. David Leon's rage at the actual perpetrator only deepened when he learned he had identified the wrong man. At Cruise's sentencing, David's sister told the judge, "I . . . wasted most of my life hating Larry Youngblood. We, without options, were given life sentences."

The rape left David feeling, in his words, "dirty and useless." As a young man, he was in and out of jail, usually on assault charges related to his anger issues. He struggled with drugs and alcohol. In 2004, while intoxicated, he was killed by a train near downtown Tucson. It was never clear if his death was suicide or an accident. He was thirty.

The tragic saga of *Youngblood* should have been a warning to the Supreme Court. Rulings on *Brady* matters are not mere legal decisions that change the outcome of cases. They change lives, for better or worse. The justices' desire to make sure they did not overburden police—however inept officers might have been—took a serious toll in this case alone.

The majority's callous mistake regarding Larry Youngblood's guilt didn't just steal his best years and smear his name. It also helped ruin the life of David Leon and his family.

But the Court never apologizes. This abiding love of finality by the legal system is another reason why *Brady* has been so ineffectual. Finding a violation requires the justices to acknowledge a serious error and to overturn a settled case. Whenever possible, despite the human cost, they avoid that option.

In the years since *Youngblood*, the majority opinion has been regularly derided by legal analysts for its flawed reasoning. Before that decision "virtually no state or federal court held that subjective bad faith on the part of police was required to find a fundamental fairness violation of the federal or state constitutions."[13] The state of mind of the police had been just one factor to consider in deciding whether there had been a denial of due process, along with such things as the nature of the evidence in question and its importance to the case.

Youngblood made bad faith the sole touchstone for due process analysis, despite the lack of any precedent. Rehnquist could not cite a single case to support his position that "the state's good faith precluded an analysis of the materiality of the evidence" at issue.[14] As Daniel R. Dinger put it in the *American Journal of Criminal Law*: "The majority opinion in *Youngblood v. Arizona* created a rule with no basis in historical or legal precedent."[15]

The best Rehnquist could do was make the debatable claim that decisions in "related areas have stressed the importance . . . of good or bad faith." But the two supposedly similar cases he named in his opinion concerned preindictment delays caused by state actions. Neither had anything to do with lost or mishandled evidence.

Since *Youngblood*, at least ten state courts have rejected its holding and have provided greater due process protections to criminal defendants.[16] These states have interpreted their constitutions to require that police and prosecutors preserve potentially exculpatory material evidence.

Despite its flaws, *Youngblood* remains the law.

The Arizona Court of Appeals had it right: *Youngblood* should have been a *Brady* decision. It wasn't. The Supreme Court majority simply did not want to broaden the rule's reach. Their ruling, and the reasoning behind it, would have a major impact on the course of *Brady*.

On its face, the opinion was a simple refusal to expand *Brady* to include possibly exculpatory evidence. A closer look shows it was a full-bore rejection of the rule's underlying principle.

Brady's foundation was the belief that "our system . . . of justice suffers when any accused is treated unfairly." In line with that precept, its test for a possible due process violation focused on the outcome. How had the state's behavior impacted the case? Regardless of intent, if actions by the police or prosecution resulted in an unfair trial, due process had been denied.

In contrast, the credo of the *Youngblood* majority was that imposing an "absolute duty" on the state to preserve potentially favorable evidence would be too great a burden. Their first concern was fairness to the police and the prosecution, not fairness to a defendant. The single determinant for a due process violation was whether the state had acted in bad faith.

Youngblood did not overrule *Brady*. But the questionable legal basis for the opinion weakened the rule by undermining its foundation. It also sent a clear signal that conservatives on the high court were determined to make sure *Brady* was a narrow remedy, giving relief only in cases of nondisclosure of patently favorable, material information.

In 1993, as *Brady* entered its fourth decade, there was little reason to hope a future case, decided by other justices, might push the rule in a different direction.

On the afternoon of January 5, 1990, nineteen-year-old Leanne Whitlock borrowed her boyfriend's blue Mercury Lynx.[17] Whitlock was a sophomore at James Madison University in Harrisonburg, Virginia. Her boyfriend, John Dean, worked at the nearby Valley Mall. At about 6:30 p.m., she left her apartment to take the car back to Dean at the mall.

Whitlock never returned the Lynx. Around 7:30 p.m., a witness saw the car some twenty-five miles south of Harrisonburg, in Augusta County. He later testified the car was muddy and he had seen it turn off the main road onto a small dirt road.

At about 9:00 p.m. that night, Tommy David Strickler and Ronald Henderson walked into Dice's Inn, a bar in nearby Staunton, Virginia. The two men stayed for at least four hours, drinking and dancing with several women. Strickler eventually left the bar in the blue Lynx with a woman named Donna Kay

Tudor. The two spent the next few days together, mostly in Virginia Beach.

They abandoned the car when they returned to Augusta County. Police discovered the Lynx on January 11 and identified it as Dean's. Inside was a jacket with ID papers belonging to Henderson. Officers found fingerprints from Strickler and Tudor on the car and arrested both.

Two days later, a farmer found Henderson's wallet in a cornfield, not far from where the witness had seen the Lynx. In a search of the area, officers discovered Whitlock's frozen, nude body under two logs in some woods. A sixty-nine-pound rock, spotted with blood, was lying next to her. An autopsy showed the cause of death was "multiple blunt force injuries to the head."

At his trial in May 1990, Strickler admitted taking part in the crime but said Henderson did the actual killing. Strickler was found guilty of abduction, robbery, and capital murder. On the recommendation of the jury, he was sentenced to death.

Ronald Henderson fled from Virginia after the killing and was later captured in Oregon. In March 1991, he was tried and found guilty of the same charges.[18] He was given three life sentences.

The star witness at Strickler's trial was a woman named Anne Stoltzfus. She testified in vivid detail about seeing Strickler and Henderson two different times at the Valley Mall on January 5, 1990, and then watching them kidnap Whitlock in the parking lot.

Stoltzfus told the jurors she and her daughter were in the Music Land store looking for a CD when Strickler, Henderson, and a blond woman came in. Stoltzfus called Strickler "Mountain Man" for his size, facial hair, and "multi-layer look." Henderson was "Shy Guy," based on his demeanor. "Blond Girl" had "blue eyes, a real sweet smile, kind of a small mouth."

Stoltzfus said that inside the store, Mountain Man was acting "revved up." He made her feel uneasy, so she left. A few minutes later, she passed the three as they were exiting the mall. She was so troubled by Mountain Man's behavior that she tried to follow. But she lost them.

Stoltzfus testified that as she and her daughter were leaving the mall, they saw a shiny blue car. The young Black woman driving it was "beautiful," "happy," and "singing." When the car stopped at a stop sign, "Mountain Man came tearing out of the Mall entrance door," looking "just really mad." He ran to the car, pulled the passenger door open, and jumped in the front seat. Shy Guy and Blond Girl got in the back seat.

Stoltzfus said she pulled up next to the Lynx and looked over. Mountain Man was hitting the driver, who seemed "frozen." The driver mouthed the word "help." As the blue car headed out of the mall, Stoltzfus followed briefly. Then she went home. Her "gas tank was empty" and she had "three kids . . . waiting for supper."

On the stand, Stoltzfus identified Whitlock from a picture as the driver of the blue car. She pointed to Strickler as the person she called Mountain Man. When asked if publicity about the killing had influenced her identifications, she said "absolutely not." "I have an exceptionally good memory," she told the jurors. "I had very close contact with [Mountain Man] and he made an emotional impression with me . . . So I have absolutely no doubt of my identification."

As proof of her excellent memory, she recited the license number of the Lynx without hesitation: "West Virginia NKA 243."

Anne Stoltzfus was the only eyewitness to testify about Whitlock's abduction. Her dramatic, detailed story—the product of her apparently superb recall—was the heart of the prosecution's case. She painted Strickler as a wild, dangerous man, the ringleader of the entire horrific crime.

The truth was rather different from her bold claims.

Stoltzfus had not called police the night of the crime. Or ever.

Twelve days later, she mentioned the incident to some friends.

One of them contacted the police. An officer came to Stoltzfus's home. On January 19, two weeks after the murder, she went to the station for the first time and spoke with Harrisonburg police detective Daniel Claytor. Over the next few months, he interviewed her four more times, and she wrote him several letters.

Details in Claytor's notes and Stoltzfus's letters contradicted most of her trial testimony. Initially, she could not recall even being at the mall on January 5, until "my 14-year-old daughter Katie . . . helped me [jog] my memory." She could not pick either Strickler or Henderson out of photo lineups, despite claiming later she was 100 percent certain of her identifications of them.

Similarly, she did not recognize Leanne Whitlock until she spent several hours "looking at current photos" of her with Dean, Whitlock's boyfriend—a fact she never mentioned in her trial testimony. At the trial she ID'd Whitlock "beyond a shadow of a doubt." And her description had expanded to include Whitlock's clothing and demeanor.

As for the abduction, Stoltzfus said she first "totally wrote this off as a trivial episode of college kids carrying on." Then she told Claytor: "I have a very vague memory that I'm not sure of." She described a "wild guy" running up to a bus as it pulled off, then someone "running up to the black girl's window." In a postscript she added that her daughter "doesn't remember seeing the 3 people get into the black girl's car."

Stoltzfus later sent a note to Claytor with a long description of the Lynx. But she never mentioned the license plate she so proudly recalled at the trial. Overall, she thanked the detective for his "patience with my sometimes-muddled memories." She avowed that if her friend hadn't called the police, "I never would have made any of the associations that you helped me make."

Prior to Strickler's trial, the prosecutor told the defense there was no need to file a motion for discovery, or for *Brady* material, because he had an open-file policy. He subsequently claimed, under oath, that he had shown his "entire prosecution file to Strickler's defense counsel."

Somehow, most of these Stoltzfus materials never made it into the prosecutor's files. Strickler's lead defense counsel later testified he had never seen any of them.

Strickler appealed his convictions in the Virginia courts, without success.

In March 1996 he filed an appeal in federal district court. His new defense team got an order allowing them to examine and copy all the police and prosecution materials related to his case. Their review led to the discovery of the previously unknown Stoltzfus exhibits.

Armed with this new information, Strickler argued—for the first time—that his convictions should be reversed because the prosecutor had violated *Brady*. After reviewing all the filings, Judge Robert Merhige Jr. agreed. He ruled that—as a matter of law—the undisclosed items were material. The prosecutor's failure to disclose them undermined confidence in the jury's verdict.

"[Stoltzfus's] memory of the events to which she testified appears muddled at best," he wrote.[19] "This information, at a minimum, would likely have been extremely valuable in attacking her credibility with the jury." He even suggested that because the materials "contradicted or impeached her trial testimony in so many crucial aspects," her entire testimony might have been barred.

Judge Merhige vacated Strickler's convictions and death sentence and ordered a new trial.

But Strickler's victory was short-lived. In June 1998, a three-judge panel of the Fourth Circuit Court of Appeals reversed the lower court ruling.[20] In their opinion, the undisclosed Stoltzfus evidence didn't come close to being material. That information, they said, "would have provided little or no help to Strickler in either the guilt or sentencing phases of the trial." The prosecution's failure to divulge the information did not give them any doubts about the verdict.

Strickler appealed their ruling, and the Supreme Court agreed to hear his case.

Based on the *Bagley* decision thirteen years earlier, the Court now had a standard framework for deciding *Brady* claims. Three factors were necessary for a reversal: (1) the evidence at issue must be favorable to an accused; (2) the evidence must have been suppressed by the state, either willfully or inadvertently; and (3) the withheld evidence must be "material."

The first two steps were fairly simple. But the third step, deciding whether the evidence was material, was anything but. The definition adopted in *Bagley*—evidence was material "if there is a reasonable probability that, had [it] been disclosed to the defense, the result of the proceeding would have been different"—had proven to be quite resilient. It had also, as Justice Marshall warned in his dissent, proven to be quite elusive.

For starters, *Bagley* hadn't really defined "material." Rather, the opinion proffered only an outcome-based determination. It required a prosecutor to decide, before a trial, what evidence—if withheld—might later be deemed to have made the trial unfair. It required a court to decide, often long after a trial, what impact the evidence might have had. And "reasonable probability" was always a judgment call. It depended as much on the judge as on the facts.

Even after repeated efforts, the Court had been unable to agree on a clearer formulation. The *Bagley* test persisted, despite often leading to confusing, conflicting results. In the legal realm, where clarity and predictability are prized, *Brady* rulings had become remarkable for their inconsistency and uncertainty. *Strickler* would be another prime example.

In June 1999 the Supreme Court upheld the Fourth Circuit decision in a 7–2 ruling.[21]

In his majority opinion, Justice John Paul Stevens acknowledged the enduring problem of deciding whether evidence was material. "The differing judgments of the District Court and the Court of Appeals attest to the difficulty of resolving the issue" of materiality.[22] The high court then proceeded to demonstrate just how hard it was by disagreeing with both lower courts.

The justices faulted the Fourth Circuit panel for claiming that the Stoltzfus information would have been of "little or no help to Strickler." "Without a doubt," Stevens wrote, "Stoltzfus's testimony was prejudicial." It made Strickler's conviction more likely than if Stoltzfus had not testified. The court went so far as to say that "discrediting her testimony might have changed the outcome of the trial."

But the majority also concluded that the district court had made the Stoltzfus evidence *too* important. That court, they agreed, "was surely correct that there is a reasonable *possibility* that . . . a substantial discount of Stoltzfus's testimony might have produced" a different verdict at the trial. But the necessary standard was a "reasonable *probability* of a different result." And they found "strong support" in the record to conclude Strickler would have been convicted of murder and sentenced to death even if Stoltzfus had been "severely impeached."

Strickler had satisfied the first two parts of a *Brady* violation. The prosecution had withheld evidence that was clearly favorable to him. But he had narrowly failed to meet the third. By the difference between *possible* and *probable*, he had not shown the evidence was material.

His convictions and sentence stood.

Justice David Souter wrote a biting dissent and was joined in part by Justice Anthony Kennedy.[23]

Souter called the "reasonable probability" standard "familiarly deceptive." Using the word "probability," he said, risked "treating it as akin to the higher standard, 'more likely than not,' " because that was how the word was used in other legal contexts. He suggested replacing "reasonable probability" with "significant possibility."

He believed that term would make it easier for appellants to prove materiality.

Justice Souter did not believe the withheld evidence would likely have changed the verdict. But it might well have changed the punishment. "I cannot," he wrote, "accept the Court's discount" of Stoltzfus's testimony as regards the sentencing calculus, based on "the undeniable narrative force of what she said."

> Her evidence presented a gripping story. . . . Its message was that Strickler was the madly energetic leader of two morally apathetic accomplices, who were passive but for his direction. One cannot be reasonably confident that not a single juror would have had a different perspective after an impeachment that would have destroyed the credibility of that story.[24]

The ruling was announced on June 17, 1999. Despite the issues around the case, Virginia moved quickly. Strickler was executed by lethal injection at the Greensville Correctional Center in Jarratt just five weeks later, on July 21.[25]

Tommy David Strickler didn't deserve sympathy.

He admitted he took part in the cruel, vicious murder of Leanne Whitlock. Aside from Anne Stoltzfus's testimony, there was independent evidence—such as his fingerprints in the car Whitlock had been driving—that confirmed his involvement. What he did deserve, like every criminal defendant, was a fair trial with honest evidence. And he did not get that.

Stoltzfus's story was the heart and soul of the prosecution's case. Strickler's quick conviction and death sentence were fueled by her riveting testimony. Nearly everything she said in court was dubious, based on her own words to Detective Claytor. From the nicknames she gave the accused to the tales she told, her strong suit was clearly creativity, not accuracy.

The federal judge who first reviewed the case believed that

Stoltzfus's undisclosed admissions made her credibility nil. In his view, the state's serious *Brady* violations required him to vacate Strickler's convictions and sentence without even holding a hearing.

Yet a unanimous panel of the Fourth Circuit Court of Appeals ruled that the entire body of withheld evidence was immaterial. They found no *Brady* violations whatsoever. And a divided Supreme Court, for different reasons, agreed.

The *Strickler* opinions laid bare how "impossible"—to use Justice Marshall's word—the materiality standard now was.[26] Three courts looked at the same evidence. Each one reached a different conclusion on what impact the hidden information might have had on the trial.

In this case, as in many others, even experienced judges—with the benefit of hindsight, with the entire trial record available, with time for reflection—could not agree on whether certain evidence was material. So why do we think prosecutors can make such judgments correctly? They must decide, before any trial, with limited knowledge, under time and work pressure, if some piece of information is or isn't *Brady*.

It's crazy to expect a procedure like that to work well.

In hindsight, the *Brady* rule was likely doomed from the start.

It was a new rule for a new, cooperative day. But that day never dawned. The combative nature of our criminal legal system was more entrenched than Justice Douglas knew. No judicial decision, by itself, could transform a well-established, competitive process into a joint search for truth and fairness. Or turn former opponents into teammates.

Once the *Agurs* court affirmed that *Brady* was not a broad discovery mandate but a very limited disclosure rule, the adversarial system remained intact. The two sides were not going to sit down, exchange information, and settle a case together. They would continue to battle.

And while *Brady* didn't change the duty of prosecutors to zealously prosecute criminals, it did require them to share favorable evidence with the defense. That often made it harder to earn convictions. Of course they didn't like the rule. They're human. They wanted to win.

Ideally, they're supposed to believe that "society wins" whenever an accused is treated fairly. Regardless of guilt or innocence. But in an adversarial system, that's not easy to do. As things stand, prosecutors equate justice with guilty verdicts. For them, *Brady* is not a boon to fairness. It is a block to justice.

In this climate, the only way the rule *might* have worked was if an ongoing Supreme Court majority made sure its requirements were clearly defined and consistently enforced.

The Court did the opposite.

The justices' imprecise definition of materiality in *Bagley* and its offspring made *Brady* decisions complicated and confusing for even the most conscientious prosecutors. At the same time, their lax enforcement made it enticing for prosecutors to withhold exculpatory information, knowing they would likely pay no price.

In theory, at least, a prosecutor's *Brady* obligations were meant to be plain. They were to disclose any evidence that was favorable to the defense. Period.

Prosecutors were also admonished to be generous in fulfilling this mandate. As the *Agurs* court noted, since decisions about the value and use of evidence are "inevitably imprecise, . . . the prudent prosecutor will resolve doubtful questions in favor of disclosure."[27]

If a prosecutor failed his *Brady* obligations by withholding favorable information, a reviewing court would decide whether any of that evidence was material. If it was, there was a constitutional violation. The appellant was entitled to relief.

If the court said the undisclosed information was not material, however, the judgment stood. Such a ruling did not mean the prosecutor had complied with *Brady* or that his transgression should be excused. It meant only that the breach was not constitutional.

That was how the rule was intended to work.

Two things transformed this process into a godsend for prosecutors who wanted to evade the rule's demands. First, the Court continued to endorse a slippery, malleable definition of materiality that could support almost any decision. Second, it failed to clearly distinguish a prosecutor's pretrial *Brady* obligation from a judge's posttrial decision about materiality.

Prosecutors exploited these lapses to devise and justify a procedure for evaluating evidence that seemed to honor *Brady* but was contrary to the rule's intent. When they turned up potentially favorable evidence, instead of disclosing it, they questioned it. Where did the information come from? Did it seem credible to them? Was the source reliable? Did *they* believe it? Would it make a difference in the outcome of the case if they handed it over?

In short, they asked themselves whether the evidence was "material." If, on their own, they decided it wasn't, they could rationalize withholding it from the defense.

Prosecutors were specifically not supposed to evaluate evidence that way. They were not supposed to judge whether information was material. There was supposed to be a careful distinction between their pretrial duty to share all favorable evidence, and a court's posttrial ruling on whether any evidence that had been withheld was material.

As the DC Court of Appeals (DCCA) explained: "It is not for the prosecutor to decide not to disclose information that is on its face exculpatory based on an assessment of how that evidence might be explained away or discredited at trial, or ultimately rejected by the fact-finder." [28]

In a 2011 *Brady*-related argument, several Supreme Court justices—including conservatives Antonin Scalia and Anthony

Kennedy—emphasized this crucial difference. They directly reproved a prosecutor who said her office made disclosure decisions based not just on whether the information was exculpatory but also on whether they believed it was material.

"[W]ith all respect," Kennedy said, "[y]ou don't determine your *Brady* obligation by the test for the *Brady* violation. You're transposing two very different things. And so, that's incorrect."[29] Their obligation was to disclose all favorable evidence. The test for a violation—to be applied only by a court—was to decide whether any undisclosed evidence was material.

But prosecutors have continued to merge these "two very different things" because the Court never wrote this distinction into law. Nor did they punish prosecutors who knowingly conflated the two. In many offices this procedure has become standard. Before disclosing any exculpatory evidence to the defense, prosecutors assume the role of judge, do a solo review, and withhold favorable information if they alone believe the evidence isn't material.

In *Strickler,* Justice Stevens seemingly blessed this illicit practice.[30] He wrote that "[s]trictly speaking there is never a real '*Brady* violation' unless the nondisclosure was so serious that there is a reasonable probability that the suppressed evidence would have produced a different verdict."

Almost certainly that was not his intent. He had earlier emphasized that prosecutors have a "broad duty of disclosure." Even when the outcome of a trial may not be unjust, he said, withholding favorable evidence is still a "breach of the broad obligation to disclose" this type of information. Such behavior does not comport with the rule. It is cheating.

Nevertheless, prosecutors seized on his use of the word "real" to say that withholding favorable evidence, if they deemed it immaterial, was not a "real" *Brady* violation. In fact, it was no violation at all, except in those rare cases when a court later said the evidence was material.

That's precisely how prosecutor Jerry Goren handled the

exculpatory evidence in the Fuller case. And later, in defending his actions, the Office of the Solicitor General would follow his lead and deliberately conflate those "very different" roles of disclosing favorable information and deciding materiality.

As Bidish Sarma, an assistant district attorney in the Orleans Parish civil rights division, explained:

> Although there is no dispute that the [Fuller] prosecution failed to turn over several categories of exculpatory evidence, the Government's brief on the merits states '[t]he government complied with its obligations under *Brady*. . . . Nondisclosures violate *Brady* only when withheld information is both favorable and material.' See how easily the Government elides that distinction between a *Brady* obligation and a *Brady* violation.[31]

In the years that followed, *Strickler* proved to be no outlier. Quite the contrary. It neatly illustrated how the rule would typically be applied. *Brady* claims would play out in court as a predictable farce, with a common series of scenes and a predetermined ending.

Here's how it would go: Prosecutors would find favorable information they didn't want to disclose, usually because it could hurt their case. They might deliberately ignore the rule. More likely they would convince themselves the evidence wasn't really material. They would withhold it. There would be a trial, and the defendant would be convicted.

Then—often months or years later—the hidden information would come to light. The convicted person would ask for relief under *Brady*, arguing that the nondisclosure made the trial unfair. The government would reply that the evidence at issue was overlooked or misunderstood or irrelevant. But no matter. It wasn't material. It would have made no difference in the verdict.

A court would consider the *Brady* claim. The appellant would present the buried evidence and plead for a new trial. The prosecution would defend the conviction, often saying "sorry" for the mistake/poor judgment/oversight, and would promise to do better next time.

After reviewing the record, the court would find that the undisclosed evidence *was* favorable to the defense. It *should* have been handed over. The prosecution had failed its *Brady* obligations and might get a scolding. But in the end, maybe with a tone of reluctance, the judge would side with the government. The evidence wasn't material. The verdict would stand. The prosecutor got no punishment. The appellant got no relief.

That scenario plays out regularly in courts across the country.

A joint study from the National Association of Criminal Defense Lawyers (NACDL) and the VERITAS Initiative of Santa Clara University School of Law, a program designed to "advance the integrity of the criminal justice system through research," quantified just how common this story line is.[32]

Together, the organizations analyzed a random sample of *Brady* claims litigated in federal courts between August 2007 and August 2012. They detailed their findings in a report titled *Material Indifference*. While court decisions on the materiality of *Brady* claims were often random and arbitrary, the rulings skewed strongly in one direction: toward the government.

In this five-year period, the defense won just 21 rulings out of 145 cases where the state violated its *Brady* obligations by failing to disclose information a judge later said was favorable to the defendant. Eighty-six percent of the time, after finding that a prosecutor had concealed evidence that should have been shared, the court excused the breach by saying the information wasn't material.

This default position for courts handling *Brady* litigation serves two purposes: It lets prosecutors appear to be embracing the rule, and it lets judges appear to be enforcing it. In reality, it means that when prosecutors fail to meet their *Brady* obligations, courts routinely allow them to do so with impunity.

The report's conclusion was not hopeful.

> This study provides empirical support for the conclusion that the manner in which courts review *Brady* claims has the result, intentional or not, of discouraging disclosure of favorable information. . . . Courts are impeding fair disclosure in criminal cases, and in so doing, encouraging prosecutors to disclose as little favorable information as possible.[33]

By keeping the *Brady* rule both narrow and confusing, by excusing the great majority of nondisclosures as immaterial, and by seldom punishing even the worst violations, judges have allowed—and enabled—injustice.

That's how, over time, the principle intended to promote fairness mutated into a muddled process that does the opposite.

6

THE LARGEST MURDER
TRIAL IN DC HISTORY

The Fuller murder trial began on October 16, 1985, a warm
Washington, DC, day.

Presiding was Robert M. Scott, a sixty-three-year-old white
midwesterner who'd been a judge in DC Superior Court since
1977.[1] Ten people were charged with first-degree murder for a
crime that—even in the official version—lacked premeditation
and deliberation. Both acts are usually required for a conviction.
How could that stand?

The answer lies in the felony murder rule. DC, like many states,
had broadened the definition of first-degree murder through this
tenet. It holds that any killing in the course of certain felonies,
even if accidental, becomes first-degree murder. Anyone who par-
ticipates in such a felony is liable for a death that occurs during the
crime.

The rule dates to the sixteenth century. In 1573, an Englishman
named John Saunders decided to kill his wife so he could marry
another woman.[2] He gave his wife a baked apple he had poisoned
with roseacre, an early derivative of arsenic.

After taking one bite, Saunders's wife passed the apple to their
hungry three-year-old daughter. The girl ate it and died. The judges
reasoned that although he did not mean to kill his child, Saunders's malicious intent could be transferred from his intended victim to his actual victim. That made him guilty of the first-degree
murder of his daughter.

This concept of transferred intent became the legal basis for the felony murder rule. The intent to commit a felony becomes the intent to commit a killing that occurs during that felony. Under DC law, any killing during an arson, rape, robbery, or kidnapping is legally considered felony murder.

It didn't matter whether the defendants had planned or intended to kill Fuller. If they had played any part in the robbery, the rule made them guilty of first-degree murder.

Jury selection took four days to complete. It was now thirteen months since Catherine Fuller had been killed. Six women and six men—all Blacks—would decide the fate of those accused of her murder.

The prosecution always leads off with opening statements. Jerry Goren was ready to spotlight his powerful narrative.

"It was the first of the month," he began.[3] On this rainy, "unseasonably cold" Monday, October 1, 1984, Catherine Fuller went out around 4:30 p.m. to do some shopping. The defendants were in the park, "playing and joking and . . . singing Chuck Brown's song about money, getting paid." The talk turned to robbery. They saw Fuller, and someone said, "She's got big money." They crossed the street and attacked her.

Goren described the assault in three stages. As Fuller went up 8th Street, Levy and Fella grabbed her from behind and pushed her into the alley. The others joined in. One after another, the men hit her, and "she fell to the ground." They picked her up and carried her to the middle of the alley by a garage. The attack continued, despite her screams for help. Finally, she was dragged into the garage, sodomized with a pipe-like object, and left to die.

At this point in a typical trial, defense attorneys tell their story of the case in an opening statement, an alternative version of events in which their client is not guilty. This gives jurors something to consider as the prosecution presents its narrative and—hopefully—helps them keep an open mind as to the facts.

But despite the requirements of *Brady*, prior to the trial Goren had decided to withhold three key pieces of favorable evidence from the defense: Ammie Davis's report of James Blue's attack on Fuller, Willie Luchie's statement about his walk through the alley, and the three identifications of James McMillian at the crime scene.

The effect of Goren's nondisclosures now became clear. The defense had no counter to his graphic opening. Goren had kept hidden the facts that could have given the accused a credible story of innocence to oppose the prosecution's gripping story of guilt. All they could offer were their shaky alibi claims.

Five of the defense attorneys opted to give statements after the prosecution's opening.[4] They agreed the killing was horrific, but they each said their client played no part in it. All of them noted that no physical evidence linked any of the defendants to the murder.

Their brief openings illustrated two serious problems that would plague the defense throughout the trial. Monk's lawyer, Michele Roberts, directly credited the prosecution's basic story. She said the evidence would show there were "other crew members who participated in the killing," some of whom "admitted their involvement." With claims like this, she and other defense lawyers became what trial attorneys call "second prosecutors," because their arguments help the government make its case against their client's codefendants.

The other problem was inherent in any alibi defense. The only evidence that's directly relevant to your case is identification testimony. If your client wasn't there and played no part in the crime, it doesn't matter what happened or how it happened.

Bobo's lawyer summed things up neatly when he said: "The [only] issue for Russell Overton is was he present?" As a result, "many of the things in evidence we're not contesting." He told the jurors he wouldn't: "waste your time . . . examining witnesses as to which there is no issue."

This meant that at literally dozens of points during the trial, gaps in the government's case would not be explored, inconsistencies would be ignored, mistakes would be passed over. By asserting alibis, the defendants' lawyers gave up their chance to point out the many serious questions about the credibility of key witnesses and the major contradictions in their stories. The prosecution's narrative would essentially go unchallenged.

The first witnesses were brief.[5] Detective McGinnis described getting the radio call about the murder, going to the alley, and seeing Fuller in the garage. He identified pictures and diagrams of the area.

Patrick Curtis, a police evidence technician, took the stand to detail the recovery of Fuller's raincoat, umbrella, and scarf from the alley on the afternoon of October 2. His short testimony seemed inconsequential. There was virtually no cross-examination. But the condition and the location of these items raised major questions about the government's story.

Fuller's umbrella was broken and the spokes were crooked. Inside the umbrella was a Velicoff Vodka bottle and the detached liquor tax stamp. The raincoat was neatly folded.

The empty half-pint bottle and the torn tax stamp meant Fuller had drunk her vodka in the alley. That would explain her high blood alcohol concentration at the time of death. But it wouldn't fit at all with a gang attack starting on 8th Street as Fuller walked home from shopping.

Barbara Wade, Fuller's sister, had said the spokes of the umbrella "were all bent up like she had been trying to fight with it."[6] How did it get damaged? None of the alleged eyewitnesses said anything about Fuller having an umbrella during the attack or using it to defend herself.

And what of the "neatly folded" raincoat? After a violent group assault, with kicking and punching and dragging and worse, no assailant would take time to carefully fold Fuller's clothing. Her jeans and underwear and pantyhose were scattered around the body in the garage. The folded raincoat, the bent umbrella, and the empty vodka bottle all suggest a crime scenario very different from the one the prosecutor had just detailed.

In addition, these items were in a nook near the 9th Street end of the alley, about 150 feet from the garage. Goren, and all his witnesses, would say Fuller was attacked at the opposite end, the 8th Street end, then carried to the garage. No one would say she was ever forced into the half of the alley between the garage and 9th Street. If the official story was correct, her raincoat, umbrella, and scarf would not have been found near 9th Street.

None of the defense lawyers raised any of those issues because they weren't relevant to an alibi defense. But they had everything to do with whether the official story was true, whether the defendants were guilty as charged.

William Freeman, the vendor, testified that when he went to urinate and found Fuller's body, he did not see the "two dudes."[7] They were by the garage when he went back to wait for the police. They ran up the side alley toward I Street when the squad car arrived.

Before cross-examination, the defense lawyers requested a break to ask Goren about any identifications Freeman had made of the two men. Goren argued no disclosure was required.[8] He told the judge—wrongly, as he would later concede—that the two were in the alley "one and a half hours after" Fuller was killed.

"It didn't seem to me that that was *Brady* in any way," he said.[9] He even refused to confirm whether the government had done any ID procedures with Freeman. Having decided to withhold this information, he was fighting to keep it hidden.

Neither the judge nor the defense lawyers realized what was at stake. Only Goren did. Disclosing that Freeman—and two other witnesses—had identified the runners as James McMillian and an associate would give the defense a plausible alternative to his gang theory. Even at this late date, it could have changed the course of the entire case.

After hearing brief arguments, Judge Scott wasn't sure Goren was correct. But he had a full courtroom and a jury waiting. His primary concern at that moment was efficiency; he wanted to keep things moving.[10] He didn't want to take the time to resolve a legal dispute about *Brady*. And he was willing to believe Goren's promise to consult with him if he had any uncertainties.

So Scott told the lawyers, "We'll take that up later."[11] They never did.

Freeman's stand was just a few steps from the 8th Street entrance to the alley. On cross-examination, he looked at each of the defendants and confirmed he didn't see a single one of them at any time on the day of the murder. He heard no shouts, no cries for help, no sounds of fighting in the nearby alley. And he said no one in the park, just across 8th Street, was playing a boom box and singing, "Let's get paid."[12]

If Fuller and the young men who supposedly followed her had gone into the alley from 8th Street, as the government claimed, they would have passed by Freeman's stand. The whole gang scenario had to have happened all around him without him seeing or hearing anything.

At the end of the trial, coverage in the *Washington Times* would raise that very point. How, reporter Michael Hedges would ask, could Mrs. Fuller "be struck down on a drizzly afternoon within sight of dozens of her neighbors" with no one noticing?[13] This question, he said, was "never sufficiently answered by witnesses describing the killing during the trial."

The government called its first apparent eyewitness to the crime— Derrick Bennett—on November 5. He'd agreed to testify against the others in exchange for a sweet deal. Now it was time to pay up.

The *Post* said Derrick looked "drawn and pained" as he

testified.[14] He talked so softly Judge Scott had to ask him over and over to speak up. He often had to repeat his answers. But he implicated every one of the accused except Cliff Yarborough, and he sketched, in considerable detail, the picture the government wanted to put before the jury.[15]

During their cross-examination, the attorneys made Derrick the target, not his version of the crime. None of them highlighted the many factual errors in his testimony. When he was asked why he joined in the attack and punched "that lady in the alley," he answered simply: "I don't know."

Calvin Alston took the stand two days later, on November 7. After being sexually assaulted at the DC Jail, and fearing a long prison sentence, he had flipped again at the last minute and agreed to cooperate. The *Washington Times* was bullish about his testimony, saying Calvin had "an aggressive, clearly stated style," unlike Derrick, who had "mumbled through" his account.[16]

In his narrative, Calvin incriminated all the defendants except Lisa Ruffin.[17] He even got down from the witness stand to demonstrate the final violation. In Hedges's story for the *Times*, he said: "Crouching, he held an imaginary foot-long pole and thrust from his shoulders." His "grisly account shocked the filled courtroom, drawing frequent groans."

On cross-examination, Calvin, like Derrick, could give no details of what he claimed he had done. He couldn't remember how many times he hit or kicked Fuller or where on her body. He couldn't recall if she was conscious or not. He could only say, "I just participated."

Two talkative jurors later told the *Washington Post* they had been skeptical about Derrick's and Calvin's testimonies. "The general consensus," one said, "was the two snitches did very well sentence-wise."[18] But because the defense was alibi, none of the lawyers challenged their stories.

Fourteen-year-old Maurice Thomas was a surprise government witness. When he took the stand on November 13, he told the jurors that on the Monday afternoon of the murder he had passed the alley behind H Street as he walked home on 9th Street.[19] When he looked down toward 8th, he saw a group of young men standing around another person.

Maurice said he saw Snotrag patting down the person in the middle. He swung once, and the person fell. Then the other young men joined in the assault. After the person said: "Could someone please help me?," Maurice walked on.

Along with Snotrag, Maurice said he recognized Levy, Fella, and Cliff. He was unsure whether Chris and Hollywood were part of the group.

All of Maurice's claims were suspect. He hadn't told his story to anyone until the police unexpectedly found him in July 1985. He was very effeminate, and several of the defendants had earned his enmity by teasing him unmercifully. In interviews he repeatedly changed the details of what he had seen in the alley and what his vantage point had been.

But the defense lawyers focused on Maurice's identifications, not his inconsistencies. As a result, he seemed like a neighborhood kid with little to gain from his testimony.

Michael Bray, the assistant medical examiner who had done the autopsy on Fuller, was the last witness in the government's initial case presentation.[20]

Bray described Fuller's three major injuries but could not give a sequence for them or say how many persons inflicted them. None of the lawyers asked whether Fuller's wounds might have been caused by a single assailant. When questioned later about his autopsy findings, he said it was possible.

Overall, Bray told the jurors, it was the "most brutal case" he'd ever seen.

The government's final piece of evidence was an edited version of Cliff's statement from the day of his arrest. On that video, Cliff said he was at the scene as a bystander. He described a brutal group attack, but the details in his story differed markedly from those of Derrick and Calvin.

In his opening statement, Cliff's lawyer had made a serious mistake. He told the jurors his client had an alibi. He named the witnesses who would support it. As a result, Judge Scott decided to let the government use the video statement to counter his defense.

Since Cliff wasn't going to testify, under the law nothing he had said could be used against any of the other defendants. All the names of other assailants had to be redacted. And the judge told the jurors the statement could be used as evidence against Cliff only.

The tape was devastating for Cliff. In his own words, he put himself in the alley during the crime. His alibi was incredible before the jurors even heard it. For the others, it was very bad, despite the edits and the judge's instruction. Watching a defendant tell the government's basic narrative made it seem more real and made it more difficult to imagine any other scenario.

When Cliff described a group assault, did any juror not see most of the accused at the scene? When he talked about the pole, did any not picture Levy as the attacker?

Three weeks into the trial, starting on Tuesday, November 20, the defendants finally got their turn to talk.

Chris Turner was excited about his defense. It wasn't just blind optimism, or his belief that innocent people didn't get convicted of murder. He'd paid careful attention to the trial. He'd taken pages and pages of notes. When he added up the prosecution's case, it seemed pretty weak. He felt sure he would be home for Christmas.

Unfortunately, Chris didn't fully understand two key factors. He knew lots of people were talking about Fuller's brutal murder. But he'd been locked in jail for a year and wasn't aware the case had been front-page news for weeks. He didn't know the public had heard the official story of the crime so many times it was considered gospel.

Second, Chris didn't realize how hard it is to overcome the doubts jurors typically have about an alibi, especially one from family or friends. A few days earlier his lawyer had met with his potential witnesses for the first time. It had not gone well.

Robert DeBerardinis learned that all four women—Hollywood's grandmother, mother, and sister, plus a neighbor—had already spoken to the detectives. They had testified in the grand jury. Their thirteen-month-old memories regarding the events on October 1, 1984, were neither very clear nor very complete. His lawyer never told Chris about those meetings.

It wouldn't have mattered. Chris was determined to offer his alibi, to stick to the facts. He remained foolishly naive about one thing: he thought his innocence would save him.

Monk—Alphonso Harris—and Levy Rouse testified before Chris did.

As Chris watched Levy offer his flimsy alibi, for the first time his confidence began to sag. He saw something new. The jurors wouldn't look at Levy. Chris could see—and feel—their disgust when he talked. "One woman turned almost completely around in her seat," he said later. "They acted like having to listen to Levy was the biggest insult they had ever encountered."

In that moment, Chris thought: "They're not hearing the evidence. Their minds are made up." If they had decided Levy was guilty, maybe they had decided he was guilty, too.

He hadn't been worried before. Now he was.

Chris's defense struggled from the start.

His first witness was Hollywood's sister, LaTonya. She was now nineteen and a freshman at the University of the District of Columbia. She said that on October 1, 1984, she got back from school around 2:30 p.m.[21] She stayed home until about 9:00 that night, and Chris and Hollywood were there the whole time.

She had trouble with specific details. She told the jurors Chris was asleep when she came in. He woke up around 4:00 p.m., after her grandmother was home. But six months earlier, LaTonya had told the grand jury that Chris was awake when her grandmother got in. The prosecutor used that incidental inconsistency to great effect.

It was worse with Denise Riddick, Hollywood's neighbor. She testified she was visiting Hollywood's family when he yelled downstairs about a killing.[22] She *thought* this was between 5:20 and 5:45 p.m. All she knew for sure was that it was the evening of October 1.

Riddick didn't know Fuller's body had not been found until after 6:00 p.m. Or that Hollywood said the call was between 7:00 and 9:00 p.m. Or that giving an estimate would make both men look like killers. In his closing, Goren would ignore what Hollywood said and argue—repeatedly—that Riddick's timeline proved both Hollywood and Chris were guilty. They knew about the crime before police even discovered the body.

Watching this carnage was frustrating, but instructive, for Chris. Only one issue was truly relevant: whether he and Hollywood were inside between 5:00 and 6:00 p.m. the day Fuller was killed. Their witnesses testified unequivocally that both were at Hollywood's house at that time. Whether Chris was asleep or awake at 3:30 p.m., whether Hollywood heard about the murder at 5:20 or 7:00 or 9:00 p.m., makes no difference to that point.

But the prosecutor was able to use their uncertainties and any differences in exact times and minor events to make their entire testimony seem untrue. Chris saw how indecision could ruin a witness. He would have to convince the jurors his alibi was true.

Chris began his testimony with a brief biography.[23] He'd wanted to join the air force after finishing high school in 1983. A dislocated shoulder delayed that plan. He'd been working full-time at the Center (Northeast Neighborhood House) until the Friday before Fuller's killing.

Chris said he got up about 2:00 p.m. on October 1. For the

rest of the afternoon he was in the house playing video games and watching TV. LaTonya returned from school. Hollywood's grandmother and mother got in from work. Riddick came over to visit.

Sometime that evening Hollywood came out of his room with news from a phone call: a "little girl" got killed on H Street. He wanted to go down there and check things out. But "his grandma say you'd better not go down there because you know they are going to try to put you in there."

Unlike his codefendants, Chris's testimony about that Monday had specific times, thanks to the TV programs that were on. He said that at 2:30 p.m., he and Latonya watched *One Life to Live*. At 3:30 p.m. he turned on cartoons and saw *Inspector Gadget*. He ate a bowl of cereal and played *Donkey Kong*. Between 5:00 and 6:00 p.m.—the very time Fuller was attacked and murdered—he was watching *Love Boat*.

The details about the TV programs could easily be confirmed. So the prosecutor used a different approach to challenge his credibility. He said Chris remembered things *too* well. Near the end of his cross-examination, he tried to build support for an argument that Chris's alibi was made up.

He started with the post-arrest interview.[24]

Q: He [the officer] asked you about the murder, didn't he?
A: Yes. . . . I told him, yeah, I didn't know nothing about it.
Q: He asked you where you were on the day Mrs. Fuller was killed and you told him exactly where you were and who would be your alibi witnesses, didn't you?
A: I didn't say nothing about no alibi witnesses. . . . I say you can call these people, and they will tell you I was there all that day.

As a final flourish, the prosecutor made his fabrication claim explicit.

Q: And when you were arrested, you had your alibi ready, didn't you?

A: No, sir.

Q: And that is why you could remember that day so well?

A: I can remember that day so well because when I was arrested, I kept an open mind about it, and I knew that I would have to remember that date for the rest of my life.

Chris felt hopeful once again when he finished testifying. He'd told his story without being intimidated or impeached. One of the other defense lawyers agreed, telling the *Post*: "He was very good. He looked like a Rhodes scholar compared to the rest."[25]

Chris knew the jury would have the final say.

In its rebuttal case, the government's primary witness was Katrina Ward, Levy's former girlfriend. In October 1984 she had been seventeen and pregnant with Levy's child.

She told the jurors that in early December, Levy told her he was present for Fuller's killing but didn't take part.[26] Soon afterward, she said, he made a shocking admission: " 'Girl, . . . I did the worst thing to that lady in the alley.' He looked at me," she said. "Then he laughed."

The *Post* reported that as Ward quietly described this alleged conversation, Levy "moved to rise from his seat and mumbled."[27] When the marshals lunged forward, he sat back down. Levy stared briefly at Ward, then "rarely looked at her as she completed her testimony."

Katrina had testified in the grand jury twice—on December 13 and 27, 1984—and said nothing about Levy making any admissions of guilt. When confronted on that, she said she'd lied to the grand jurors because Levy was her baby's father. She hadn't wanted to get him locked up.

Her claim, true or not, gave a powerful close to the government's case. In her telling, Levy hadn't just done the "worst thing" to Fuller. He'd laughed about doing it.

He was now the most hated man in DC. That taint infected his codefendants as well.

"A dollar bill is a friend of mine, a nickel, a dime, it's love boat time. I need some money. I've got to have some money."[28]

On the morning of December 4, Goren began his closing argument like he'd started his opening statement: with the Chuck Brown go-go lyrics the defendants had supposedly been singing the day of the crime. "It all began with a song in a park in northeast Washington," he said, "and it ended in a brutal, senseless murder."

He called the killing a "very fast-moving, a very confusing, a very emotional, a very shocking event." No one person would see everything. No two people would describe it the same way. Those facts, he would later argue, explained away all the differences and discrepancies in the witnesses' accounts.

He next retold a longer version of the government's narrative, emphasizing graphic details and picking out the starkest claims from the many witness stories. He made sure every defendant had a role. He described how Fuller was sodomized, how the assailants fought over her purse, how they argued about her rings and chains. Then, finally, "the carnival was over."

When he turned to the alibis, Chris and Hollywood got special attention. Goren said their witnesses could not be trusted. All of them "were family members of—or good friends of—the two of them, all close relations." The details they gave were not consistent.

"Most importantly," he told the jurors, Hollywood claimed to know about the murder "before the police ever discovered the body."[29] He couldn't have known about it at that time unless he had been part of it.

Goren was misstating the evidence to make his big point. But

Chris's lawyer did not object. Goren's claim stood. He would repeat it in his rebuttal.

In the defense closings, the lawyers all argued their clients were innocent. They also helped the prosecution by bolstering questionable witnesses and implicating other defendants.

The way they described Maurice's testimony illustrates the problem. Maurice had said he looked down the alley and saw the faces of Levy, Snotrag, and Cliff. By clothing or body build he thought he recognized Hollywood, Derrick, Fella, and Chris. He didn't see Steve.

Steve's lawyer argued that "[Maurice] has no motive to lie. . . . He is just coming here to tell you what he saw."[30] Snotrag's lawyer said the very opposite: "Either [Maurice is] wrong or all the other people are wrong. Because under no stretch of the imagination did [the murder] happen where he says it happened; nor . . . the way he says it happened."[31]

If all the defense lawyers had argued Maurice was not believable, their words might have carried weight with the jury. But they'd never had a unified strategy, largely because they all had embraced the government's gang theory. Every defendant couldn't be innocent. Their defense had to be "not my client, but maybe the others." They felt compelled to say any witness who had not implicated their client was credible, while any who had was incredible. That caused severe collateral damage to the entire defense case.

Goren was easily able to turn these arguments against the defendants. "The defense lawyers say: Believe the people who help me," he later told the jury. "Don't believe the people who hurt me. That's totally wrong."[32]

The closing arguments underlined what had been going on throughout the trial. Rather than attack the government's theory together, or point out the myriad problems with the evidence, each lawyer had tried to distance his or her client from the crime and the other suspects.

When it was Chris's turn, his lawyer focused on the identification testimony of Derrick and Calvin.[33]

The government was claiming they were "honest murderers"
who had given trustworthy testimony. He argued that since both
admitted they hadn't initially told the truth about their involvement in the crime, or put Chris on the scene, they were "lying
murderers" with no credibility.

He defended Chris's alibi by pointing out the government
wanted things both ways. If, like Chris, "you've got a lot of details," they say, "you've got to be lying." But if you don't, they say,
"that's no good. He doesn't know enough details." He told jurors
that while Chris's witnesses differed in their specific recollections
about the day of the murder, all of them said he was inside during
the afternoon and early evening when the crime occurred.

But DeBerardinis never contested Goren's claim that the crucial phone call about the murder had been as early as 5:20 p.m. He
didn't say that both Hollywood and his grandmother had testified it came at 7:00 p.m. or later. He finished on a rather neutral
note. "I have taken Christopher Turner as far as I can take him,"
he said. "His fate is now in your hands."

All Chris could do was to hope he had taken him far enough.

Goren got the final say. His rebuttal closing was nearly twice as
long as his initial closing.[34]

He began by admitting that despite an intensive investigation,
the police had found no physical evidence linking any of the accused to the crime. But he called arguments about that just "a
smokescreen," an attempt to shift the focus away from what he
called the "real believable evidence," the testimony of his witnesses. He needed to make that claim, since manufactured words
were all he had.

Goren went down the list of defendants and said none of their
alibis were credible. Again, he focused on Chris's and Hollywood's testimonies, returning to his earlier false claim: the two

had an "impossible" alibi based on the timing of the phone call about the police finding a body.

Goren claimed Chris's demeanor was too eager, and his recollections were too good. Why, he asked the jurors, did Chris "get his alibi ready and was ready the day he got arrested? Because he was there. He participated and he's guilty."

His final summation had a defensive tone. After acknowledging the flaws of his witnesses, he argued that "[t]here is no reason why anybody would come in here and lie about these people. There is no reason the government . . . would create the testimony and the events that you have just heard unless it was true. Thank you." [35]

But there were reasons. Lots of reasons.

Calvin and Derrick faced first-degree murder charges. Others, like Katrina, said the detectives told them they could be charged if they didn't provide helpful information. There is no way to know how many teenagers had faced that stark choice. They could be prosecution witnesses and get favorable treatment. Or they could be defendants and face a lifetime in jail. To no one's surprise, some chose the first option.

For the detectives, and later the prosecutor, once their gang story went public and the arrests hit double digits, there was no going back. Proving their theory and solving the crime merged. The testimonies of their witnesses, however coached or coerced they may have been, were all for a noble purpose: to convict the people they felt sure were guilty of murder.

The jury began deliberating on Monday, December 9. For Chris and his codefendants it was a time of hope and a time of dread. They knew what they faced if the jury found them guilty.

The jurors were also under pressure. The graphic, disturbing details of the killing were now public. They had spent five weeks hearing the case. Christmas was sixteen days away. People wanted a conviction and closure. They were eager to get on with their lives.

Because Goren had violated his *Brady* obligations, the jurors had just one story, one crime scenario, to consider. No one, not even the defense attorneys, was publicly saying the 8th and H Crew were innocent. The only issue seemed to be whether *all* of them were guilty.

And yet. When it came to actually deciding, more than a few jurors were troubled by the government's case. They had questions about the official theory. They weren't sure the two snitches had been truthful. They wondered why no one from the neighborhood had seen or heard anything related to a gang attack.

To the surprise of nearly everyone, their deliberations continued all week with no resolution.

The Fuller jury debated the case through the week of December 9, including Saturday.

On Monday, December 16, the jurors sent a note saying they'd reached unanimous verdicts for eight of the ten defendants. They had deliberated seven full days.

Within minutes, the courthouse was buzzing with the news. Once the lawyers were assembled, Judge Scott called in the jurors to receive the verdicts. First, he addressed the spectators. "I want to admonish the members of the audience and anybody else that there will be no display of emotion when any verdict is announced."[36]

Before a jammed, hushed courtroom, the proceedings moved in alphabetical order, as always. First, Snotrag: guilty on all charges. Monk's verdict: not guilty on all the charges. Levy: guilty on all. Lisa: not guilty. Hollywood, Fella, Steve, and Cliff: guilty.

When the foreman pronounced Hollywood's verdict, Chris covered his face and began to weep for his best friend. When his brother, Fella, was also found guilty, Chris sobbed openly. It barely registered when the judge said the jury had been unable to reach unanimous verdicts on him and Bobo.

The next day's *Post* had a column titled "Bring Back the Death

Penalty." [37] Courtland Milloy wrote that for such a heinous crime, sending someone to prison to "watch soap operas all day, this is not justice." It was time "to fire up 'Ole Sparky.' " He predicted—wrongly, as it turned out—that "at least one of them will be back on the streets before Fuller's 13-year-old son finishes high school."

Once the courtroom quieted, Judge Scott told the jurors to keep working.

Later that afternoon, he received a note from juror number seven.[38] "I personally don't want to deliberate anymore on Russell Overton or Christopher Turner. We have taken a vote on these two defendants more than 10 times, with most of the people never changing their decision."

The judge called in the attorneys to discuss the note. Chris's lawyer moved for a mistrial. He argued that asking this juror to keep deliberating would coerce him into making a decision. Bobo's lawyer did not join the motion. He was hoping for an acquittal. Goren didn't want a mistrial. Judge Scott never replied to the note.

On Wednesday, December 18, the jurors sent a note saying they had reached agreement on Chris and Bobo. When everyone was assembled, the jury filed into the courtroom for the last time.

In a strong voice, Lucas, the foreman, announced the final verdicts: guilty on all charges.[39]

Chris broke down. His sister, Charlene, from her third-row seat, whispered: "Chris, don't cry. Don't cry." Then she started crying, too. Bobo appeared stoic at first. But as he took off his black bow tie, tears began to run down his face.[40]

Both defense lawyers asked for a poll. The jurors stood to respond individually. Lucas spoke his "guilty" loudly each time. Others, however, barely whispered. To the watching reporters, they looked drained.

Afterward, two unnamed jurors spoke to the *Post*. They reported that, following the initial verdicts, they voted forty to fifty times more on Chris and Bobo.[41] They said "more than one" juror had been holding out for acquittal on the last two defendants.

"But you'd be surprised what happens when the pressure is on you," one said.[42] According to the *Post*, they "did not explain what broke the impasse." The other juror said he didn't vote to find them guilty "until the last day. I had a real hard time with that."[43]

It was the most depressing moment of Chris's life. Speaking to a *Post* reporter later that night, he said: "I feel like dying."[44] For him, the hardest thing was not facing decades in prison, but "having people look at me as though I'm the worst person in the world when I know I'm not."

His lawyer was equally dramatic. "He knows his life is over now," DeBerardinis said.

Not quite a month later, on January 14, 1986, Snotrag was sentenced to twenty years to life for armed robbery/felony murder and to fifteen years to life—consecutive—for kidnapping; a total of thirty-five years to life.[45] Steve got the same on January 28.

On the next sentencing day, February 4, Bobo and Fella said they were absolutely innocent. "I didn't rob Mrs. Fuller and I didn't kill Mrs. Fuller," Bobo told Judge Scott. "I am charged for a crime I didn't commit," Fella said. "That is all I have to say." They both received the maximum of thirty-five years to life.[46]

When it was his turn, Chris questioned the government's evidence. He reminded Scott the witnesses had first said he "didn't do nothing." He became part of the case only after the police showed Calvin Alston a list of names and Calvin put him in it.

He told the judge anyone who knew him would say he would never "participate in anything like that. . . . [M]y character witnesses came in here and told you what kind of person Christopher Turner is. And he always will be."[47]

Because Chris had no criminal record, Scott gave him slightly less time than he gave the others: twenty-seven and a half years to life. "You will be . . . just under 50 when you get out," the judge told him. "You will have a chance to do something at that time."

Levy's day came the next week, on February 11. Goren made the most of it. He described Levy's actions as "among the most disgusting and reprehensible that I or anyone in the U.S. Attorney's Office has ever heard or seen in the District of Columbia or anywhere else."[48]

When he spoke, Levy came right to the point. "I'm not no gang leader," he said. "I never hung with no gang." As for the crime: "I didn't do what they said I did. Whatever they said I did, I didn't do." Any leniency was out of the question. Levy got thirty-five years to life.

On February 18, Scott sentenced the last two defendants, Cliff and Hollywood. Goren had particularly harsh words for Cliff, who had given police a statement about the incident but refused to testify for the government.[49] Because of Cliff's silence, Goren said angrily, "there is another of Ms. Fuller's killers walking the streets today." He was referring to Monk.

Cliff, now seventeen, spoke in a barely audible voice. He said he lied to the police about being in the alley and seeing what happened. "I was afraid," he said. "I said anything that I thought would get me out of the situation . . . that I was in at that time."[50] Hollywood said nothing. Scott gave them both thirty-five years to life.

Two months later, in April, there was different news: Goren was resigning from his job as an assistant U.S. attorney.[51] He never tried another case.

Chris and his codefendants, except for Fella, appealed their convictions. Given the number of appellants and the length of the record, the case was not argued before the DC Court of Appeals until November of 1987, nearly two years after the trial ended. Seven months later, in June of 1988, a unanimous three-judge panel upheld all the convictions.[52]

Goren had won the guilty verdicts he'd sought so fervently. He had violated his *Brady* obligations and withheld evidence the defendants could have used to demonstrate their innocence. It remained hidden. They continued to say they had nothing to do with the crime, but they saw no way to prove it. And since no physical evidence had linked them to the killing in the first place, none could show they hadn't been involved.

The government believed the Fuller murder case was finally over. It wasn't. Not even close.

7

AN EPIDEMIC OF VIOLATIONS

K enneth R. Olsen was an odd duck, as he freely conceded.[1]
Olsen was a chemist at Agilent Technologies, a manufac-
turer of analytical laboratory instruments in Liberty Lake, Washington. In August 2001, a coworker using a shared office printer
found a document describing explosives.

Company security personnel identified Olsen as the person
who had printed the document. When they interviewed him and
examined his computer, they found he had made repeated internet searches related to poisons and killing, including such phrases
as "undetectable death pill." He explained that he just had "an ir-
responsible sense of curiosity" about "strange and morbid things."

The investigators concluded that Olsen's explanations for these
various internet browsings were not credible. He claimed, for example, that he gathered information on poisons to help his son's
Boy Scout troop avoid potentially dangerous berries.

After the investigation, Olsen was fired. A search of his cubicle
disclosed a wealth of printouts on methods of harming people. He
also had test tubes, several bottles of medicines, a bag of mysteri-
ous beans, and various other chemistry paraphernalia.

Agilent passed these items to the police. A forensic scientist at
the Washington State Patrol (WSP) crime lab, Arnold Melnikoff,
found that the test tubes contained castor oil. The beans looked
like castor beans. This raised the possibility Olsen might have
been making ricin, a lethal poison derived from the beans.

Melnikoff's lab could not test for ricin, so he sent the evidence to the FBI. Twelve items from Olsen's cubicle proved positive for the poison. They included four capsules of Equate allergy medicine, with one having "a high concentration." Since the pills had to be liquefied for testing, the lab could not say whether the ricin had been put inside the capsules to disguise it or had been on only the surfaces of the capsules.

In July 2002, Olsen was indicted for knowingly possessing a biological agent or toxin for use as a weapon, based on the allergy pills in his cubicle. A second charge of possession of a chemical weapon was added in April 2003. Three months later, after a twelve-day trial, a jury found him guilty of both charges. His convictions were affirmed on appeal. He was eventually sentenced to ten years and one month in prison.

At his trial, Olsen admitted he made and possessed ricin. But he denied doing it for "use as a weapon" or as a "chemical weapon," which were essential parts of the charges. He said he was just curious.

To prove otherwise, the prosecution offered evidence he'd researched not only how to make poisons but also how to convey them. A key piece of their case was the claim Olsen had spiked an Equate capsule with ricin as a means of delivering it. Melnikoff testified for the government about his handling of Olsen's items and the tests he had conducted on them.

Six years after Olsen's convictions, while working on an appeal, his lawyers learned that prosecutors had suppressed evidence regarding Melnikoff's honesty and professional competence. After getting complaints about him, WSP had conducted an internal probe of Melnikoff's conduct at two previous jobs. They found examples of contamination of laboratory materials and sloppiness in his work, which raised doubts about his "diligence and care in the laboratory." Not long after Olsen's trial, in late 2003, WSP had fired Melnikoff.

In 2009, Olsen's lawyers filed a motion challenging their client's convictions. They argued that the government had violated the *Brady* rule by failing to disclose Melnikoff's misdeeds. After the federal district court denied Olsen's motion, without holding an evidentiary hearing on the *Brady* issue, Olsen appealed to the Ninth Circuit Court.

Although Melnikoff had not tested any items himself, he "handled and extensively manipulated" them before sending them to the FBI. Trial testimony established that

> he examined the Equate capsules not by individually removing them from the bottle with forceps, but rather by dumping them onto his laboratory bench . . . after he had examined other items on the same bench—which including scraping ricin-positive powder from some of the items. Melnikoff also does not appear to have changed gloves between handling each item.[2]

Olsen's lawyers asserted that if they had known of Melnikoff's long record of carelessness and incompetence, they could have undercut his trial testimony and argued he inadvertently contaminated the Equate capsules himself. They submitted an expert affidavit that concluded, based on the trial evidence, it was "highly probable" Melnikoff contaminated the capsule after handling other items containing ricin.

The court agreed the WSP investigation report was "clearly favorable to Olsen." It should have been disclosed. The defense could have used it to attack Melnikoff's testimony and to support their contamination theory. But the three-judge panel deferred to its default position: the evidence was favorable, but it wasn't material. It was unlikely the jury would have reached a different verdict even if they had known of it. Olsen's convictions were affirmed.

After the panel's ruling, Olsen's lawyers asked the entire Ninth Circuit Court to rehear the case. A significant majority of the judges voted no. The petition was denied in 2013. But Chief Judge

Alex Kozinski, supported by four others, dissented.[3] He did not do so quietly.

Kozinski was an unlikely *Brady* crusader.

He was a conservative-cum-libertarian, with a brash, outspoken style. After his 1985 appointment to the federal bench by Ronald Reagan, he had risen to become chief judge of the nation's largest appellate court. For nearly three decades he watched prosecutors break the *Brady* rule and the courts do little about it. By 2013 Kozinski had had enough.

His dissent was not subtle. "There is an epidemic of *Brady* violations abroad in the land," he began. "Only judges can put a stop to it."[4]

In his argument, Kozinski detailed the significant record of Melnikoff's ineptitude and untruthfulness that had been hidden. If the jurors had learned of the WSP report, he said, and of Melnikoff's history of "contaminating samples," they might have doubted whether Olsen poisoned the allergy pills.

"On these facts," he wrote, "I would easily find a *Brady* violation."

But Kozinski's sights were on a bigger issue. The last section of his opinion focused on how prosecutors would interpret the court's decision.

> The panel's ruling . . . effectively announces that the prosecution need not produce exculpatory or impeaching evidence so long as it's possible the defendant would have been convicted anyway. This will send a clear signal to prosecutors that, when a case is close, it's best to hide evidence helpful to the defense, as there will be a fair chance reviewing courts will look the other way, as happened here.

He called the fact that most violations remain unknown "a serious moral hazard for those prosecutors who are more interested in winning a conviction than serving justice."

Kozinski concluded his dissent with an appeal to his judicial colleagues. "We must send prosecutors a clear message: Betray *Brady* . . . and you will lose your ill-gotten conviction. Unfortunately, the panel's decision sends the opposite message."[5]

Brady infractions were epidemic. The fact that a jurist of Kozinski's experience and position had grown outraged about how the rule was being abused showed the depth of the problem.

It should not have been a surprise. In his *Bagley* dissent back in 1985, Justice Thurgood Marshall had issued a bleak prediction about the likely path *Brady* would now take. The majority's new "rigorous test of materiality," he said, showed they were "apparently anxious to assure that reversals are handed out sparingly."[6]

Over the next decades, that prophecy became fact. Under the narrow, murky materiality standard the courts were using, defense lawyers routinely lost *Brady* claims even when they uncovered serious, deliberate violations. With rare exceptions, judges did nothing.

For prosecutors, the more they won, the more tempting it became to break the rule. The problem worsened. *Brady* was the central criminal procedure rule designed to ensure trials were fair. Its breakdown was doing serious damage to the justice system.

As Kozinski asserted, judges—with or without the help of prosecutors—could have stemmed this epidemic. But over the years, courts high and low repeatedly passed on chances to clarify or strengthen *Brady* or to rigorously enforce its requirements.

Several things contributed to this reticence. The judicial system loves finality above all. There is a deep reluctance to disturb a settled verdict decided by a unanimous jury. Reversals and retrials for *Brady* violations are costly in time, money, and court resources. Legal inertia is powerful; the longer a decision has stood, the harder it is to overturn.

Further, state and federal prosecutors, along with their respective state and national organizations and the Department of

Justice, have all been united in claiming *Brady* violations are rare, exceptional events. They say the rule is working just fine. No reforms are needed. Most judges have been hesitant to take a stand against this powerful tide of opposition or to push for changes.

A crucial but less visible factor that feeds this reluctance to address *Brady* infractions is the makeup of the judiciary. Many judges are former prosecutors or attorneys who worked as government proponents in other contexts, such as tax or civil rights or regulatory litigation. Only a relative few are former public defenders or have ever done criminal defense work.

A 2021 study by the Cato Institute, a libertarian think tank with a focus on public policy, found that of 880 federal judges, 36.1 percent were ex-prosecutors and 27.6 percent had been non-criminal courtroom advocates for the government.[7] Just 6.6 percent had been public defenders, while another 8.6 percent had criminal defense experience. Overall, previous government proponents outnumber former opponents by more than four to one.

As president, Donald Trump made a significant contribution to this inequity. Of his 227 judicial appointments, 39.2 percent had been prosecutors, while just 1.7 percent had been public defenders. Before Ketanji Brown Jackson was approved as an associate justice-designate of the Supreme Court in 2022, there had not been a lawyer with criminal defense experience on the Court since Justice Thurgood Marshall retired in 1991.

No reliable figures are available on ex-prosecutors who have become state, county, or municipal court judges. But those numbers would likely resemble the breakdown in the federal courts.

President Joe Biden has made a deliberate effort to remedy this imbalance.[8] Of the forty judges confirmed in his first year, nearly 30 percent were former public defenders. But overall, the numbers still don't come close to any sort of parity.

Previous experience as a prosecutor *does* affect judicial rulings. Decisions over the last decade, from the Supreme Court on down, have shown the powerful impact of personal beliefs and ideologies.

On matters such as voting rights, access to abortion, immigration policy, and death penalty appeals, judges regularly rule differently on the same issue or evidence, depending on whether they are liberal or conservative, on whether they were appointed by a Republican or a Democratic president.

As *Brady* law stands, decisions on materiality are judgment calls. Assessing what impact a piece of undisclosed evidence might have had on a jury's verdict is always a subjective activity. With almost any *Brady* claim a judge can find reasons to rule for the prosecution or for the defense.

Prosecutors-turned-judges can understand and empathize with the challenges current prosecutors face. In the not-so-distant past, many might even have committed a *Brady* violation or two themselves—or been sorely tempted to do so. They're often reluctant to second-guess their former colleagues, or to impose harsh judgments on them, or to act in ways that might incite their opposition. Even on the bench, these factors pull them in a pro-prosecution direction.

As long as ex-prosecutors dominate the judiciary, it's unlikely judges will ever be the source of serious *Brady* reform.

Judge Kozinski's screed in *Olsen* gained wide notice. The reactions were predictable.

Defense lawyers agreed and applauded. Prosecutors and some judges pushed back. Many claimed he vastly overstated the problem by terming it "epidemic." After all, his dissent cited only thirty cases where prosecutors had committed serious *Brady* violations.

In response, Kozinski told *Bloomberg News*: "I could have cited 300 cases, easily. I just didn't have the time." [9]

The hubbub soon subsided. Nothing changed. But Kozinski wasn't done. If his colleagues wouldn't join his crusade, he'd press on alone.

In line with their heavily progovernment *Brady* rulings, Kozinski thought courts were far too protective of erring prosecutors, far too timid about exposing their misdeeds. They were typically shielded from censure even after serious violations. Judges rarely identified the guilty parties, choosing to avoid a practice lawyers call "shaming by naming." Time and time again they seemed more concerned about embarrassing a prosecutor than about enforcing the rule.

At the end of his *Olsen* dissent in 2013, Kozinski wondered aloud whether the prosecutor should be sanctioned for hiding exculpatory evidence. Writing in the *Georgetown Law Journal* in 2015, he noted that "[n]aming names and taking prosecutors to task for misbehaving can have magical qualities in assuring compliance with constitutional rights." [10]

In 2016, his majority opinion in *Frost v. Gilbert* put this preaching into practice.

The Ninth Circuit ruled Joshua James Frost deserved no relief from his robbery and burglary convictions on *Brady* grounds. The prosecutor had not disclosed evidence that one of his witnesses had a plea agreement. He'd permitted the witness to lie about it on the stand. But given the weighty evidence against Frost—he made three confessions—the court said the hidden information was not material.

Kozinski was unwilling to excuse the prosecutor's misdeeds. After detailing the legal basis for the ruling, he trained his fire on the key government actors.

Though the court had denied Frost's arguments, Kozinski said: "We find the facts giving rise to his *Brady* . . . claims most troubling." [11] He called the prosecutor's actions of withholding favorable evidence and allowing a witness to lie about it "deliberate tactic[s]." "So far as we are aware," he wrote, "the individuals involved have never been held to account for their conduct."

Kozinski called out three people by name: two deputy prosecuting attorneys and one public records officer. He concluded by saying that "[t]he individuals we have named may wish to furnish a copy of this opinion to the state bar and seek to clear their names by providing an explanation for its consideration. This would seem to be the prudent course."

His colleagues responded quickly.

Of the eleven judges who heard the case, only one joined that part of his opinion. Five others specifically dissented. They seemed far more troubled by Kozinski's disclosure of the names than by any possible misconduct on the part of the officials in question.

The dissenting judges accused Kozinski of launching "a groundless, personal attack against several King County employees" who had no way to defend themselves. They said he had "tarnished" the officials' "character and integrity." "Thankfully," they wrote, "a majority of the court has refused to join in his indefensible and intemperate attack." [12]

Kozinski's words prompted an investigation by the Office of Disciplinary Counsel for the Washington State Bar Association into the attorney who had prosecuted Frost, Zachary C. Wagnild. But after reviewing the matter, the organization declined to sanction Wagnild.

As a result, the initial *Frost* opinion that discussed his behavior was "WITHDRAWN and REPLACED" (emphasis in original) by a unanimous amended opinion.[13] It did not name any of the officials or raise any questions about their actions.

Kozinski remained convinced that this kind of judicial inaction had led to prosecutors feeling little shame when they got caught cheating. In an interview on CBS's *60 Minutes* in April 2017, he had this exchange with reporter Lesley Stahl:

Q: How much of a stigma is it to not turn over exculpatory evidence? Is it a huge blemish on a prosecutor, on a lawyer?

A: I don't think so. I think they consider it feathers in their caps.[14]

Judge Kozinski resigned in disgrace from the federal bench in December 2017, after his lengthy, aggressive history of sexual misconduct was widely reported.[15] His behavior toward women, including his own law clerks, had often been reprehensible. His sordid actions didn't change the fact that his analysis of the dismal state of *Brady* had been correct. But they did effectively silence him.

None of his colleagues has since taken up the issue.

But others have, despite the challenges. In 2021, when a group of law professors called out some erring New York City prosecutors by name, they ran into fierce headwinds.

In March 2021, a judge in Queens freed three men who'd spent twenty-four years in prison for a murder they did not commit. The prosecutors "deliberately withheld . . . credible information of third-party guilt," Justice Joseph A. Zayas said. They "completely abdicated [their] truth-seeking role in these cases."[16]

This serious, intentional *Brady* violation was one of several that had recently come to light in Queens County alone. Neither the district attorney nor the New York attorney grievance committees, the state offices charged with monitoring legal misconduct, seemed to be taking any action. Six law professors decided to do something to publicize—and to try to help stop—such behavior.[17]

In partnership with Civil Rights Corps, a nonprofit organization that works for progressive legal reform, the professors filed grievances against twenty-one Queens prosecutors. Each of the prosecutors had been subject to judicial findings of misconduct. The professors formed a coalition with other professors, attorneys, and activists called Accountability NY. The group built a website and published the information about the prosecutors online. Their aim was to publicize the violations and to prod the grievance committee to act.

The response was swift and severe. A lawyer with the Office of the Corporation Counsel, which handles New York City's legal affairs, termed the grievances "an abuse of the system." He accused the group of "misus[ing] . . . the grievance process to promote a political agenda" in a way that "should not be countenanced."

The lawyer argued that publicizing this misconduct broke a New York law intended to keep complaints about attorney behavior secret. He threatened to take additional steps against the professors if they kept filing grievances. He asked the committee to deny the group access to any further proceedings related to their complaints. The committee complied.

In response, Accountability NY filed a public lawsuit. They asserted the secrecy law was a violation of their free speech rights. They asked a judge to declare it unconstitutional. They also requested that their rights as complainants be restored so they could monitor any actions taken by the committee.

On June 13, 2022, a federal district judge ruled that New York's anti-disclosure law violated the First Amendment.[18] The professors had a constitutional right to publicize their complaints without having to fear retaliation from the state. As of July 2022, the other aspects of their suit remain unresolved.

The reactions to Accountability NY from the city's lawyer and the state's grievance committee show that confronting misconduct by prosecutors is risky. The legal establishment seems keener to protect their culpable colleagues than to find ways to end their widespread violations that—too often—put innocent defendants away for decades.

In this climate, would-be *Brady* reformers could be forgiven their pessimism. History kept saying "don't hope." Prosecutors and judges, together or separately, had the power to initiate substantive changes in the law. But for their own reasons, neither had shown the interest or the will to do so.

Prosecutors are fine with *Brady* law as it is. They control the government's evidence. They can decide what to share and what to withhold. If they fail their obligations, if they hide information, there's a good chance no one will ever know. If their violation comes to light, the odds are that the courts will excuse it. What's not to like?

For judges, finding a *Brady* violation requires doing two things they'd rather not do: reopening a previously settled case and—at least implicitly—reproving a prosecutor (who's often a former colleague). A broader rule, with stepped-up enforcement, would mean they'd have to find and punish more violations. So with few exceptions, they aren't eager to support reforms.

But amid this bleak landscape, a path to real progress emerged outside the normal legal processes.

On April 14, 1995, police found the body of Allen Ray Jenkins inside his home in Aulander, North Carolina.[19] Jenkins, a fifty-six-year-old truck driver, had been killed by two shotgun blasts to his chest at close range.

Jenkins was known to have a fondness for "underage girls." In 1990, he'd been convicted of the statutory rape of a fourteen-year-old. Detectives soon learned he was friendly with two local fifteen-year-olds, Crystal Morris and Shanna Hall. Jenkins would let them use alcohol and drugs in his home. The girls later told police that on the day of Jenkins's murder, the three of them were drinking wine coolers together.

In July, Morris and Hall led officers to some nearby woods where the shotgun that killed Jenkins had been tossed. Both were charged with first-degree murder. After telling several conflicting stories about the crime, they claimed the real killer was Hall's boyfriend, a twenty-year-old named James Alan Gell.

The girls said Gell came to Jenkins's place on April 3 after a phone call from Morris. He allegedly snuck into the house, found Jenkins's shotgun, and killed him as he walked with Morris from the kitchen into his bedroom. After the killing, Gell supposedly took $400 from a cabinet in Jenkins's house, along with the gun and some shells.

Gell denied any involvement in the crime. Based on the stories of Morris and Hall, he was charged with first-degree murder, robbery, and conspiracy to commit both. After agreeing to testify for the state, Morris and Hall were allowed to plead guilty to the lesser charges of second-degree murder and robbery.

At Gell's trial in February 1998, the two teens were the state's star witnesses. Morris said she saw Gell shoot Jenkins twice after hiding behind his bedroom door. Hall said she was outside at the time but heard one shot. She went into the house and saw Gell holding the gun.

The April 3, 1995, date was crucial for the prosecution. The very next day, Gell and Hall had driven to Virginia and Maryland in a stolen pickup truck, hoping to buy drugs. Their mission failed. They returned on April 6. Gell was arrested that same day on a car theft charge. He was still locked up on April 14, when Jenkins's body was found. For Gell to be the killer, the crime had to have occurred on April 3.

A forensic pathologist testified for the state that, based on the condition of Jenkins's body, April 3, 1995, was a realistic date of death. On March 3, 1998, Gell was convicted of all four charges. He was sentenced to death for Jenkins's murder.

In October 2000, as they prepared Gell's appeal, his new attorneys received access to the prosecution's case files. In reviewing these materials, they made some startling discoveries.

During the initial investigation, no fewer than eighteen witnesses told police they had seen Allen Jenkins—alive!—*after* April 3, 1995. These people included his brother (on April 8), a neighbor (April 8), a couple walking by his house (April 9), a former coworker, a waitress, and a shopkeeper (all April 10).

Before the trial, Gell's defense lawyer heard rumors about these sightings. He specifically requested access to any such statements. Prosecutors disclosed nine of the statements but withheld the other nine. Still, the testimony of Morris and Hall, along with that of the pathologist, convinced the jury of Gell's guilt.

The appellate lawyers also found the transcript of a recorded telephone call from 1995 between Crystal Morris and her then boyfriend. On the call, Morris twice failed to answer when her boyfriend asked if Gell really killed Jenkins. Then she told him she "needed to make up a story" to tell police about the murder.

Based on these *Brady* violations, Gell's lawyers asked that the case against him be dismissed. In 2002, after a short hearing and a review of the undisclosed information, a North Carolina superior court judge vacated Gell's convictions and death sentence.

Despite the prosecution's misdeeds and the new exculpatory evidence, the state decided to retry Gell. They didn't want to admit the first trial was a mistake. "A man was murdered in cold blood," Attorney General Roy Cooper said. "We want justice." [20]

This time around, many of the witnesses who had seen Jenkins alive after April 3, 1995, testified in Gell's defense. So did the forensic pathologist. After deliberating two and a half hours, the jury acquitted Gell on all charges.

Later in 2002, Gell was officially exonerated. In 2009, North Carolina and insurers for the state bureau of investigation paid James Alan Gell a civil settlement of $3.9 million in compensation for his unlawful convictions and the nine years he spent on death row.

When details of the prosecution's blatant *Brady* violations in Gell's case became public, there was widespread outrage. [21] People wanted action.

Discovery reform was already brewing in North Carolina. It started with death penalty cases. [22] Prosecutors claimed appellate lawyers were up to all manner of actions to stall capital proceedings. They were. The appellate lawyers replied that the process could be greatly streamlined if prosecutors would disclose all their available information. In 1996 the two sides struck a deal, and the legislature approved it. Prosecutors in capital cases would open their files; appellate lawyers would accept deadlines.

These disclosures were a boon for appellants. Their lawyers found an array of serious *Brady* violations. As more infractions came to light, prosecutors in the state lost standing. The need for open-file discovery, and its potential benefits, became obvious.

Defense lawyers mounted a major lobbying effort, bolstered by the wide publicity about Gell's wrongful convictions. In 2004, the North Carolina state legislature passed a bill codifying and extending pretrial disclosure requirements in criminal cases.[23]

The new law required prosecutors to share their investigative files with defense attorneys in all felony cases. The statute applied to police investigation notes, defense and witness statements, test results, and the names of likely witnesses for a trial. In return, defense lawyers were to give the prosecution their witness lists and divulge their trial defense.

Along with the mandated disclosure, the law provided a variety of sanctions for failure to comply. These included granting a recess, barring any previously hidden evidence, declaring a mistrial, or even dismissing the case.

Three years later, this law compelled the disclosures that helped exonerate three Duke University lacrosse players falsely accused of rape. The prosecutor in that case, Michael Nifong, had withheld DNA test results from the alleged victim that did not match any of the students.

Texas was another surprise success story.

For decades the state mandated only minimal discovery in criminal cases. Reform efforts were unsuccessful. Then in late 2011, Michael Morton was released from prison and exonerated after serving nearly twenty-five years for allegedly murdering his wife, Christine, in 1986.[24]

New investigation showed that the prosecutor on the case, Ken Anderson, hid crucial evidence that would have proved Morton's innocence. This included the police report of a suspicious man lurking in the area and someone's use of Christine's Visa card *after* her murder. The state never tested a blue bandanna from the scene for blood or DNA and fought defense requests to do so.

In 2011, Morton finally won the right to test the bandanna. Along with Christine Morton's blood, it contained DNA from an unknown male. The DNA was entered into a national database. It matched a convicted killer named Mark Norwood. In 2013 he was convicted of Christine Morton's murder and sent to prison for life.

The outrage over Morton's wrongful conviction was widespread. New voices called for change. A nonprofit public interest law center, Texas Appleseed, joined with the Texas Defender Service to publish a paper titled *Improving Discovery in Criminal Cases in Texas: How Best Practices Contribute to Greater Justice.*[25] This report, along with a major lobbying effort headed by Morton himself, led to passage of the Michael Morton Act in 2013.

The act, which took effect on January 1, 2014, mandated open-file discovery. Specifically, the state was required to "promptly disclose" any information that could be considered exculpatory, impeaching, or mitigating without a request from the defense, even if discovered after a conviction. This evidence also had to be disclosed prior to any plea.

Texas Appleseed monitored the reforms and in 2015 issued a follow-up report titled *Towards More Transparent Justice: The Michael Morton Act's First Year.*[26] While they found some compliance problems, the writers' conclusion was positive. They believed that, over time, the act would "improve the fairness, accuracy and efficiency of the Texas criminal justice system, as it was designed to do."

Anderson, Morton's prosecutor, had become a judge in 2002. In September 2013 he resigned his judgeship after a Texas court ruled he "should face criminal contempt and tampering charges for failing to turn over evidence pointing to Morton's innocence." Two months later, after agreeing to disbarment, he was sentenced to ten days in prison for contempt.[27]

With time off for good behavior, Anderson spent ninety-six

hours in prison. By contrast, his crime had sent an innocent man to prison for twenty-four years, seven months, and eleven days.

The discovery reforms in both North Carolina and Texas also included a vital time element: they required prosecutors to disclose their evidence *before* any plea agreement.

That obligation was a giant step toward fairness. Defense lawyers had long argued *Brady* should apply to plea negotiations as much as to trials. Fully 97 percent of criminal cases are currently resolved through pleas.[28] The vast majority of defendants—anyone who's taken a deal—haven't been covered by the rule.

The Supreme Court has never directly considered whether *Brady* applies in pre-plea discussions. But their opinion in *U.S. v. Ruiz* (2002) made it clear that if anyone asked, the justices' answer would be an emphatic no.[29]

Angela Ruiz was stopped as she entered the United States from Mexico. Police found sixty-six pounds of marijuana in her luggage. The prosecutor offered a "fast-track" plea. He'd recommend a reduced sentence if she gave up her right to a trial and to two types of *Brady* material: evidence that could be used to impeach any witnesses against her and information supporting a defense. Ruiz declined the plea because of the required *Brady* waiver.

Ruiz later pled guilty and asked for the old sentencing offer back. The government refused. A federal judge took the prosecutor's new recommendation and gave her a standard guidelines sentence. Ruiz appealed. A divided panel from the Ninth Circuit Court of Appeals ruled the fast-track waiver was unconstitutional. The majority said *Brady* rights could not be surrendered, even in exchange for a plea.

A unanimous Supreme Court disagreed. Justice Stephen Breyer, writing for the Court, said *Brady* was meant to guarantee a fair trial. The rule had nothing to do with the validity of a guilty plea. In his concurrence, Justice Clarence Thomas emphasized that *Brady*'s sole concern was "avoidance of an unfair trial."[30]

Thomas's assertion was one more illustration of the Court's determined effort to keep the rule narrow. While most *Brady* cases involve trial-related issues, the rule itself had no explicit confines. Its founding principle was "justice suffers when any accused is treated unfairly." [31] But the Court gets to say what the rule means. Setting this limit was a way for the justices to simply shut the door on any consideration of pre-plea disclosure requirements. And one more reason to look outside the judicial system for real reform.

Breyer bolstered the Court's dubious holding by citing practical concerns. Requiring pre-plea *Brady* disclosures, he said, would "force the government to devote substantially more resources to trial preparation" and would "seriously interfere" with securing "guilty pleas that are factually justified, desired by defendants, and help secure the efficient administration of justice."

The *Ruiz* court also waded into deeper water by noting the Constitution "permits a court to accept a guilty plea . . . despite various forms of misapprehension under which a defendant might labor." [32] Among other things, this means a plea can be valid even when defendants know little or nothing about the case against them.

A common—and somewhat cynical—claim is that suspects accused of crimes don't need the details of the government's evidence, favorable or otherwise. They know what they've done. Or have not done.

That view, however logical, doesn't match the reality of the system.

Eyewitnesses can be uncertain or mistaken. People in trouble make false accusations to protect themselves or to earn favors or leniency. Police lie. Because of limited discovery laws and *Brady* violations, innocent defendants often don't know what evidence the prosecutor has that may help or hurt them. What they know is if they're convicted after a trial, they'll almost certainly get a far longer sentence than if they take a deal.

Many innocent people in this situation choose to plead. Of 354 DNA exonerees since 1989, 11 percent had pled guilty to serious crimes they didn't do.[33] Figures from the National Registry of Exonerations are similar. Over the past three decades, of more than 2,300 exonerees, 18 percent had pled. From that group, 65 percent were people of color.

These numbers illustrate why disclosing evidence before a plea is so important. When defendants know what kind of case the government has and what evidence they are facing, they can make informed decisions on how to proceed. They don't have to make blind guesses. That holds for guilty folks as well.

North Carolina and Texas did what the Supreme Court will likely never do. By mandating discovery prior to plea negotiations, they extended the benefits of full disclosure to thousands of criminal defendants who were previously excluded. They made the system fairer and far more transparent.

Down the road, the results of North Carolina's open-file rules would show that the Court's concerns about the dangers of pre-plea disclosure were unfounded. The opposite would prove true. This requirement would benefit the system in ways the justices never imagined.

Following North Carolina's lead, Ohio (2010), Louisiana (2013), and California (2015) also adopted broader discovery rules for criminal cases, along with sanctions for noncompliance.[34] None of their reforms were as sweeping as North Carolina's or Texas's. But to some degree they all required prosecutors to share investigative files and information prior to trial.

The embrace of expanded criminal discovery rules was by no means universal, however. Virginia had long had some of the nation's most restrictive discovery laws, which dated from 1972. Criminal defendants there were given a "trial by ambush," as one defense attorney put it.

To address the issue, in 2012 the Virginia Supreme Court, which sets rules for the state's courts, appointed a Special Committee on Criminal Discovery to recommend possible revisions.[35]

The committee—a representative group of prosecutors, judges, law professors, defense lawyers, police, and victim advocates— spent a year studying the issue. They proposed major reforms, with broad reciprocal discovery requirements that included providing witness lists, statements, police reports, and expert notice. Prosecutors would also be required to issue a certificate of compliance with *Brady*.

The committee members approved the recommended changes with only one dissenting vote: the representative of the Virginia State Police. Officers there, like most of their colleagues elsewhere, were concerned that any reforms requiring greater disclosure would make it harder to win convictions. The proposal was then circulated for public comment. The defense bar strongly supported the proposed new rules.

The Virginia Association of Commonwealth's Attorneys, the statewide organization of prosecutors, opposed the proposal, even though the group's members on the committee had voted for it. In November 2015, the Virginia Supreme Court "summarily and without explanation" dismissed the committee's report.[36] They left the rules as they were.

Virginia wasn't the only place where discovery reform ran into strong opposition. When a bipartisan group of U.S. senators tried to replicate North Carolina's success at the federal level, they ran into a prosecutorial buzz saw.

In the fall of 2008, only weeks before the November elections, Senator Ted Stevens (R-AK) was found guilty in a Washington, DC, federal court of seven felony counts of lying on ethics forms.[37]

Friends of the senator allegedly provided thousands of dollars of work on his Alaska home without being paid. Stevens had not reported these "gifts." At the time, he was the longest-serving Republican senator in history and was seeking his eighth term.

Following his convictions, Stevens narrowly lost his race.

Before he was even sentenced, his defense lawyers learned—from an anonymous FBI whistleblower—that prosecutors had committed a potpourri of serious *Brady* violations.[38]

They hid evidence that their key witness had previously made inconsistent statements, and had suborned perjury from an underage sex worker. They used business records they "undeniably knew were false." They gave the defense a series of intentionally inaccurate document summaries. They did not disclose a statement from a potential witness that supported Stevens's testimony that he had actually paid—or intended to pay—for the work.

When this information came to light, the federal trial judge, Emmet Sullivan, set aside Stevens's convictions. "In nearly 25 years on the bench," he said, "I've never seen anything approaching the mishandling and misconduct that I've seen in this case." He called the government's actions "systemic concealment of significant exculpatory evidence."[39] He also appointed an independent attorney to investigate other possible prosecutorial violations.

After the reversal, Stevens said his faith in the criminal justice system had been restored. Still, he wanted to "encourage the enactment of legislation to reform laws relating to the responsibilities and duties" of prosecutors. His hope was "that others may be spared from similar miscarriages of justice."

Six prosecutors who had worked on the case were investigated. Two were briefly suspended. The government's lead attorney was found to have exercised poor judgment. But none of them were prosecuted for the violations. Stevens died in a plane crash in 2010, before the investigations—which uncovered additional prosecutorial misdeeds—were completed.

In March 2012, Stevens's colleague Lisa Murkowski (R-AK) introduced the Fairness in Disclosure of Evidence Act.[40] At a hearing on the bill before the Senate Judiciary Committee three months later, she explained why she was promoting this legislation.

Murkowski said the Stevens's prosecution was "truly one of the darkest moments in the Justice Department's history."[41] The department's malfeasance "permeated every aspect" of the prosecution. "We are no longer able to do justice to Senator Stevens," she testified, "[b]ut we can . . . through reforms, make a start in ensuring that the same fate does not befall other defendants."

Her bill was not as far-reaching as North Carolina's law. But the key provision required federal prosecutors to disclose "information, data, documents, evidence or objects that may reasonably appear to be favorable to the defendant in a criminal prosecution."[42]

The bill's aim, as Murkowski explained, was to "eliminate the materiality requirement . . . and end the practice through which prosecutors rationalize their way out of disclosing material evidence by claiming that it is not material."

The bill addressed two other significant *Brady* issues: timing and sanctions. It required disclosure "without delay after arraignment and before the entry of any guilty plea," so that the information could be used to make decisions on any plea offers or plans for a trial. And it provided a range of remedies and punishments, depending on the facts of each situation.

A number of disparate organizations endorsed the bill, including the American Bar Association (ABA), the U.S. Chamber of Commerce, the American Civil Liberties Union (ACLU), and the Constitution Project, a think tank that tries to build bipartisan consensus on important legal questions.[43] The ABA president called it "an important step towards consistency and fairness in our justice system." He added that the "history of wrongful convictions because of unclear guidance is an entirely preventable tragedy."

The National Association of Criminal Defense Lawyers embraced the legislation as well. The group saw it as a "giant step forward in improving the fairness and accuracy of our criminal justice system." The proposed rules provided prosecutors with "the clear statutory guidance necessary to ensure the full and prompt disclosure to the defense of favorable evidence."

But the bill had powerful enemies: the Department of Justice (DOJ) and the U.S. attorneys who worked there. Even though DOJ employees had been responsible for the many abuses in Senator Stevens's trial, the department opposed any change in federal disclosure rules.

The deputy U.S. attorney general, James M. Cole, spoke for the DOJ at the June 2012 hearing on the legislation.[44] Robert Gay Guthrie, president of the 5,600-member National Association of Assistant U.S. Attorneys, sent a letter for that organization.[45] Their two-pronged arguments against the proposed bill echoed each other.

Cole acknowledged the misconduct in the Stevens case and said it was "unacceptable." Guthrie conceded there had been "[m]istakes of poor judgment and management." But both were adamant that these *Brady* violations were "aberrations." Both insisted there was no "systemic problem" with federal prosecutors related to discovery issues.

The two asserted that Murkowski's bill would not fix anything. On the contrary, they said, it would lead to "very real dangers to safety and privacy" for both victims and witnesses.

This alarmist claim is suspect at best. But it merits a closer look, because prosecutors and police officials and conservative politicians raise the issue of witness safety again and again to justify their opposition to substantive changes in discovery laws.

To support his argument, Cole offered four instances where witnesses to crimes had been threatened or killed to prevent them from testifying. All four were federal cases. All four had been handled according to the long-standing disclosure rules in effect for federal courts.

These examples had no link to Murkowski's bill. It was still just a proposal. But Cole alleged that it "fail[ed] to recognize the need to protect" witnesses and victims. If enacted, he warned darkly, the new law "would likely lead to an increase in such tragedies."

Participants in criminal cases can face threats and violence intended to silence them. It's an unfortunate feature of our adversarial system. There will always be some defendants brazen enough to try to intimidate or harm witnesses against them. It's vital to make sure that—when necessary—both victims and witnesses are protected.

But as Cole well knew, Murkowski's draft specifically provided that if prosecutors had legitimate safety concerns, they could request a protective order and could limit any disclosures that might endanger a witness. Every state with open-file discovery has a similar provision.

Empirical evidence also debunks the claim that open-file discovery makes witnesses less safe. "[T]hat hasn't happened in the jurisdictions that use it," wrote Avis Buchanan, director of the Public Defender Service in Washington, DC.[46] "In studies by some of the states and cities with open-file discovery . . . no causal link between the practice and witness intimidation has been found."

Researchers who studied North Carolina's rules reached the same conclusion. "We also found little evidence," they wrote, "that open-file discovery endangers the safety of witnesses, a common argument against the practice."[47]

Nowhere in their communications did Deputy Attorney General Cole or Assistant U.S. Attorney Guthrie mention any of the hundreds of defendants who were wrongly convicted because of the restrictive disclosure rules they were defending—rules that allowed prosecutors to withhold favorable evidence with near impunity.

Likewise, neither Cole nor Guthrie brought up the biggest reason members of the public are often afraid or unwilling to cooperate with the police. It has nothing to do with discovery rules.

New York Times reporter David Kocieniewski wrote a series of stories in 2007 about crime witness problems in Camden, New

Jersey.[48] "An array of powerful forces converges here," he said, that "discourage people from cooperating with the investigation of crimes—crimes committed against their own homes, their own neighbors, their own children."

The chief cause for this silence, he found, was the prevalence of "deep distrust of the local police and prosecutors and politicians . . . racial profiling, police corruption, and the excesses of the war on drugs have made them [community members] suspicious of virtually any arm of government."

New Jersey's deputy attorney general Hester Agudosi, who supervised all the state's prosecutors, agreed. "[T]he number of witnesses who remain silent because they fear for their safety," she said, "is probably less than one-tenth the number who refuse to talk because they fear the social repercussions."

"A lot of white Americans from suburban communities can't understand why people won't talk to law enforcement," said Harvard law professor Charles Ogletree, who studied witness intimidation issues for the National District Attorney's Association and who is Black. "In a lot of inner-city communities, there is so much hostility to the police that many people of color can't fathom why someone would even seriously consider helping them."

If Cole and Guthrie and the DOJ and its federal prosecutors truly want to increase witness safety and cooperation, they should be working to build better ties to the communities where people of color live and to increase the levels of trust. Not opposing discovery reform.

Claims by Cole and Guthrie that open-file discovery would "result in the unnecessary and harmful disclosure of national security-related information" and would "compromise intelligence . . . sources and methods" were equally dubious.[49]

Robbery or rape or murder cases almost never involve classified information. And for the tiny fraction of criminal matters related to national security issues, Murkowski's bill specifically provided—as Cole acknowledged—that classified evidence be

treated "in accordance with the Classified Information Procedures Act (CIPA)," the law that details how criminal cases involv-
ing classified information should be handled.

Even if the proposed legislation became law, information related to national security would be treated the same way it was
currently being handled.

Despite their flimsy arguments, the strong opposition of the
DOJ and its prosecutors overcame the bipartisan support for
Murkowski's proposed law and sank it.

Finally, the insistence of both Cole and Guthrie that there is no
"systemic problem" with *Brady* should not pass unremarked. They
must make that claim. If they conceded otherwise, they'd have to
admit the need for some serious reforms. So even as the violations
have mounted into the high hundreds, they continue to call them
"aberrations."

In Guthrie's letter opposing the bill, he called current *Brady*
practice part of "an already fair, well-known and well-understood
discovery process." Virtually every defense lawyer would find that
characterization funny were it not so sadly mistaken. And a variety of observers, from across the political spectrum, have noted
the irony of how a rule designed to increase fairness has ended up
doing the opposite.

Ex-judge Kozinski's view was that "[a]ll the incentives prosecutors confront encourage them not to discover or disclose exculpatory evidence. . . . Some prosecutors don't care about *Brady*
because courts don't make them care." [50]

In a brief supporting the Fuller appellants, the right-wing Texas
Public Policy Foundation agreed. *Brady*, they said, is "an invitation to withhold favorable evidence based on an asserted percep-
tion that the evidence against the defendant is overwhelming, or
to not look for such evidence in the first place." [51]

The joint study from the National Association of Criminal Defense Lawyers (NACDL) and the VERITAS Initiative of Santa

Clara University School of Law, which examined how the judiciary handled *Brady* claims, concluded that courts were "impeding fair disclosure in criminal cases" and "encouraging prosecutors to disclose as little favorable information as possible." [52]

Law professor and *Brady* scholar Bennett L. Gershman echoed the point: "As interpreted by the judiciary, *Brady* actually invites prosecutors to bend, if not break, the rules." [53] An overview of *Brady*'s history in the *University of San Francisco Law Review* argued that the rule not only "failed to protect factually innocent defendants" but it "facilitates the suppression of evidence" that leads to wrongful convictions.[54]

And in summarizing a study of unjust convictions through official wrongdoing, law professor Samuel Gross noted that "[m]isconduct by police, prosecutors and other law enforcement officials . . . [has] produced a steady stream of convictions of innocent people." [55]

Rather than promoting fairness, *Brady* had become a rule that "imped[es] fair disclosure." That "encourag[es]" and "invites" and "facilitates" the suppression of favorable evidence. That produces a "steady stream" of unlawful convictions.

That's the definition of a systemic problem.

8

THE LONG WAY HOME

The early years in prison were the toughest for Chris.

Gone were his dreams of an air force career, of a home and a family. His beloved grandmother, Mimi, died of cancer before the trial. He kept thinking his arrest hastened her death. He was only twenty. He couldn't imagine spending more time locked up than all the years he had lived. Or the possibility he might never be free.

Worst of all, Chris felt like he'd betrayed everyone who believed in him. He'd promised Mimi he would make something of his life. He'd vowed that his children wouldn't grow up like he had, with parents who were often missing. Now he was an absent father to his two small sons—and branded as a killer besides.

He was angry, too. Angry at himself for believing the system was fair, that being innocent would save him from a murder conviction. Angry for going along with his lawyer and for not fighting harder. Angry at Calvin and Derrick for lying on the stand and for saying he was part of this terrible crime. Angry at society for putting him in prison and for stealing his future.

Chris felt that in the whole world no one was as unlucky as he.

One of the few good things about his time at the DC Jail was that it prepared him for what lay ahead. When he was first arrested, he didn't think he could survive a single day behind bars. Then he didn't think he could take it for a week, until his detention hearing. When he was denied release, he couldn't imagine being locked up until his trial. But he made it, hour by hour.

It helped to have friends on the outside and on the inside. Neighborhood folks wrote or visited when they could. People he knew kept saying they had faith in him, even after he was convicted. At the jail, he and his codefendants encouraged one another.

They needed all the support they could find. As the awful details about Catherine Fuller's murder became public, folks in the community—and many of their fellow inmates—were understandably outraged. From what they heard, people assumed the 8th and H guys were guilty. They deserved whatever they got.

All the defendants faced constant pressure. Men at the jail spit on them. One day when Chris was at court, someone got into his locker and ripped up pictures of him with his friends. A guard threw a burning piece of cloth into Steve's cell so other officers could come with fire extinguishers to spray everything down and ruin all his belongings.

More serious threats were in the air. After the convictions, a *Washington Post* columnist wrote that "[f]rom the day of the arrests in the Fuller murder case, according to informed sources, death contracts were being circulated and signed within the D.C. Jail and down at Lorton, where two of Fuller's sons [from her first marriage] are doing time."[1] Lorton was the prison for DC inmates, located nearby in Virginia.

One evening, as Chris walked back to his tier in handcuffs, a guard he'd known slightly on the street pushed him hard and called a Code Blue—attack on an officer. Other guards came running. The one who started things tried to bash Chris in the head with a big flashlight. Chris managed to dodge the blow. Back in his cell, he realized he could have been seriously hurt or even killed. He didn't feel safe after that.

Chris knew he was hardening. But he couldn't let that incident go. A few days later, he passed the guard who had tried to harm him. "I know where you live," Chris said quietly. He promised to kill the man when he got out. Chris had no such plan. But he wanted to make it clear no one could threaten him without paying a price.

Because Lorton had limited space, most DC prisoners with long sentences went into the federal system. Chris's time came in mid-1986. He was sent to the U.S. penitentiary in Ashland, Kentucky. It was still difficult, despite his experience.

Inmates talked, and stories spread. Other convicts soon knew why Chris was there. At mealtimes, when he got his tray and sat in an empty seat, anyone at the table would move to another one. When he passed guys in a hallway or on the yard and offered a greeting, he would meet a hard stare. They didn't want anything to do with someone they thought helped brutalize and kill a small defenseless woman.

Chris knew he would carry that mark forever. If he had a future, it was a bleak one.

A book changed his mind—and his life.

Kaffir Boy was the autobiography of a South African named Mark Mathabane.[2] He was raised in extreme poverty during the apartheid era in Alexandra, a Black township on the edge of Johannesburg. Violence, sadistic police officers, and roving gangs were an everyday part of his childhood. Still, he taught himself to read and to play tennis. With help from U.S. pro Stan Smith, he got a tennis scholarship. He came to the United States and became a writer.

The book was a revelation for Chris. Mathabane's early life had been far worse than his. Despite long odds, Mathabane had achieved success. He hadn't let himself be poisoned by bitterness or by anger over his bad luck. It got Chris thinking. Maybe he could be that kind of person.

The first step was developing a new mindset. He tried to see his situation as an opportunity, not as a punishment. He decided to stop acting like a victim or letting officers treat him like a number.

Chris decided to move, in his words, "from being agitated to being educated."

He started taking all the classes and training programs he could. He got involved in the policies and politics of whatever institution he was in, working to make conditions better. Over time, Chris built a reputation with his fellow inmates, and even a few prison administrators, as a reasonable advocate for progress. In the process, he changed himself.

Chris was moved repeatedly. Long-term federal inmates are typically transferred every two or three years so they won't get too comfortable in any prison. Chris was delighted when he and his brother, Fella, were both at the prison in Allenwood, Pennsylvania, for a year in the late 1990s. They became cellmates and grew closer than they had ever been on the street. Being together eased part of the hurt of the separation from their family.

All the men were shocked by Steve Webb's sudden death on July 30, 1999.[3] He was at the U.S. penitentiary in Terre Haute, Indiana, playing a baseball game for the prison championship. He caught a foul popup and collapsed on the field. Hollywood and Bobo had been watching from the stands. When Steve fell, they ran to his side.

"Man, don't do this," Bobo yelled. "We're going home, man. Don't leave, Steve. We're going home." But Steve was gone. The cause of death was an aneurysm. He was thirty-four years old.

As the years passed, any chance for legal relief seemed to dim. Chris and several of the others contacted groups that helped wrongly convicted prisoners. They tried to find someone, somewhere, to take another look at their plight. But they couldn't point to anything concrete that might exonerate them. The case was so sprawling any review would be daunting.

Hope seemed wasted. Then there came an unexpected ray of light.

———

The source was a tenacious, fearless *Washington Post* reporter named Patrice Gaines.

She was in the courtroom on December 16, 1985, when the first Fuller verdicts were announced. She later wrote, "The foreman said 'guilty' so many times I stopped counting." [4] Each one hit her "with the force of a hammer."

Gaines's reaction was unusual for a member of the media. She'd grown up just outside Washington, DC, in Prince George's County, Maryland. [5] She knew the neighborhood of the murder because her family shopped at the businesses on H Street NE in her teen years. And on visits to her grandma's home in DC she would change buses at 8th and H Streets.

During high school, Gaines drifted into trouble: skipping classes, shoplifting, using drugs. She had a daughter. At twenty-one, she was arrested in North Carolina on a heroin charge. She spent the summer in jail. She ultimately pled guilty in exchange for five years' probation.

Gaines wanted desperately to be a writer. She took college classes, worked part-time, and eventually landed a job as a researcher/writer for the *Charlotte News*. From there she went to the *Miami News*, then to the *Washington Star*. After freelancing for the *Post*, in 1985 she was hired as a staff reporter.

The *Post* sent Gaines into the 8th and H neighborhood to gather background on the Fuller case and the suspects. The more she learned, the more troubled she became. She started with a vague sense that something was amiss in the official story. She ended with the conviction it was just wrong.

Her unease was fed by what she had lived through. After her arrest, alone and afraid and lost, officers said she could give up her suppliers or "we can see to it you never get out of here." She came close to making up information to save herself. Now Gaines saw that nearly all the evidence against the defendants in the Fuller case came from kids with problems. Kids like herself. Kids who were told they could talk or disappear in prison.

But no one else seemed bothered by these concerns. After eight of the defendants were convicted, the case was considered closed. Gaines had other stories and a career to focus on. She tried to put the whole thing behind her. For nine years, it mostly worked.

In 1994, Gaines published her autobiography *Laughing in the Dark*. She told the story of her personal and family problems, her troubles with the law, her struggle to find success—and fulfillment—as a Black woman and as a writer. The book was widely praised. One review, in *USA Today*, caught Chris's attention.

He wrote Gaines a letter, which she later lost. But she could remember, almost word for word, the part most important to her. "Dear Mrs. Gaines," Chris had written from his prison cell,

> I would never have guessed we had anything in common. I used to pray that something bad would happen to you because you were part of the media that put me here. But I long ago learned that praying is not for bad. . . . But I want you to know I am still innocent.[6]

Gaines called Chris. At his suggestion she met with a group of mothers of the convicted men. A few weeks later she went to see him at the penitentiary in Allenwood, Pennsylvania. As they talked, he showed her a letter Derrick Bennett had sent him.

"I want to have one good night's sleep before I die," Derrick had written. "I have ruined a lot of people's lives with my lies." He said his trial testimony against Chris and the others was false. He offered to testify again, this time on Chris's behalf.

After the meeting, Gaines spoke to Derrick by phone at his Wisconsin prison.[7] He said simply: "I lied on those dudes and myself." Derrick told Gaines that after hours of interrogation, he agreed to talk to avoid a possible life sentence.

"The detectives basically fed me information about the murder," he said, "and I just repeated what they told me when they turned on the video camera."

Gaines talked next with Calvin Alston at the federal prison in Ashland, Kentucky. He told a similar story. He lied because the detectives told him that if he didn't help them, he would spend the rest of his life in prison.[8]

Calvin said he knew the outlines of the crime from being in the neighborhood. In the interrogation room, the detectives kept going over it. They offered "bits and pieces" of a story, "an outline of what they thought took place." After a lot of prompting and revising, they turned on the video. He said his statement—which had broken the case—was simply untrue.

Gaines was hooked. She persuaded her editors to let her do an in-depth feature about the Fuller case ten years after. From what she had seen of the trial, and from what Derrick and Calvin said, she believed more than ever the defendants were innocent. She needed proof.

With help from a colleague, Bill Miller, she put together a list of people from the case: witnesses, detectives, prosecutors, defendants, jurors. She got the *Post*'s lawyers to request the relevant police documents. One by one, Gaines began tracking down the young people who testified for the prosecution.

Gaines met with Katrina Ward, Levy Rouse's old flame. She wouldn't say directly she'd lied under oath.[9] But she contradicted key parts of her testimony. Levy never told her he "did the worst thing to that lady." She said she was just a scared teenager who testified as she did because McGinnis and Sanchez threatened to charge her with murder.

Gaines caught up with Maurice Thomas at the hair salon where he worked. He said he hadn't lied on the stand.[10] But he couldn't recall how he ended up being a witness. Or where he was coming from or going to that day. "It was so long ago. I can't remember what I saw."

To many of the jurors, Maurice seemed to be the least-biased prosecution witness. When Gaines asked Katrina—his first

cousin—about Maurice, she had a very different take. She told
Gaines Maurice didn't really know anything about the crime. His
testimony was payback—his chance to get even with the guys who
disrespected him and teased him for being gay.

Katrina didn't believe he would ever come clean. "Maurice has
no heart," she said.[11] "He told me the other day he doesn't care if
he goes to hell. He's not telling the truth."

These interviews deepened Gaines's belief that the Fuller investigation had been seriously flawed.

Virtually all the government's evidence came from repeated,
relentless interrogations of teenagers as young as thirteen. Only
after officers threatened them with murder charges, followed by
offers of leniency in exchange for help. It seemed like the police
weren't looking for the truth. They were trying to prove their
theory.

Gaines talked to the detectives and the prosecutor about her
concerns. They denied any wrongdoing. Gossage said he wasn't
surprised or bothered by the recantations. He called it "business
as usual" among convicted killers.[12] The officers, he said, always
followed procedures "within the confines of all the laws."

Sanchez laughed at the memory of the playacting he had done
to scare information out of sixteen-year-old Cliff—banging on
the door and yelling like a bull and tearing his T-shirt.[13] He insisted he never solicited false testimony.[14] "There is no humanity
in these people," he said of the defendants. "If they had capital
punishment, they deserve it."

Goren said he had "no reason at all to believe" that Derrick and
Calvin had lied when they testified. "I can speculate about why
they might now want to change their minds . . . But I don't think
they are recanting because now they're telling the truth."[15]

Gaines's files on the murder got thicker and thicker. She felt a
wave of excitement when she found Ammie Davis's statement telling police she had seen James Blue attack Fuller. But she couldn't

follow up that lead. Blue had killed Davis in 1985 and died in prison in 1993.[16]

Her belief that the men had been wrongly convicted never wavered. But as months turned into years, support from her superiors did. Gaines submitted several story proposals and met resistance. Her editors agreed she had unearthed major problems with the case. But she had no convincing proof of the men's innocence.

Gaines finally got permission to publish her piece, on one condition. She had to frame any conclusions as opinions, not facts.[17] That caveat devalued her narrative and made the substantive doubts she raised seem more like quibbles. But it was her only option.

Gaines's six-year odyssey with the case took a serious toll, personally and professionally. Her story ran in the *Post* on Sunday, May 6, 2001. The next day she resigned.

She didn't give up. Gaines had learned two lessons. She'd have to go outside the *Post* to make anything happen. And the case wasn't just a matter for a reporter; it needed lawyers.

Gaines sent a copy of her story to the Mid-Atlantic Innocence Project (MAIP) in Washington, DC, the local arm of the national organization that works to exonerate the wrongly convicted and to promote criminal legal reform. She followed that up with a letter, giving more details about what the detectives had done in their investigation and about the favorable evidence that had been hidden by the prosecution.

A few weeks later, Gaines was elated when MAIP agreed to take the case.

In the meantime, Chris Turner was nearing a major milestone: mandatory parole eligibility.[18] He wasn't optimistic about his odds. Parole wasn't exoneration, but it would mean being out of jail.

Along with the notoriety of the killing, Chris faced another huge roadblock. To be paroled, an inmate needs to show he has been rehabilitated. Most parole boards believe a major part of rehabilitation is admitting guilt and expressing remorse—typically called "acceptance of responsibility." [19]

A person's refusal to acknowledge guilt can be seen as a refusal to be rehabilitated. After two and a half decades, Chris was not about to deny what he had said from the start: he had nothing to do with the crime. Even if it meant not going free.

Once Chris got a July 2009 date for his parole hearing, he began consulting with his new lawyers. They needed an uncommon approach for any chance at success. Together they decided to supplement his application with two kinds of materials: (1) information supporting his innocence, including the recantation affidavits from Calvin and Derrick; and (2) a statement of sympathy for Catherine Fuller and her family. Chris could not, and would not, admit to any part in the killing.

He knew that if he'd been willing to say he was involved in the crime and to express remorse, he would likely have been released years earlier. Despite his exemplary prison record, and one of the longest lists of awards, honors, and educational achievements the parole board had ever seen, it took twenty-four years to even get a hearing.

So he was shocked when—after a long period of consideration—the examiners voted to grant him parole. They gave him a presumptive release date for April 2010.

On a sunny Thursday morning, September 9, 2010, Chris Turner walked out of the high-security section of the U.S. penitentiary in Atwater, California. He had been in prison for 9,405 days and nights.

As officials processed Chris out, they gave him $50, a surplus pair of pants, a shirt, and a voucher for a Greyhound ticket to Washington, DC. He withdrew the $87 in his prison account. He had a few pictures, his release papers, and his glasses. He wore jail shoes and socks and underwear.

Chris was forty-four years old. That was everything he owned in the world.

He'd dreamed of being free since the day he was locked up. He wasn't sure it would ever happen. In late 2009, when the parole board unexpectedly gave him an April 2010 release date, he was still uncertain. As the time drew near, he couldn't lose the fear that something—a change in the rules, an alleged infraction, an administrative mistake—might keep him inside.

He'd seen that happen to others. His concern only grew when the board pushed his date back to September 2010 to review his application further. It ramped up when the Federal Bureau of Prisons refused to grant him early release to a federal halfway house. They told Chris his crime was so serious he would be held until his final day.

Next the parole office in DC told Chris to report in person by noon on September 10, the day after his release. He couldn't possibly get across the country that fast by bus. His case manager at the prison called them to say Chris needed a few days of grace. Now he was worried about starting off on the wrong foot.

But the moment came. He was released. He felt no wild joy. Just relief, mostly.

A low-security inmate drove Chris to the bus station in Modesto, where he traded his voucher for a ticket. He got to Los Angeles and changed buses for Dallas.

They traveled east through the desert, with the air-conditioning blasting nonstop. Chris had only his thin pants and a short-sleeved shirt. He got so cold he started shaking. When the bus stopped in Lordsburg, New Mexico, the driver announced a short break. Chris saw a Family Dollar Store across the street. He decided to run over and get some warmer clothes.

As he left the store, he saw the bus easing out of the parking lot. He sprinted after it, but he was too late. The bus headed toward Texas with his few belongings but without him. He had to wait a whole day for the next one.

After seventy-five hours on the road, Chris finally reached DC. Despite repeated calls to Greyhound, he never got his property back. He had nothing from his old life to bring into his new one.

Chris's bus trip home wasn't exactly a metaphor for what would follow. Still, it was hard adjusting to life outside.

At the parole office the next morning, Chris got stringent conditions. He had to report in person every week. He had to submit urine samples for drug and alcohol testing twice a week. He had to find regular employment and provide proof of work hours and copies of pay stubs. He had to get permission anytime he left DC. He had to wear an electronic monitor and observe a daily curfew.

Chris had no money, so his first need was a job. Within two weeks he was hired as a parking attendant at the Washington Hospital Center. Neither the pay nor the hours were good, but it was a start.

His top personal goal was to reconnect with his two sons. Both had been in trouble with the law. One was sent to DC Jail for a drug offense the day after Chris's homecoming. More than anything, he wanted to talk to them about what he had learned. He wanted to help them avoid his mistakes.

Forming a bond proved difficult. They didn't really know him. They weren't in the mood for life advice from a stranger. They told him he didn't understand the modern world. And who was he, anyway, to tell them how to live after the way he messed up his whole life.

It was hard for Chris to be patient with them. But over the months, they were able to spend more time together. His sons realized he was going to be around for the long haul now. Their rapport slowly improved and evolved into a source of pleasure rather than a cause of pain.

One of the toughest adjustments was getting used to the pace of life in the free world. Everyone and everything moved so fast.

In prison, Chris always had time to sit and think about things. Outside was the opposite.

It wasn't easy to simply relax, to spend a few hours doing nothing. So much of his life had been taken from him. He'd sit down to rest and immediately start thinking he should be working, or studying, or doing something. He should be making up, somehow, for all those lost years.

He also had to decipher the mechanics of everyday life. Inside, he didn't worry about meals or bills or appointments. He didn't need transportation or groceries or utilities. He never thought about buying toilet paper or toothpaste or sheets. He'd never owned a car or had insurance or paid for gas or repairs. It took time to adapt.

His efforts to find a better job were discouraging. Over and over, the first interview would go well. People would promise to get back to him quickly. When they checked his history, they'd learn he'd recently been released after serving twenty-six years for a terrible murder. Usually, he never heard back.

Over time, though, things got easier. Chris figured out his cell phone. He learned how to shop and drive and use the internet and an ATM. He got his own apartment with cable TV, so he could watch his beloved Dallas Cowboys. He mastered the ins and outs of owning his own car. He did what he could to help the lawyers working on his case.

The Fuller murder was unlike many cases MAIP worked to reopen.

There was no DNA evidence, no smoking gun to conclusively exonerate the accused. There were seven living defendants. The trial had taken five weeks. Along with hundreds of pages of police reports and records was a trial transcript of nearly nine thousand pages. Gaining even a basic knowledge of the proceedings required a serious commitment.

MAIP was able to attract lawyers from several of DC's biggest firms. For the first time, the defendants had competent counsel who believed in their innocence. These law firms also had deep pockets. They paid investigators to track down trial participants and other potential witnesses who had spoken to the police. They amassed a wealth of material.

Among the most significant—and disturbing—pieces of evidence were sworn statements from the two key government snitches. In an affidavit on February 13, 2009, Derrick Bennett summed up his actions at the trial.

> I lied when I testified. I did not see anyone attack Mrs. Fuller or see anything related to her assault and murder; my testimony about the assault on her was untrue. . . . As far as I know, none of the defendants had anything to do with killing Mrs. Fuller.[20]

Derrick said he was a "young and inexperienced teenager" who was "scared and intimidated" into testifying. He asserted that Goren and McGinnis and Sanchez "told me what I should say about what happened, and what I should say about who did what."

Calvin Alston had made a similar statement in his affidavit almost a year earlier, on March 7, 2008.

> I lied when I testified that I witnessed any part of the attack and murder of Mrs. Fuller, as I was not in the park or the alley by H Street that afternoon, and I never saw anything with respect to the attack and murder of Mrs. Fuller. . . . I provided false testimony in exchange for being able to enter a guilty plea to a second-degree murder charge.[21]

Through MAIP's efforts, the pace of discovery picked up. The government turned over more and more information. The lawyers learned how Ammie Davis's statement about James Blue's attack on Fuller had been misplaced. How after it resurfaced, it was deliberately withheld.

They learned new facts from experts in forensic pathology and crime scene examination. Fuller's injuries, though serious, did not match the details of the attack offered by the alleged eyewitnesses. The location and type of her wounds were most consistent with an assault by one or two people, not twenty or more.

In early 2010, reviewing prosecution files, the appellate lawyers learned that James McMillian was at the crime scene near the time of the murder. They found the accounts of the three independent witnesses who'd told police he was by the garage—acting suspiciously, hiding something under his coat, running when the police came. Goren had kept that secret, before and during the trial.

Chris's lawyers filed their first motion to vacate his convictions on January 6, 2010.[22] After finding the McMillian information, they filed a new motion three months later.[23] The primary claim was that the government had violated *Brady* by deliberately withholding evidence of McMillian's presence at the scene and Ammie Davis's report of seeing James Blue attack Fuller.

Attorneys for the other defendants—Tim Catlett, Levy Rouse, Charles Turner, Kelvin Smith, Russell Overton, and Cliff Yarborough—made similar filings soon afterward.

The lawyers asked the court to set an evidentiary hearing where they could present their new evidence. The government opposed any hearing, arguing these claims were inconsequential and decades too late.

New details piled up until the information could no longer be ignored. The U.S. Attorney's Office finally agreed a hearing was needed to resolve the issues that had arisen. Robert Scott, the original trial judge, was long dead. The case was assigned to Frederick Weisberg, who'd been a DC superior court judge for more than thirty years.

The six appellants still serving time—middle-aged men now—were brought back to Washington for the hearing. Seeing them together, with Chris in a business suit and the others in orange jumpsuits, it was hard to picture them hanging out in a park or visiting the go-go clubs. Or committing a street robbery, for that matter.

Some of them had never been close, or even friends. There were strained relationships among a few. Levy, in particular, still blamed Cliff for giving a video statement to the police, implicating him and most of his codefendants. Others understood Cliff's limitations and cut him a bit of slack. As at the trial, they sat there together, sharing the same fate.

To a non-lawyer, the recantations seem like the best evidence of innocence. The prosecution's star witnesses, Calvin and Derrick, flatly swore they had lied at the trial to help themselves. Both said they hadn't even seen the killing. They didn't know how it happened or who did it.

As compelling as these affidavits were, recantations get short shrift in our system.[24] One reason is the law craves finality. Revisiting a long-resolved matter, decided by a jury, is inefficient and costly. Judges fear they'll be asked to reopen a case every time some new information, some new piece of evidence, comes to light. There's a strong reluctance to even start down that path, which works against any *Brady* claim. As Justice Louis Brandeis noted: "[I]t is more important that the applicable rule of law be settled than that it be settled right."[25]

The other main concern is judging the truth of a recantation. The most common reason for telling a new story is that at the time of the old story, the person was facing serious punishment and lied to get leniency. The witnesses in this case said that's what they'd done.

But people recant for other reasons as well—reasons that can apply to previous truthful testimony. They may be sorry about the effect of their words. They may regret seeing former friends or associates wasting away in jail. They may feel guilty about how easily they got off.

That's why recantations are always iffy. When a person tells one version of events under oath and then recants and tells a different version, we know at least one of the stories is false. Judge Weisberg put it succinctly: "[W]ith any recantation, the court is necessarily confronted with a witness who has demonstrated a willingness to lie under oath."[26]

Despite their power, the legal weight of the recantations was minimal. Alone, they would not be nearly enough to win an appeal.

The lawyers believed their best grounds for winning a reversal were the government's *Brady* violations. They had proof the prosecutor had deliberately buried several pieces of information favorable to the defense.

Most prominent were the statements of the three witnesses putting James McMillian at the crime scene near the time of the killing. A close second was Ammie Davis's report about seeing James Blue "beat the fuck" out of Fuller. Both suggested a different crime scenario and countered the idea the assault was a gang attack.

The pleadings asserted that if this information had been disclosed, the trial attorneys would have had strong, credible alternatives to the prosecution's theory. The jurors deliberated seven full days. A clear optional narrative would likely have resulted in different verdicts.

As the hearing date neared, the lawyers cycled between hope and doubt. They knew their arguments and their evidence were solid. They also knew they were challenging a story that had been accepted as the gospel for nearly twenty-eight years.

The new trial hearing began in DC Superior Court on April 23, 2012.

Cliff Yarborough was the first witness. He'd been only sixteen when officers picked him up in October 1984. He testified he didn't remember making *any* statement that night, that the detectives just wrote what they wanted.[27] He signed and initialed the pages they typed.

Cliff also swore the video confession he made two months later, after his arrest on December 9, 1984, was false. He talked because he was afraid. He said McGinnis and Sanchez pushed him around the interrogation room, slammed him into the wall and a cabinet, and put his head in a toilet bowl.

During his testimony, Cliff struggled to remember facts and sometimes seemed confused and uncertain. That wasn't surprising, given the passage of time. He was a sympathetic witness but not an especially credible one.

Calvin Alston and Derrick Bennett took the stand to repudiate—under oath—their video statements and their trial testimonies. Both said they did not see the crime or have any part in it. They knew details about the killing only because the police fed them information.

Calvin testified that the detectives went over his story with him ten to twelve times before turning on the video. "It was basically like they were coaching me."[28] Derrick said they would tell him what to say when the camera was off.[29] He would repeat it when the video was on. Both asserted they changed their roles from observers to participants because McGinnis and Sanchez said they had to make themselves guilty to get their plea bargains.

Derrick was still a wild card. He claimed that at one point in the interview, where static lines show up on the video, he actually "jumped up . . . and told them 'Look, this is a lie. This is not the truth, and I'm through with the interview.' " He said the detectives got mad, stopped the tape, and began the process "all over again."

Neither Calvin nor Derrick were particularly convincing on the stand. Their memories were incomplete and their recollections selective. At times they seemed to be straining to make amends for trading false testimony for leniency.

The appellants found firmer ground with their next two witnesses. Richard Callery, the chief medical examiner for the state of Delaware, testified about Fuller's injuries as an expert in forensic pathology. Like the original ME on the case, he couldn't say for sure how many assailants there had been. But both the type and the location of Fuller's wounds suggested to him just one to three attackers, not a group of ten or more.[30]

Larry McCann, a veteran police officer who spent years investigating murders and sexual assaults for the Virginia Bureau of Criminal Investigation, testified as an expert in violent crime analysis and crime scene reconstruction. He agreed with Dr. Callery. The facts of the crime were most consistent with just one or two offenders.[31]

McCann based his conclusion on three facts:

(1) Fuller's clothes were near the body, undamaged. With multiple offenders, her clothing likely would have been "stretched, torn, ripped and farther away."

(2) She had only one injury to her torso. With many attackers, the frenzy and peer pressure would have led to extensive injuries "all over her body."

(3) There had been only one sexual assault. With a group, there would have been multiple assaults.

McCann's testimony contradicted other parts of the government's case as well. From the location of Fuller's scarf, raincoat, and umbrella, McCann said she was likely attacked near the 9th Street end of the alley. At the trial, both Derrick and Calvin said Fuller was pushed into the alley from 8th Street and assaulted at that end.

He also testified that the blood and clothing at the crime scene showed Fuller had been sodomized behind the closed left door of the garage, where her body was found. That conclusion directly conflicted with what Calvin and Cliff had said about where the attack took place.

The lead prosecutor, Jerry Goren, was the government's first and most crucial witness. His aim was to explain—and justify—his investigation and prosecution of the case and to rebut as many of the appellants' claims as possible. The bulk of his testimony was cross-examination about the favorable information he'd failed to disclose to the defense.

Goren said McGinnis first told him about Ammie Davis's statement in August 1985, two months before the trial. Inexplicably, the information had been "lost in the shuffle," as he put it, for ten months. Once he had the report of her interview, he made a deliberate decision not to disclose it. He conceded he had looked at Davis's story through the lens of the prosecution's theory. It didn't fit with a gang attack. He deemed it incredible.[32]

The sharpest questioning focused on James McMillian. Goren acknowledged he had chosen to withhold the identifications of McMillian and his associate, Gerald Merkerson, even though three independent witnesses had placed them at the scene and said they were acting suspiciously.

During the trial, Monk's lawyer specifically asked about the identities of the two men who ran from the garage. Goren would not answer. He told the judge the information was not relevant because they were at the scene only long after the killing. On the stand now, Goren admitted he had been wrong about that timing.[33] It was twenty-seven years too late.

Chris and the others were optimistic when the government finished its case. They felt sure they had met the first two requirements for a *Brady* violation: (1) the prosecution had found evidence favorable to the defense, and (2) the evidence was never disclosed.

But they needed to show how the hidden information was material.

In closing arguments, the appellate lawyers used the recantations, the previously withheld information, and the expert testimony to present a new scenario.[34]

Given all the evidence now available, an attack on Fuller by one or two assailants was far more credible than a gang attack by twenty or more teens. To prove materiality, and win relief, they had to show Weisberg that the official theory of the crime—which had been assumed to be true for almost three decades—was simply wrong.

First, they argued that the police and the prosecutor had too quickly embraced the gang narrative, then molded the evidence to fit their story. They pointed out that Goren admitted, under oath, he ignored facts and leads that pointed elsewhere. And nearly every government witness claimed to have been coerced into talking.

Second, they said that without the now-recanted confessions, the evidence could not support a scenario of dozens of assailants. As their experts had testified, Fuller's actual injuries were most consistent with one or two attackers. And the circumstances of the crime scene were not typical of a group assault.

Third, they highlighted the many inconsistencies and factual errors in the stories of the supposed eyewitnesses, which the original trial lawyers had never done. These mistakes and contradictions, plus the recantations, supported a conclusion that the two key witnesses were not even present during the crime.

Their concluding argument was that the prosecution actually had a weak case, with little credible information to support it. If the defense attorneys had known about the *Brady* evidence and been able to use it at the trial, the result would have been different.

In its response, the government at last conceded the obvious: clearly exculpatory facts had been withheld from the defense. But their bedrock claim remained. The evidence against the men was "overwhelming." None of the hidden information would have made a difference in the outcome of the trial. So none of it was material.

Throughout the hearing, and in later arguments, the strength of the prosecution's evidence would be a highly disputed point.

This was far more than a question of semantics. It went to the legal heart of the matter. The more powerful the government's case, the heavier the burden to show that any new evidence undermined confidence in the original verdicts and required a reversal.

In its 1988 opinion upholding the convictions, the DC Court of Appeals (DCCA) had included a footnote about the assault. In it, the judges opined that while there were conflicts in the testimony, there was "overwhelming" evidence each of the defendants had been involved.[35]

That evidence—the confessions and trial testimony of Calvin and Derrick—had since been recanted. Nevertheless, this footnote adjective became a mantra for supporters of the verdicts. They used it repeatedly. In its brief, the government said none of the *Brady* claims were material because they were "overwhelmingly contradicted" by evidence that Fuller had been brutally killed by a large group of assailants.[36]

In contrast, the defense lawyers repeatedly asserted that the prosecution had an underwhelming case.[37] No physical evidence ever linked any of the defendants to the killing. All the alleged eyewitnesses were young and vulnerable to police pressure and had changed their stories repeatedly. Not one neighbor or passerby who was unconnected to the case had seen anything related to a group assault. It had taken the jury a week to reach the first verdicts.

The appellants had another strong counter to the DCCA footnote: Goren himself. He knew the case best. In 1997 he told the *Post* he'd been "skeptical" about his trial witnesses. He said the case "easily could have gone the other way."[38]

———

That would not be Judge Weisberg's view. Two months after the hearing ended, on August 6, 2012, he denied all the claims raised by the appellants.[39] The recantations and the new evidence had not even slightly dented his faith in the official theory of the murder.

Near the start of his thirty-eight-page opinion, Weisberg noted the DCCA claim that the evidence of guilt was "overwhelming." Then he cut to the chase: his belief that the recantations "are at the heart of all of petitioners' claims. Unless the court credits the recantations, petitioners . . . cannot demonstrate that any of the information that was not disclosed . . . meets the test for 'materiality' under *Brady v. Maryland*."

Weisberg didn't just discredit Calvin's and Derrick's recantations. He called them "nothing short of preposterous."[40] But in opting to credit their trial testimonies rather than their recantations, the judge passed over the full context of their words. He revealed more about his state of mind than about the state of the evidence.

Both Calvin and Derrick initially denied knowing anything about the murder. After intense questioning and threats of life in prison, each of them said he saw the crime. Only after more time and more threats and more promises did they agree to say they took part in the killing and would testify against the others.

For their cooperation, both snitches got reduced sentences. In prison, they apologized to several of the others for giving false testimony. Later, they signed sworn affidavits and testified under oath that at the trial they had lied about participating in or even seeing the murder.

The testimonies of Calvin and Derrick the judge credited were not the first or even the second version of the crime they had given. It was just the one that fit the official story. Based on the new evidence and the many conflicts and errors in their claims, Weisberg could easily have called their trial testimonies preposterous and their recantations credible. What he could not do was entertain the notion the gang theory might have been wrong from the start.

Weisberg next turned to the *Brady* claims. They were "not so easily dismissed," he said, before proceeding to dismiss them.[41]

In his view, Davis's story was "thoroughly discredited" by "numerous eyewitness accounts and other evidence proving the crimes were committed by a large group of young men acting in concert." Since he believed the gang theory was fact, Davis's report could not be true.

Weisberg agreed that the duty to disclose evidence favorable to the accused was not trumped by the government's lack of belief in the evidence. But rather than chastising Goren for doing just that, the judge excused him. He said it was "understandable why . . . this careful and fair-minded prosecutor" did not consider Davis's information to be credible.

In Weisberg's view, the McMillian evidence would be material only if he and Merkerson did the crime by themselves. And "that possibility flies in the face of all the evidence."

What he meant by "all the evidence," of course, was the prosecution's *trial* evidence. The appellants had just given him a wealth of new information showing the crime was most likely the work of one or two men. But he could not—or would not—imagine that possibility.

Judge Weisberg's ruling was painful but not surprising. The hill was getting steeper.

Even though the new trial hearing confirmed the government hid crucial pieces of favorable evidence from the defense, the appellants still lost. The presumption of innocence is only for those charged with a crime. After a conviction, there is the presumption of guilt. Courts give deference to any past decisions by juries and judges.

The attorneys appealed Weisberg's ruling to the DCCA and tried to stay hopeful. Two years later, in April 2014, the case was heard by a three-judge panel of that court.

During the argument, the judges seemed troubled by the

prosecution's actions in concealing exculpatory information. But thirteen months later, in a forty-one-page opinion, the DCCA affirmed the lower court's ruling.[42]

One of the judges called Ammie Davis's story "very compelling" and expressed the view that an eyewitness account of an alternate perpetrator is "always material."[43] But that point was moot. Davis had been murdered before the Fuller trial. She "was unavailable to testify at it."

If Blue hadn't killed Davis, her potential testimony might well have been material. Since she was dead, Goren was off the hook.

The heart of the ruling came in the third paragraph. The *Brady* claims "fail because appellants have not shown a reasonable probability that the outcome of their trial would have been different had the government disclosed the withheld evidence in timely fashion."[44]

The judges understood that the hidden evidence went directly to the key point of disagreement: "[t]he basic structure of how the crime occurred." The opinion carried this point to its extreme conclusion.

> This makes the burden on appellants to show materiality quite difficult to overcome, because it requires a reasonable probability that the withheld evidence (in its entirety, and however appellants would have developed it) would have led the jury to doubt *virtually everything* that the government's eyewitnesses said about the crime. (italics in the original)[45]

A bar that high was nearly impossible to clear.

The DCCA's ruling was one more loss in a long line of failures. The appellants' final option was the U.S. Supreme Court. Despite having lost their previous claims, the attorneys decided to try. They believed their clients were innocent.

In briefs submitted on June 10, 2016, the attorneys asked the high court to review the Fuller case. In legal jargon, this is called a petition for a writ of certiorari.[46] Or for short, a cert petition. As in the lower courts, the attorneys said the government's *Brady* violations required reversal of all the convictions.

In particular, the MAIP lawyers argued that if Ammie Davis's statement about James Blue, and the three identifications of James McMillian, had been disclosed, the appellants would have had a strong counternarrative to the government's theory. That would have changed the outcome of the trial.

Given their losses so far, they had small hope the justices would choose to intervene. But on December 14, 2016, lawyers on both sides—along with most court watchers—were surprised when the justices granted the appellants' cert petition. It was another unexpected turn in an improbably long, torturous trip.

Chris Turner was delighted to get the news, though it took time to sink in. His excitement—and that of the other appellants—was tempered by the past. So many of their hopes had ended in so many disappointments. No one was sure why the justices had agreed to hear the case. The Court never explains.

Still, as the argument date neared in the spring of 2017, anticipation began to build.

The MAIP attorneys had a reason for optimism. After all the evidence, old and new, had been marshaled, after a lengthy evidentiary hearing, and after multiple lower court arguments, they finally had what the trial lawyers had lacked: their own powerful story of innocence.

Unlike the government's narrative, the MAIP attorneys' narrative didn't rely on "manufactured" evidence: the long-recanted words of scared teens in police custody. It came from the information the prosecution had hidden, from a careful study of the crime scene, from the police reports, from the myriad of conflicting details in the confessions, from the recantations. It came from the solid expert testimony.

Their story was as compelling as the prosecution's theory. And far more credible.

Catherine Fuller just wanted to drink in peace.

She was always rushing: cleaning, cooking, shopping, doing laundry. Caring for her three children and her semi-invalid husband. Working from 6:00 to 11:30 p.m. weeknights. It often felt overwhelming.

On this Monday, October 1, 1984, Fuller's leg was hurting from a fall the previous week. Not too much, but enough to skip her cleaning job at the World Bank and to get $50 for medicine from her husband, Junior. She brought him an early dinner. She went downstairs and set out food for the children. She changed into jeans and a sweater and said goodbye to seventeen-year-old David III. It was time to do something for herself. She went out around 4:30 p.m.

Fuller liked vodka. That afternoon she was headed for nearby Family Liquors. On the way she chatted briefly with James and Maggie Pendergrast, who were sitting out on their front porch on 9th Street. Then she walked through the alley behind the 800 block of H Street NE to reach the store.

At Family's, she bought a half-pint of Velicoff Vodka. She walked back to the alley. Near the 9th Street end, on the south side behind Meadows Garage, was a small nook. It was protected from the rain that was falling softly. She closed her polka-dot umbrella, took off her blue raincoat, and found a place to sit.

In the next hour, her last minutes alive, she drank her bottle. Perhaps it eased the pain that was to come.

As Fuller was drinking, Ammie Davis and a girlfriend came into the alley to shoot heroin. They ran into James Blue. That's what Davis told the police, anyway. But her report was misplaced.

Maybe they all met Fuller and shared a drink. Maybe they just asked if they could. Maybe that led to an argument. Fuller was feisty, despite her size. So was Blue, who had a history of assaults.

Fuller's umbrella ended up bent and broken, like she had used it to defend herself. Later, Davis told police Blue "beat the fuck out of her [Fuller]." Somebody sure did.

Davis said Blue grabbed the woman and pulled her into the alley. That would explain the two pink curlers that were later found at that end, across from the nook where Fuller's raincoat and umbrella and the vodka bottle were. Blue left her there, battered, "for just a few dollars."

It's a plausible scenario, based on all we know. No one—now—can say for certain it's what happened. Months later, when the report from Davis resurfaced, there was minimal investigation. Officers never found her girlfriend. When Blue shot Davis to death, that was that. Blue died in prison before the prosecution ever disclosed Davis's story.

If Blue wasn't the one who beat and robbed Fuller, James McMillian, along with his associate, Gerald Merkerson, probably was. And based on the evidence we have now, almost certainly it was McMillian who sodomized and killed her.

He was living on 8th Street, in a row home that backed onto the alley. The rear door afforded easy access. It was just a few houses down from the garage where Fuller's body was found. Around the corner from where she drank her vodka.

Passing through the alley that rainy afternoon, McMillian and Merkerson would have seen Fuller. She might have been sitting and drinking. More likely she was lying injured. Either way she would be alone, vulnerable. To someone like McMillian, that would not elicit sympathy. It just meant she was easy prey.

The probable crime sequence: McMillian needed someplace more private for what he wanted to do. He took Fuller's ankles and dragged her down the alley into the empty garage. The friction scraped her back raw and pushed her sweater and bra up toward her neck.

Inside the garage, he closed the wooden doors. When Fuller

struggled, McMillian kicked her as hard as he could. He pulled off her jeans and underwear, found a pipe or pole and rammed it up her rectum. When he was done, he left her to die.

The crime was not a frenzied gang attack, cheered by dozens of watching teenagers. It was a cold abomination by one deeply twisted young man.

Why is this scenario much more likely than the official theory?

McMillian knew these alleyways from living on 8th Street. The day of the murder, he was cruising the neighborhood. William Freeman, the street vendor, saw him and Merkerson pass the corner of 8th and H Streets several times. They were together at the garage when the police came. McMillian was hiding something under his coat. Then they ran. The object used to sodomize Fuller was never recovered.

Freeman, and two independent witnesses, later identified the runners as McMillian and Merkerson. All three confirmed their suspicious actions.

Unlike the government's version of events, this story fits with the physical evidence. It explains how Fuller could have a blood alcohol concentration of .20, two and a half times the legal limit for driving, at the time of death. It explains why her raincoat was neatly folded, why her umbrella was broken, and why both these items, plus two hair curlers and her blue head scarf, were all at the 9th Street end of the alley. It's also consistent with Ammie Davis's statement.

It even explains how two of Fuller's pink curlers could suddenly appear in the garage the day after the killing. McMillian lived so close he could have been there and back in a minute.

This story also fits with the statements of Willie Luchie and his friends. They didn't see anyone as they walked down the alley about 5:30 p.m. Three of them heard a low moan from the closed garage. The assault was still going on. When Freeman got to the garage just after 6:00 p.m., Fuller was dead. Whoever killed her had left. The right door was open slightly.

What Luchie and his friends heard was the crime in progress inside the small garage. It could not have involved a large group.

As for the sodomy, why would anyone inflict such horror on a tiny woman just to end a robbery? McMillian's seriously troubled psychology could explain it.

He was young but deeply disturbed. He'd been physically abused by his mother and in and out of foster homes since the age of five. He'd had multiple run-ins with the law. He already had a record of extreme violence against women. One young woman he dated briefly said later that "all he wanted was oral and anal sex." [47]

Within two weeks of Fuller's murder, McMillian committed two daytime robberies of women walking alone not far from 8th and H Streets. Both were punched multiple times in the face. He was arrested soon after the second crime and pled guilty to both robberies. On March 15, 1985, he was sentenced to eight to twenty-four years in prison.

When *Post* reporter Patrice Gaines first talked to McMillian in 1992, he denied being in the area of 8th and H the day of the killing.

After MAIP took over the case, Faheemah Davillier, an investigator working for the new lawyers, spoke to McMillian at a federal prison in Kentucky.[48] She told him MAIP was reexamining the killing. They had information he was at the garage near the time of the crime.

In that conversation McMillian admitted—for the first time—he'd been in the 8th and H neighborhood that day. He continued to deny any involvement in the murder. But Davillier said when she told him MAIP intended to retest items of evidence for DNA, his tone changed.[49] He anxiously asked if they'd gotten any results. He repeatedly probed as to whether she'd talked to his old sidekick, Merkerson.

Davillier later spoke to Merkerson. He was hard to find because he had changed his name to Sonny Baker. Merkerson/ Baker declined to say anything about the crime. He did ask Davillier whether McMillian had tried to learn where he was living and whether McMillian would spend the rest of his life in prison. To her, Merkerson seemed frightened of his former friend, even though he was behind bars.

If the detectives had investigated McMillian in the months after the killing, who knows what they might have learned? None of their hundreds of interviews included him.

Then McMillian provided one more terrible reason to believe he had sodomized and killed Catherine Fuller.

He served almost eight years for his two brutal robberies in the days after her murder. He was released to a halfway house in DC on July 23, 1992. He was scheduled to be paroled on September 11. The date was pushed back because McMillian had several curfew violations and had signed out for work "under false pretenses."

Not quite two months later, on September 15, a twenty-two-year-old woman was walking home from work around 8:00 p.m.[50] A block from her apartment, she was dragged into the alley behind the 500 block of 8th Street NE and brutally assaulted.

Shortly afterward, two men walked into the alley to get their car. As they opened the door, a man stood up from behind the car. He was pulling up his pants with one hand and holding something in his other hand. He mumbled what sounded like "excuse me," and quickly left the alley.

When the two men checked behind the car, they saw legs sticking out. Thinking the person might be dangerous or sleeping off a hangover, they went back to their apartment and called 911. Both later identified McMillian in a lineup as the person they had seen in the alley.

The woman died three days later without ever regaining

consciousness. An autopsy showed the cause of death to be "blunt force trauma to the head and torso." The skin around the anus had "radiating tears," and there were rips and bruises extending up into the rectal mucosa. These wounds, according to the report, "clearly indicated sodomy or forced penetration."

The medical examiner noted that the injuries were so severe and extensive they were "analogous to what I typically see in a frontal vehicle collision."

The parallels between the two murders are obvious. Both victims were small women; both were attacked in alleys close to 8th and H Streets NE. Both were horribly beaten, with injuries more like a car crash than a typical assault. In both cases, the assailant focused his fury on the women's anal area. At the new trial hearing, Dr. Callery testified that anal sodomy was rare even in rape-murder cases, occurring in "considerably less than one percent."

In 1993, James McMillian was convicted for the murder. He was sentenced to life in prison without the possibility of parole.

The appellate lawyers believed that at point after point after point, their story of James McMillian committing the murder—with a single associate—fit with the facts far better than did the prosecution theory of a gang attack.

Their story explained the location and condition of the physical evidence, the lack of any independent witnesses, the reason why the apparent eyewitnesses continually contradicted both the evidence and one another, and the source of the unspeakably brutal sodomy.

That symmetry alone did not make their story true. But every one of those points of agreement made their narrative more likely, just as every gap and inconsistency and mistake and discrepancy in the official narrative made it more unlikely. The McMillian story was so strong it could not be ignored.

Would it be enough to change what had been accepted as the truth about the case since its very beginning?

———

The Supreme Court argument on March 29, 2017, was unusual. To decide whether the undisclosed evidence raised doubts about the verdict, the justices needed a clear understanding of the facts.

They quickly got down to basics. Anthony Kennedy wondered why James McMillian, if he really was the killer, would have kept hanging around the crime scene after the murder.[51] Samuel Alito asked what he called "kind of a picky question": How many assailants could fit inside the small garage where Fuller's body was found?[52]

Cliff's lawyer, John Williams, from the powerhouse DC firm Williams & Connolly, led the argument for the appellants. He was opposed by Michael Dreeben, an assistant solicitor general and one of the most experienced litigators in Supreme Court history. Dreeben had argued more than one hundred cases before the Court, and the justices treated him almost like a colleague.

Williams wove the McMillian information into a story.[53] Given the evidence now available, he was a far more likely suspect than any of the appellants. Had the defense lawyers known of his actions around the time of the killing, they could have challenged the prosecution's narrative and changed the entire case.

Dreeben conceded it would have been "good practice" to disclose the McMillian identifications, as well as the other favorable information, prior to the trial.[54] He said that would be the practice of the U.S. Attorney's Office today.

But he insisted that none of it would have affected the outcome. The confessions, plus the limited supporting evidence, would still have carried the day. Dreeben went so far as to question whether the lawyers would have used a McMillian defense even if they had known about him.

Overall, it was a low-key argument. Several of the justices said little. Clarence Thomas was silent as usual. Stephen Breyer—who the appellants hoped would be on their side—asked just one question. The same was true for Chief Justice John Roberts Jr.

By the end of the argument, it was clear the Court had no intention of revisiting basic *Brady* law. Several of the justices seemed to have a minimal interest in the case itself.

Fewer than three months later, on June 22, 2017, the Court denied the appellants' claims by a 6–2 vote.[55]

It was a dispiriting result for the convicted men. They hadn't even come close. It was particularly galling that Breyer had written the majority opinion.

The ruling detailed the seven pieces of favorable evidence that had been suppressed at the trial, including the McMillian identifications. This information, the Court said, should have been turned over to the defense. "Such evidence ought to be disclosed . . . as a matter of course." The majority also agreed the hidden information could have been used to support an alternative-perpetrator narrative. That, in turn, would have undermined the group assault theory that was the "cornerstone of the Government's case."

But none of the accused had actually mounted a defense that "McMillian did it." And so, using a curious twist of logic, the majority deemed the withheld evidence "too little, too weak, or too distant from the main evidentiary points" that had been argued at the trial to meet the *Brady* materiality standard.

In dissent, Justice Elena Kagan, joined by Ruth Bader Ginsburg, wrote that this reasoning only proved her point. "The defendants didn't offer an alternative-perpetrator defense because the Government prevented them from learning what made it credible."[56] She argued that they had been in an impossible bind: because the prosecutor had hidden the supporting evidence, they couldn't use the very defense that might have earned them a reversal.

In Kagan's view, a "McMillian did it" defense "had game-changing potential exactly *because* it challenged the cornerstone of the Government's case," i.e., that the killing was a gang attack. If they had known of the withheld evidence, "the whole tenor of the trial would have changed." It would have offered "a way to view the crime in a different light . . . that could well have flipped one or more jurors—which is all *Brady* requires."

More than three decades after the trial, that was a hard argument to make. Despite all the facts being tossed about, too much time had gone by to be sure of anything. A majority of the justices did what they typically do in such a situation: they let the verdicts stand.

For the appellants, it was a final, wrenching loss. The Court had essentially agreed with their arguments. The justices had explicitly affirmed that the favorable evidence Goren had hidden should have been disclosed. They still refused to grant any relief. The information wasn't material.

9

THE FAILURE AND THE HOPE

Following the Supreme Court's decision, there were good reasons to despair for *Brady*.

The Court majority said nothing about any problems with the rule. They just settled into their default position for *Brady* claims. The prosecutor's violation wasn't material, so it didn't matter.

Since deciding Fuller in 2017, the Court has not taken a single *Brady*-related case.

Equally disheartening was the majority's added justification for denying relief: their eager reliance on the government's promises that any problems with *Brady* were gone now.

In his argument, Assistant Solicitor General Dreeben avowed that the evidence the prosecutor hid in the Fuller case in 1985 would surely be disclosed under current understandings of *Brady*. He said since then the DOJ "has adopted a different discovery policy that exceeds what's required."[1]

Dreeben also told the Court the DOJ "devotes considerable resources to giving guidance, training, and supervision to prosecutors to go above and beyond *Brady* and disclose information that a defendant might wish to use even if it's not [*Brady*]."

Justice Breyer seized on this guarantee. He cited it to support ruling that a reversal was unwarranted, despite the prosecution's misdeeds. "The government assured the Court at oral argument that subsequent to petitioners' trial, it has adopted a 'generous policy of discovery' . . . under which it discloses any 'information

that a defendant might wish to use,' " he wrote.[2] "As we have recognized, and as the government agrees, 'this is as it should be.' "

These rosy claims about *Brady*'s health did not reflect reality.

At the very time Dreeben was making his self-congratulatory
pledge before the Court, lawyers from the DC Office of the U.S.
Attorney (DCOUSA)—the nation's largest and most influential
prosecution office—were committing a series of egregious *Brady*
violations in a high-profile case.

On January 20, 2017, a group calling itself #DisruptJ20 staged a
protest at Donald Trump's presidential inauguration.[3] During
the event, which involved several hundred demonstrators, a small
group damaged a police car and the windows of a few businesses.
The police broke up the gathering with pepper spray, tear gas, and
Sting-Ball grenades. They arrested 234 people.

In April, 214 of the arrestees were indicted on eight felony
counts related to the DC rioting act.[4] Only a few of them had
been involved in the actual property damage. To win convictions,
the government needed to prove they all engaged in a conspiracy
to riot—that they all agreed to join a protest that included property destruction. If that were true, each defendant would be responsible for damage caused by any one of them.

A key part of the government's evidence was a video made
by Project Veritas, a far-right organization specializing in sting
operations against liberal groups and mainstream media. An
undercover operative for Veritas filmed a planning meeting of
#DisruptJ20 on January 8. In the video, organizers talked about
using blockades. One said he would turn the inauguration into "a
giant clusterfuck."[5]

There were so many defendants that they were divided into
groups for prosecution. The first six went to trial in DC Superior
Court on November 15, 2017.

The lead prosecutor, Jennifer Kerkhoff, introduced the Veritas
video to show that the J20 activists had talked about disrupting

inauguration events. She told jurors everything that occurred during the protest was planned. The tape was evidence of the conspiracy. She also assured the court the video itself was in "complete, unredacted form" and was the only tape Veritas made about #DisruptJ20.

The six defendants were acquitted of all charges.

The second trial started six months later, on May 14, 2018. After it began, defense lawyers learned Kerkhoff's claims about the Veritas video were untrue. Someone—either the prosecutor or the lead detective—had cut out a key section. In the omitted part, the Veritas mole said: "I was talking to one of the organizers . . . and I don't think they know anything about any of the upper echelon stuff." [6]

That statement directly contradicted the government's argument that the protesters had a clear plan to commit violence during the action. One defense lawyer wrote: "What better exculpatory evidence . . . than the words from the person sent to capture a nefarious meeting stating right after the meeting 'I don't think they know anything.' " [7]

Later that same week, the defense attorneys also learned Kerkhoff had failed to disclose sixty-nine more Project Veritas recordings related to the protest. Thirty-five recordings showed J20 action camps or planning meetings where attendees actually talked about how to de-escalate violence—the opposite of the government's central theory.

At a hearing on May 31, Judge Robert Morin, the superior court chief judge who was presiding, ruled that the government's actions had violated *Brady*. He dismissed the conspiracy charges against the defendants before him. In the end, none of them were convicted on any of the other counts. The government later dismissed the charges against all the remaining defendants.

Judge Morin said Kerkhoff's failure to disclose key evidence and her misrepresentations were "serious [*Brady*] violation[s]" and they had been "intentional." [8] He blocked any additional prosecutions on the conspiracy charges. Several of the protesters filed complaints against Kerkhoff with the Bar Association of the District of Columbia.

Brady expert Bennett L. Gershman called Kerkhoff's behavior disgraceful.[9] "The prosecutors in this case cheated, and they got caught."

"The shocking thing," Gershman said, "is that this case was being prosecuted under the national spotlight. The glare of public scrutiny. . . . You'd think that under these conditions, they'd feel the need to be more responsible, more careful. . . . But that's not the case."

The misleading video edit was discovered only because one of the defendants, Elizabeth Lagesse, spent "countless hours" examining the tape.[10] Lagesse, who described herself as "a slightly OCD, unemployed data scientist," scrutinized the metadata associated with the Veritas video. She told her lawyer parts had been excised.

Without that lucky break, the violation might have been missed. Innocent people might have been wrongly convicted.

In this instance there was a consequence for the case, but not for the cheating prosecutor. The judge dismissed the charges related to the video evidence with prejudice, barring any future prosecution. But he couldn't say if Kerkhoff's actions were malevolent. No sanctions for her.

How did her bosses at the DCOUSA—the people who were allegedly teaching their underlings "to go above and beyond *Brady*"—respond to Kerkhoff's violations? They promoted her to chief of the Felony Major Crimes Trial Section.[11]

Despite cases like J20 and a surfeit of violations that keep popping up around the country, prosecutors continue to insist there's nothing amiss with *Brady*. Transgressions are rare, they say. The fault of a few bad actors.

Yet a growing mass of evidence supports ex-judge Kozinski's

claim that infractions are epidemic. As the libertarian Cato Institute stated in its amicus brief in the Fuller case, "[a]n extensive body of empirical research has found that *Brady* violations occur with alarming regularity." [12] Two subsequent reports have powerfully confirmed that fact.

A 2019 study by *USA Today*, in partnership with the Chicago-based Invisible Institute, a journalism production company that supports investigative reporting and human rights documentation, looked at how prosecutors' offices around the country track police misconduct.[13] Under *Brady* law, the defense is entitled to know if a police witness has testified falsely in a previous case. The government typically has access to such information; defense attorneys do not.

Of 443 prosecutors' offices contacted by the researchers, 52 of them provided their list of dishonest officers. But 316—more than 71 percent—said they did not keep such a list. Of the others, 48 claimed they had no police misconduct to report, and 27 ignored the query.

The individual responses were telling. Two jurisdictions said they would amend their current policy and begin a *Brady* list. But most of the offices that don't keep such records said they didn't plan to start doing so. Many offices that kept a list had incomplete records.

These lax practices have a serious negative impact on criminal trials. *USA Today* "identified at least 1,200 officers with proven histories of lying and other serious misconduct who had not been flagged by prosecutors." Their report concluded that "thousands of people have faced criminal charges or gone to prison based, in part, on testimony from law enforcement officers deemed to have credibility problems by their bosses or by prosecutors."

Perhaps the most troubling evidence of *Brady*'s failure comes from the National Registry of Exonerations.[14]

In September 2020 the registry released a study of the impact of official misconduct on wrongful convictions. The authors examined all 2,400 documented exonerations from 1989 through February 2019. They focused on cases where misbehavior contributed directly to an unjust conviction.

They found that more than half of wrongful convictions— 54 percent to be exact—were caused by government misconduct. The most common sin was concealing favorable information: aka breaching the *Brady* rule. That happened in 1,056 cases: 44 percent of all exonerations. In nearly three-fourths of these cases, it was prosecutors, not police, who hid exculpatory evidence.

These figures are only for the mistakes that came to light. The writers acknowledged that "we miss a great deal of official misconduct that remains hidden." And they noted in passing that *Brady*'s materiality requirement "has been widely criticized as incoherent, inconsistent and unadministrable."

As with nearly every aspect of the criminal system, race was a significant factor. Overall, Black exonerees were somewhat more likely to have been victims of official misconduct than were white exonerees, 57 to 52 percent. But the racial disparity was significantly higher for murder cases (78 to 64 percent), especially with death sentences (87 to 68 percent). For drug crimes it was more than double: 47 to 22 percent.

The study also tracked what happened to these 770 transgressors, the prosecutors whose actions put innocent people behind bars, often for decades. How many were disciplined by their employers? Eleven. How many were disbarred? Three. How many were fired? Two. How many were convicted of crimes for their misconduct? Two.

And just one prosecutor went to jail for breaking *Brady*. One. No wonder the violations keep coming.

Almost sixty years of trying to make *Brady* work is more than enough. If history is any guide, it will never be revitalized. Whatever prosecutors and judges may say, the great majority have shown by their actions they are content with a narrow, ineffectual rule.

It's past time to declare *Brady* dead. To briefly mourn its failed promise and move on.

That is grounds for optimism, not despair. Once the rule itself is gone, the focus can turn to a workable way to realize its purpose.

When the Virginia Supreme Court killed discovery reform in that state in 2015, it seemed finished. But some members of the special committee that developed the new rules refused to abandon them. They put together an alliance to build a better justice system.[15]

The group took the ideas from the committee's earlier proposal and wrote them into legislative form. They found a Republican state senator to sponsor the law. They formed the Virginia Fair Trial Coalition and held community forums around the state to highlight the need for change in the discovery rules. In 2017, after a coordinated lobbying campaign, their bill passed the Democratic-majority Virginia Senate in a 36–1 vote.

Later that year the legislation went to the Republican-controlled House of Delegates for hearings. By then, state prosecutors had awakened and mobilized against it. Fifteen attended the hearing personally to testify against the measure.

Opponents said it would never pass. But after the hearings, members of the Courts of Justice Committee told prosecutors that supporters of the bill had demonstrated the clear need for reform. If prosecutors didn't act soon, the committee said *they* would.

In response, the Virginia State Bar formed its own committee of prosecutors and defense lawyers. In a series of meetings, both sides laid out their concerns and what any potential reforms should include. After several bargaining sessions, the group agreed on a new set of rules. In September 2018, the Virginia Supreme Court approved the proposed changes.

The new regulations did not impose open-file discovery or require pre-plea disclosures. They did mandate that prosecutors give defense lawyers access to police reports and disclose any statements they intended to use against a defendant. Both sides were to provide trial-witness lists, and written notice of any expert opinions.

The reforms were set to go into effect on July 1, 2019. But continued opposition from prosecutors led the chief justice, Donald W. Lemons, to announce in a letter dated January 29, 2019, that he was delaying implementation of the new rules until July 2020.[16]

In his letter, Lemons said discovery reform was "long overdue." Still, he argued that concerns about the use and impact of police body cameras needed to be addressed before the new rules took effect. His reasoning surprised proponents since the proposed changes had nothing about body cams. Some suspected it was another delaying tactic.

But after a one-year lag, the new rules went into effect. Doug Ramseur, a past-president of the Virginia Association of Criminal Defense Lawyers who played a key part in reform efforts from the start, says he's optimistic about the changes.[17] It's still too early to assess their impact.

Since many *Brady* issues arise from hidden police reports, Ramseur thinks requiring disclosure of these documents will decrease violations. The new rules also list the most common types of *Brady* material, and prosecutors are on notice they must disclose such evidence.

The reforms aren't everything Ramseur hoped for, but they're a step forward.

New York's path to discovery reform has been rocky as well.

The Empire State, like Virginia, had long required only minimal disclosure in criminal cases. The law on evidence sharing was known as the Blindfold Law, since it left defendants in the dark about crucial evidence against them. For at least forty years, experts and practitioners had urged the state "to reform its outdated and unfair criminal discovery rules."[18] But Republicans were able to block any changes.

Nearly a decade ago, the state bar formed a task force on criminal discovery that included judges, district attorneys, and defense attorneys. The group came up with a series of significant reforms that were approved by a large majority of the members. At the last minute, state district attorneys organized against any changes. They resorted to a tried-and-true strategy: playing on the public's fears by claiming the reforms would endanger the safety of witnesses and victims. The proposal died.

The reforms found new life when Democrats took control of the state senate after the 2018 elections. The legislature approved a major discovery-reform package similar to what the task force had initially proposed, and imposed significant limits on cash bail.[19] The changes included much broader disclosure requirements with strict deadlines. They also mandated that discovery be provided before a plea offer is made and that any offer be kept open for at least seven days.

Then-governor Andrew Cuomo was not enthusiastic about the reforms, but he signed them into law in April 2019. They were scheduled to take effect January 1, 2020.

The new rules quickly ran into heavy resistance. A vocal coalition of police, district attorneys, conservative media, and Republican lawmakers began working to amend or undo many of the changes, including a provision requiring prosecutors to disclose information from their files to defense lawyers within fifteen days of arraignment.

In June 2019, soon after the bill passed, the *Daily News* ran an opinion piece titled "Big risks in discovery reform; NY's new law tips the balance way too far in favor of defendants."[20] Although the effective date was more than six months away, the article argued that the new discovery rules would "risk endangering witnesses and crime victims." No statistics were cited to support that fear. Just the claims of two district attorneys.

The *New York Post* further stoked these fears in a December 31, 2019, story titled "Why New York criminals are celebrating the

New Year."[21] The first sentence was "It's the Year of the Perp." The piece quoted local prosecutors saying the new law would harm public safety, even though it authorized judges to issue protective orders if they could show legitimate safety concerns about revealing information.

Michael Palladino, the head of the NYPD detectives' union, said the reforms showed elected officials have "lost their minds and created a fragile situation where criminals feel comfortable, entitled and in control."[22] Republican politicians seized on the issue to paint Democrats as soft on crime and made it central to their efforts retake the state senate.

Bending to the backlash, New York attorney general Letitia James, a former public defender, quickly called for changes to the new law. "Safety should be the priority," she said.[23] In a similar vein, Governor Cuomo called the reforms a "work in progress" with "consequences that have to be adjusted for."

In April 2020, barely three months after the new rules took effect, lawmakers amended them. The rollback included relaxing the timeline for required disclosure and limiting the release of identification details for witnesses. It also strengthened the provisions regarding protective orders to block such information.

These changes weren't enough for opponents of the bill. Ronald S. Lauder, the billionaire cosmetics heir, founded and pledged $4 million to a funding group called Safe Together New York.[24]

The organization's web page claimed the reforms had resulted in "radical" policies "that are bringing violence and chaos to our streets."[25] It trumpeted the tired mantra that requiring prosecutors to "give the names of witnesses to criminals and the defense attorneys . . . could lead to witness tampering or even endanger the lives of witnesses."

During the 2020 elections, the group spent $2.9 million on TV ads targeting six senate districts, including four districts with Democratic incumbents who had voted for the reforms. All four candidates won reelection in November 2020. In the 2021 county elections, however, several Republican district attorney candidates who ran against the new laws beat better-funded opponents who had supported them.[26]

Prosecutors also kept up their resistance to the changes.

They said the disclosure requirements and deadlines were still so onerous they couldn't meet them with existing personnel and resources.[27] They claimed the new rules threatened public safety. Polling from Siena College showed that 56 percent of respondents believed bail reform, which was linked with the discovery revisions, was "bad for NY."[28]

The *Post* continued to prophesy doom by asserting—with little supporting evidence—that the state's "outrageous new rules for discovery" were "upending prosecutions as dismissals soar."[29] The editorial board claimed that "this 'liberal reform' endangers battered women's lives."

In response, Governor Kathy Hochul, who had replaced Cuomo after his resignation in 2021, included more rollbacks as part of the state budget that passed in April 2022. She defended her actions by saying "we're going to continue to work to restore New Yorkers' sense of safety," though aside from some anecdotal claims, there was no evidence the rules had led to any harms.[30] As reporter Nick Pinto commented, having been "relentlessly instructed to fear bail reform, New Yorkers were now afraid."

The biggest shift in the discovery rules was adding a "good faith" exception that gives prosecutors more time to comply with the disclosure requirements whenever necessary. While that dispensation seems reasonable on its face, no one knows yet if it will be rarely invoked or if it will become the new normal.

Defense lawyers hoped the reforms would make a significant difference. New York's Center for Court Innovation, a nonprofit organization dedicated to creating a more efficient and humane justice system, after noting the state's history of withholding vital information from the defense, called the changes "another step toward a more fair, transparent and just criminal legal system."[31]

Angelo Petrigh, training director for the Bronx Defenders, said the reforms have made things better, at least initially.[32] Prosecutors are disclosing more information. The law—like Virginia's—now lists specific types of exculpatory or impeachment information. Prosecutors are less likely to withhold that information since they can't claim to be unsure about what is required.

But Petrigh already sees danger signs. Some prosecutors have been passively resisting the reforms by saying they cannot meet the timelines for disclosure or by providing incomplete information. Some judges, in deference to these DAs, have been reluctant to enforce strict deadlines for evidence sharing or to impose sanctions for any violations. Many have let "substantial" compliance substitute for full disclosure.

Now Petrigh fears that the good faith exception could end up swallowing the new rules; that lax enforcement of the disclosure mandates will become standard practice. "It's always been difficult to get sanctions for any discovery violations," he said. He called this latest change "a huge exception that will likely make sanctions a rarity."[33]

If courts keep easing the requirements, Petrigh says, prosecutors will keep pushing the boundaries, and the reforms will weaken over time. To prevent that, the people and organizations instrumental in passing the changes need to reengage in the process, to ensure their efforts are not undone.

For now, the struggle continues. And the future of discovery reform in New York remains uncertain.

The new rules in both Virginia and New York represent substantial progress, particularly on paper. They're also limited. Neither state has open-file discovery. Although the rules detail a range of *Brady* material that should be disclosed, any decisions remain in the hands of prosecutors. They still decide what to share and what to withhold.

As with *Brady*, it is naive to think simply passing a rule, however well intentioned, will end any problems. Unless courts in those states are committed to defending the new rules and to punishing violations, prosecutors will find ways to circumvent them. It will take ongoing vigilance to make sure these hard-won changes don't end up like *Brady*.

The only way to make reforms permanently effective is with a transformation of the current culture. That was Justice Douglas's original dream when he wrote the *Brady* opinion in 1963. But it can't happen until prosecutors believe full disclosure of all relevant evidence is the best route to fairness and justice.

A climate change so profound may seem impossible. Or unlikely, at best. But there is clear evidence that when common sense open-file rules are linked with careful enforcement, the culture can shift.

After North Carolina adopted open-file discovery in 2004, there were dire predictions from opponents.[34] Criminals would find and intimidate witnesses against them. Guilty people would walk free. The streets would run with blood. Prosecutors would be buried in paperwork.

But the sky did not fall. Neither did the state's legal system.

The chief justice of the North Carolina Supreme Court was a Republican and a conservative. He and a majority of his colleagues had seen firsthand the need for serious reform. The state's judiciary knew they were expected to support—and to enforce—open-file discovery. Prosecutors knew they were expected to follow the rules, like them or not.

Once the new regime was in place, there was a period of adjustment for both sides. Richard Rosen, a longtime professor at University of North Carolina School of Law and a prime force in instituting the reforms, said both prosecutors and defense lawyers had to get comfortable with the requirements. Neither group was accustomed to sharing information with opponents.

Early on, some amendments were needed. The first law specified disclosure of prosecution files. To evade those demands, police officers would sometimes withhold particular documents or reports so they never made it to the prosecutor. The problem was remedied by changing the statute to require disclosure of all police investigation files.

Something unexpected happened on the way to the courthouse, according to Rosen. Most prosecutors stopped complaining about the reforms. They realized open-file made their jobs easier in several crucial ways. They didn't have to guess what the defense's strategy might be. They didn't have to wrestle with whether a piece of evidence was material or worry about being penalized down the road if they got it wrong.

There were more—and earlier—plea agreements. Defendants could see the case against them and make better-informed decisions. The system gained efficiency and transparency. If prosecutors had safety concerns about disclosing certain evidence or the name of a witness or victim, they could seek protective orders to keep such information confidential.

The new rules didn't magically solve all discovery issues. Police or prosecutors who were determined to hide evidence could still find ways to do it. But unlike the laws related to *Brady*, which the courts made more complex and confusing as time went on, the requirements of the statute were clear. Anyone who wanted to conceal information had to affirmatively cheat. If they got caught, they could not claim, as myriad prosecutors have (and still do) with *Brady* violations, that they really, truly didn't think the undisclosed evidence was material.

The reforms didn't necessarily improve criminal defense practice. Rosen emphasized that broad disclosure was no help to defense lawyers who weren't prepared to understand and to use the information they were now receiving. It required more training and experience to make sure defendants got the full benefit of the disclosures.

Overall, Rosen said, there's no doubt that the reforms made the criminal process in North Carolina better and fairer. And, as he wryly pointed out, they haven't stopped the state from convicting people of crimes.

Over time, open-file discovery didn't just change the way cases were prosecuted and defended. It changed the culture.

A study of defense lawyers and prosecutors in North Carolina and Virginia provides clear evidence of this transformation.[35]

During 2014 and 2015, two law professors—one from Southern Methodist University and one from George Mason University—surveyed attorneys in both states about their discovery laws. While the states are similar demographically and geographically, North Carolina had had open-file discovery since 2004. Virginia, by contrast, had very limited disclosure rules.

Of the North Carolina prosecutors who responded to the survey, 91 percent said open-file discovery worked well. Another 6 percent thought it worked "somewhat" well. Only 3 percent believed it did not work well. The researchers said many of these prosecutors "defended the policy in strong and unequivocal terms."

Curiously, North Carolina defense lawyers were less bullish than prosecutors were about the open-file rules. Of those surveyed, 67 percent said it worked well and 15 percent said it didn't. Another 18 percent went with somewhat well. Part of that discontent, however, had to do with how the reforms had been implemented rather than with the rules themselves.

Benefits of open-file discovery, as cited by prosecutors, included greater efficiency in resolving cases. There were more guilty pleas and faster resolutions. They now were protected against claims of withholding evidence. Many also said they believed it made the entire criminal process fairer.

A very real, but unmeasurable, bonus was a reduction in

wrongful convictions. It's not possible to know how much favorable evidence was hidden from the defense, or simply undisclosed, under the old rules. Or what impact that had on verdicts. Now that exculpatory information is routinely shared, it can be a part of the resolution of any case.

Asked about potential problems with the disclosure requirements, only 9 percent of prosecutors cited concerns about witness threats or intimidation. Just one prosecutor noted a specific case where that had happened. And he acknowledged it likely would have occurred even under the old rules. Commenting on that issue, the authors noted they "found little evidence that open-file discovery endangers the safety of witnesses."

Having lived for a decade with open-file discovery, there were more prosecutors who cited resource and logistical issues as a problem than mentioned witness concerns. Still, only 14 percent said it was a major disadvantage of the process.

With regard to *Brady*, the authors report that open-file discovery "does enhance" the disclosure of favorable evidence. This is particularly true for information that might not, on its face, seem exculpatory. The reforms solved one of the biggest problems the rule has always faced: the failure of prosecutors to recognize favorable evidence when they found it.

Comparisons between the attitudes of prosecutors in the two states were equally instructive.

Virginia prosecutors had significantly higher levels of concern about possible harms from open-file discovery than did their North Carolina counterparts, who had worked in that system for ten years.

Of the Virginia prosecutors surveyed, 47 percent said they worried open-file policies would pose a danger to witnesses, compared with just 10 percent of prosecutors in North Carolina. Virginia prosecutors were also two and a half times more likely to fear defense lawyers might twist or misuse the evidence they received than were North Carolina prosecutors.

As for resource and logistical issues, 25 percent of Virginia prosecutors were concerned that compliance with open-file discovery would be unduly difficult. About half that number in North Carolina (14 percent) said this was actually a problem for them.

Overall, 20 percent of prosecutors in Virginia said there were no major advantages to adopting open-file discovery. Not one of the North Carolina prosecutors surveyed agreed with that pessimistic assessment.

The qualms about open-file discovery expressed by Virginia prosecutors proved to be far less problematic in reality when this policy was put into practice in North Carolina. Prosecutors in that state had to be pushed into the open-file pool. Once there, they rather liked the water.

One more finding of note from the study: over time, the reciprocal disclosure requirements in North Carolina had led to more collegiality. There were significantly lower levels of mistrust between prosecutors and defense lawyers in that state than in Virginia.

On the subject of culture change, it's worth recalling the *Miranda* rule.

In 1966, when the Supreme Court announced *Miranda*, there was a great brouhaha.[36] Police and prosecutors and many judges, even state supreme court justices, predicted disaster. With these required warnings, nobody will confess. We won't solve any crimes. Killers and rapists and robbers will be running free.

Lifetime conservative and future Supreme Court chief justice William Rehnquist expressed such views in 1968. *Miranda*, he said, "upset the balance between the right of society to convict the guilty and safeguard the accused." He predicted it would "very likely have the effect of preventing the defendant from making any statement at all."

Those disastrous forecasts did not come to pass. Fifty-six years later, most suspects still confess. On average, about 80 percent of arrestees that police wish to question waive their rights and agree to talk without an attorney. Every one of the defendants in the Fuller case did so.

Even Mr. Chief Justice changed his tune on *Miranda*. In 2000, when voting to sustain the requirements, Rehnquist wrote that "*Miranda* has become embedded in routine police practice to the point where the warnings have become part of our national culture."

Since the failure of Senator Murkowski's Fairness in Disclosure of Evidence Act in 2012, there have been no serious efforts to reform federal discovery rules.

This lack of reform activity at the federal level has hampered similar efforts elsewhere. The DOJ and its prosecutors—U.S. attorneys—are powerful and influential in the legal community. Their defense of limited disclosure dampens reform efforts at the state and local levels. Their insistence that *Brady* is working just fine continues to enable federal prosecutors to abuse the rule.

In 2020, Congress did pass the Due Process Protections Act with bipartisan support. The name sounds promising. But its only requirement was that federal judges remind prosecutors of their *Brady* obligations, and of possible sanctions for noncompliance, at the start of a case. It did nothing to improve or enforce the rule.

With Democrats taking control of the White House and Congress in 2021, there has been some talk of new reforms. In March, the Subcommittee on Crime, Terrorism, and Homeland Security of the House Judiciary Committee held a hearing titled *From Miranda to Gideon: A Call for Pretrial Reform.*

At that hearing, Barry Scheck, cofounder of the Innocence Project, told subcommittee members *Brady* should be replaced with open-file discovery—"the Occam's razor for disclosure."[37] He urged Congress to "adopt a version" of Texas's Morton Act and called for the DOJ to "incentivize states to adopt it through a grant program."

Afterward, the chair of the subcommittee, Sheila Jackson Lee (D-TX), noted that "current [pretrial discovery] practices disproportionately disadvantage people of color."[38] She expressed interest in pursuing reforms. But so far there have been no more hearings.

The ups and downs of discovery reform, especially over the last decade, offer important lessons for proponents. They also suggest a road map to future progress.

The successful reforms in North Carolina and Texas show citizens will support change when they see—in clear, human terms—the injustice that inevitably flows from limited disclosure. Progressives in those states had long pushed for reform. But the crucial catalyst was an egregious *Brady* violation that led to a wrongful conviction.[39] When people understood the problem, they wanted to end it.

Several states demonstrate that reform efforts are most successful if they are nonpartisan and nonpolitical. Advocates in North Carolina had strong support from the state's rather conservative judiciary. In Texas the Morton Act won the backing of Governor Rick Perry, a right-wing Republican. And Virginia's progress was boosted after a Republican member of the state senate introduced and promoted the reform bill.

In New York the new rules quickly became politicized. Prosecutors and police unions, joined by most Republican state politicians and conservative newspapers, opposed them. That generated passive resistance from some judges who—perhaps concerned about a loss of their own power and control—have been reluctant to carefully enforce the rules and have let prosecutors slide without full compliance.

Open-file discovery—including pre-plea disclosure—should be

the ultimate goal. But lesser reforms like those adopted in New York and Virginia are a major improvement. Listing specific categories of favorable information that must be disclosed can significantly reduce *Brady* violations.

The drawback is that these limited changes leave prosecutors in full command of the evidence. Those with good intentions can still miss or misunderstand possibly favorable information. The only way to avoid that problem is with open-file discovery.

Even when their professional organizations back reforms, many prosecutors are reluctant participants in any new regime. To be successful, revised rules must be closely monitored for compliance by both prosecutors and judges. If they aren't fully implemented and enforced, the rules can become weak and ineffectual over time, as *Brady* did.

Logistical issues always need to be worked out. Copying and transmitting case documents, which can be voluminous, requires additional time and effort. Prosecutors in North Carolina identified administrative matters as the most vexing problem with open-file. It takes patience and cooperation from both sides to figure out how best to share information efficiently.

Finally, with expanded discovery, defense lawyers have to learn how to handle the evidence they receive and incorporate it into their work. Only then will reforms fulfill their promise.

The hopeful news is that North Carolina's experience with open-file discovery—nearing two decades now—has been so successful. Lawyers in that state have demonstrated that when broad disclosure rules are clear, and are enforced, they make the criminal system more efficient. And more collegial. And fairer. Even according to most prosecutors.

Over time, open-file discovery changed the culture for both defense attorneys and prosecutors. That's the only path to lasting reform. When the rules and the benefits of open-file discovery are internalized, enforcement becomes simpler. Ethical lawyers on

THE FAILURE AND THE HOPE 227

both sides of the aisle will generally abide by them. They make the system better for everyone.

Brady was still young when Justice Thurgood Marshall saw it was headed toward an iceberg. In his 1985 *Bagley* dissent, he did his best to change its course, to make the case it should be a broad disclosure rule.[40]

His argument began with the Court's own words: "[T]he state's obligation is not to convict, but to see that, as far as possible, truth emerges." From that simple premise, he pointed out that "when evidence favorable to the defense is known to exist, disclosure only enhances the quest for truth." Conversely, when the state fails to disclose such evidence, it "undermines the reliability of the verdict."

It's not complicated. If we want pretrial proceedings and guilty pleas to be fair, if we want juries to reach just verdicts, disclosing all the available, relevant evidence can only help reach that goal. Otherwise, the system will continue to routinely convict or acquit defendants with incomplete information.

Still, most prosecutors keep resisting discovery reforms that have proven to promote justice. The reason is simple. And shameful.

Narrow, limited rules give them control of all case information, of all investigative files. They alone decide what to reveal and what to conceal. In any dispute over materiality, courts rule overwhelmingly in their favor. They like the status quo. They don't want to give up the long-standing, unfair advantage *Brady* gives them.

But prosecutors can't admit that. They are reduced to serving up red herrings like witness safety and national security problems. Those claims are grossly overstated. Yet they are continually repeated. They're scary enough to arouse public jitters and make reforms seem dangerous. So far, that tactic has often worked.

————

The struggle over the rules of disclosure in criminal cases can seem like an abstract legal debate for scholars. The *Brady* cases show what is really at stake: the futures, and sometimes the very lives, of ordinary people caught in our criminal system.

Restrictive discovery has led to a literal stream of injustice. In the three decades from 1989 to 2019, hiding favorable evidence— aka violating *Brady*—contributed to the wrongful convictions of 1,056 people. Three innocent persons every month. That we know about. No one can say how much higher the real number is.

That stream must be cut off at the source. If we care about justice, it's long past time to bury *Brady* and make open-file discovery the law everywhere.

EPILOGUE

Thirty-eight years after it began, the Fuller murder case plods on. The last one of the defendants in prison, Russell Overton, was released in March 2022. All of them except Chris Turner remain on lifetime parole.

There won't be a happy ending. When the hidden evidence regarding James McMillian and Ammie Davis came to light, nearly three decades late, the men got a new round of appeals. Given the sad state of the *Brady* rule, they did not prevail. Their convictions stood.

An examination of the whole case record shows the Fuller defendants were almost surely innocent. But because of the prosecution's misdeeds, so many years have passed, so many facts have been forgotten, so many witnesses are gone, we can't know for certain.

Without a doubt they did not get a fair trial. How could it be fair when they were denied the chance to present powerful evidence of their innocence? They spent the best decades of their lives behind bars. Most were teens when they went to prison. They came out as middle-aged men with nothing but jail-issue clothes and memories.

For them, the case will never be over.

Taken together, the time inside for all eight defendants totaled 255 years. The cost to taxpayers, based on figures from the Federal Bureau of Prisons: $9,549,495 in 2018 dollars. If anyone is counting.

Each of them served his entire sentence. They were released only because they timed out. They would likely have been paroled years or even decades earlier—if they had admitted guilt. But they had the audacity to insist they were innocent, after the system decided they were guilty. Parole officials saw that as a refusal to take responsibility, as proof they were not rehabilitated.

It was a surreal experience: "Say you are a killer, and you will go free. But say you are innocent, and you will be deemed dangerous. We'll keep you confined."[1]

Chris Turner is fifty-six now, a little thick in the middle, with touches of gray in his hair when he lets it grow. He needs some dental work and maybe shoulder surgery. But he still has a quick smile. He still moves with the grace of an ex-athlete.

He's working for the DC school system, after stints as a parking attendant and as a flagman and as a security guard. He would like a better job; ideally, one where he could use his skills and experience to benefit society. Thanks to all the classes he took online while inside, he's only nine credits away from an associate degree in business management.

He has found ways to use the wisdom he gained in his prison decades. He's on the board of MAIP, the organization that handled his appeal. He's involved with Healing Justice, a national nonprofit that works to raise awareness of the harm caused by wrongful convictions. He's joined the advisory board for Free Minds, a DC-based group that encourages and supports creative writing projects for incarcerated men and women.

Despite all he's been through, Chris isn't bitter or consumed by the past. He's even able to see that a few positive things came out of his terrible ordeal. He says prison helped make him a man. Gave him a focus.

He does have some anger. It comes through the edges of his voice when he talks about the trial or about the men who were locked up with him.

Chris believes that as the investigation progressed, the prosecutor and the three lead detectives—Goren plus McGinnis and Sanchez and Gossage—started to realize he and the other defendants likely hadn't killed Catherine Fuller. But after proclaiming the crime solved, after seventeen arrests, after countless news stories, they couldn't admit they might be wrong. The stakes were too high.

Chris thinks Donald Gossage, in particular, was corrupt. He was the one cop who knew the suspects, the neighborhood, and the local dynamics. In Chris's view, long before the trial, Gossage knew the prosecution's narrative of the killing was not what happened. But he believed these 8th and H guys were trouble. If they hadn't done this crime, well, they had certainly done others.

If this is what it took to get them off the streets, he was fine with it.

The story of the wrongful convictions of Chris and his comrades is unusual in several ways: that so many people were involved, that a dogged reporter cared enough to reinvestigate the case, that the hidden *Brady* evidence was ultimately uncovered, that they got new hearings almost thirty years after their convictions, that they survived the long years behind bars.

One other thing about these defendants was unusual: their characters.

The men—boys, mostly, when it all began—were just guys from the 8th and H NE neighborhood in DC. They had limited education and experience and resources. They had all the human flaws that come with such circumstances and with youth. During the case, especially after their convictions for Fuller's horrific murder, they were vilified as pond scum.

But each of them had a core of basic honesty. Under immense pressure, day after day after day, that core never cracked.

They were offered leniency in exchange for statements of guilt. Confessions would have endorsed the official story of the murder and validated the officials who crafted and promoted that story. But they hadn't done the crime, so they wouldn't say otherwise.[2]

They did not want mercy. They wanted justice.

They got neither. Yet they endured. They never sold their integrity for their freedom.

The failure of justice in the Fuller case was not surprising at all.

It was business as usual for the police to decide their suspects were guilty and to generate enough evidence to convict them. So was the fact that when the prosecutor found compelling evidence of their innocence, he could easily conceal it from the defense.

That still happens regularly. Consider this *Brady*-related news from just four weeks in February–March 2022:

February 14: A judge in Avoyelles Parish, Louisiana, vacated the convictions of Vincent Simmons.[3] He'd been locked up in the state prison for forty-four years.

In 1977, Simmons was found guilty of the attempted aggravated rape of fourteen-year-old twin sisters. He was Black; the sisters were white. A judge sentenced Simmons to fifty years for each count, consecutive. Simmons said he was innocent, and no physical evidence linked him to the crime.

Beginning in the mid-1990s, Simmons's lawyers found evidence of serious *Brady* infractions. The prosecution never disclosed a medical examination of both twins, done shortly after the alleged attack, that showed no signs of any assault. And despite their positive identifications at trial, they had earlier told the sheriff they didn't know who had attacked them, that "all Blacks look alike."[4] Only, they used the N-word.

It took more than two decades to even gain a hearing, which the local DA had opposed. A review of the previously hidden evidence finally led to Simmons's vindication and release.

The sisters still say he's guilty, but the state will not retry Simmons.

February 21: A Pennsylvania judge reversed the conviction and sentence of Kevin Brian Dowling. He had been on death row since 1998 for the murder of Jennifer Myers.[5]

The only witness who put Dowling near the crime scene—a

shopping center in Spring Grove—testified she had "no doubt at all" he was in the parking lot before the killing. She'd seen him as she came out of a grocery store. Dowling said he was fishing in Muddy Run Lake, an hour away, at the time of the killing. Testimony from the proprietor of a boat rental site had supported his alibi.

A 2021 hearing showed the prosecution had violated *Brady* by withholding the witness's grocery store receipt. The receipt proved she was wrong about the time of her alleged sighting and that Dowling could not have been in Spring Grove when she claimed to see him.

February 22: A judge in Chicago set aside the conviction of Reynaldo "Scooby" Munoz.[6] In 1985, Munoz, sixteen, had been sentenced to sixty years for the murder of Ivan Mena despite denying any involvement. He was paroled in 2015 after serving thirty years.

Prior to a 2021 hearing, Munoz's lawyers had found several police reports that were never disclosed, in violation of *Brady*. One was an eyewitness statement saying Munoz was not the killer; the shooter was "Shorty," not "Scooby." Two other reports showed that the gun used in the Mena shooting had been used in an earlier crime by someone other than Munoz.

In vacating his conviction, the judge said that "if even a fraction of the allegations included in this evidence had been presented at trial . . . Munoz would likely [have] been acquitted." His exoneration was the three thousandth documented by the National Registry of Exonerations since 1987.

February 24: At a wrongful-conviction hearing in Brooklyn, New York, lawyers for Anthony Sims presented evidence of *Brady* infractions they say would have proven his innocence and should earn him a new trial.[7] As of March 2022, a decision on that issue is pending.

Sims was found guilty of the 1998 murder of Li Run Chen. But the prosecution hid evidence—including an eyewitness statement—that Julius Graves, the state's key witness against Sims, was the shooter. And they allowed Graves to testify falsely about his past behavior.

From 2014 until his retirement in 2021, the prosecutor on Sims's case, Mark Hale, had been the head of Brooklyn's Conviction Review Unit, which investigates possible prosecutorial misconduct. Under questioning at the hearing, Hale denied any wrongdoing but testified he has no memory of the state's case against Sims.

March 10: An Ohio court ruled that Isaiah Andrews had been wrongfully imprisoned for forty-five years.[8] Despite his protestations of innocence, Andrews had been sentenced to life in prison for the 1975 murder of his wife, Regina.

In 2017, Andrews's lawyers uncovered evidence of a likely alternate perpetrator whose name had never been disclosed. They also found the report of a bloody palm print from the crime scene. The first police note said tests excluded Andrews as a possible source. That had been crossed out in favor of a second note, which read "print not clear enough to compare."

Based on this previously unknown *Brady* evidence, Andrews's conviction was vacated in April 2020. The state retried him in October 2021, but the jury acquitted him after deliberating just ninety minutes. The wrongful conviction ruling will allow him to receive compensation from the state.

The *Brady* violations in these cases were eventually found. But for every infraction that is uncovered, how many stay hidden? One? Two? Five? No one can say. And you probably guessed right: of the last four cases, Dowling is white, Munoz is Hispanic, Sims and Andrews are Black. That's how it goes.

As of 2021, in this "land of the free," more than two hundred thousand men and women are serving life in our prisons.[9] Hundreds of thousands more have decades-long sentences. How many of them are innocent, locked up because favorable evidence was never disclosed? How many *Brady* violations will happen this week, this month? When, if ever, will they be discovered?

Studying various *Brady* decisions, it's tempting to focus on courtroom arguments and claims, to mull over the legal hair-splitting, to parse the difference between possible and probable. But every case is about someone's life. Every ruling determines a person's fate.

We have ways to measure time, to add up lost hours and days and months. It's easy to write the figures: 45 years, 44 years, 30 years. But we have no scale to weigh the immense human cost of all the wrongful convictions from *Brady* violations; no way to quantify how much hurt and anguish and ruin those numbers contain.

How must it feel to know you are innocent, yet hear a jury pronounce you guilty? To know the evidence that would open the prison doors is out there somewhere, yet to have no way to find it? How do you keep from slipping into rage, or violence, or quiet despair? What becomes of all the energy and beauty and creativity that's wrongly locked away, maybe forever?

There's also the collateral cost. The children who grow up without the nurture and guidance of a mother or father. The family members who must face a lonely future without the comfort and support of a partner or child or sibling. As the infractions go on and on, so do the injustice and the pain they cause. It's an ocean of misery and grief and loss with no shore in sight.

It doesn't have to continue.

Brady's sixty-year history makes one thing perfectly clear: prosecutors and judges aren't going to fix its problems. They are the cause. But we have a solution, and it's in our hands.

Open-file discovery is not a magic answer. Nor is it an instant one. But it's doable and quite effective. It can prevent most violations. We know that, not simply in theory but in practice. It's working in North Carolina and Texas. It's starting to work in Virginia and New York. The rules are changing because people in those places saw the problem and came together to educate them-selves and to raise the issue and to push their lawmakers to act.

That change never comes without a fight.

It took seventeen years for Larry Youngblood to be exonerated. By that time, as often happens, the lead prosecutor from his trial, Deborah Ward, had become a judge, in the superior court of Pima County.

There were many things Judge Ward might have said after DNA evidence cleared Youngblood. That his case showed why the county needed to be more professional in collecting and pre-serving evidence. That she should have been more careful about relying completely on a child witness with uncertain memories, or more open to allowing the defense to test crucial items. That he deserved some compensation for the wrongs that were done to him.

She could have just said, one person to another, "I'm truly sorry, Mr. Youngblood."

Judge Ward didn't say any of those things. She admitted to being "pretty shocked" by the test results that proved his inno-cence.[10] Still, she continued to defend her work on the case, as she had earlier, saying, "[w]e certainly had enough evidence to meet our burden."

In a subsequent interview, *PBS* reporter Tim O'Brien asked Ward directly: "Is Youngblood owed an apology?" She paused nearly ten seconds before replying, "You know, that's really a hard question for me to answer. I suppose on one level, certainly." [11]

Whatever Judge Ward may have meant, that didn't happen. "I never got an apology," Larry Youngblood said later. "I never got nothing from any one of them." [12]

ACKNOWLEDGMENTS

This book was conceived on the beach at Duck, North Carolina, during a wedding weekend in 2008. I told some friends I was looking for a writing project. Todd Edelman said, "What about the Catherine Fuller murder?" I'd never heard of the crime. A mere fourteen years later, here's a book featuring it.

Todd, a former colleague at the DC Public Defender Service, now a superb judge in DC Superior Court, did far more than give me the idea. He shared his knowledge and his research materials with me, which gave me a jumpstart. He also played a major role in shaping the initial appellate filings in the case and in setting it on a path to the Supreme Court.

This book would have been impossible without the courage and generosity of Patrice Gaines. Over a seven-year period in the 1990s, she researched and revived the Fuller case. She freely shared the results of the extensive investigation that she and her colleague at the *Washington Post*, Bill Miller, had done—comprehensive interviews with most of the key figures, a trove of legal documents—as well as her broad understanding of the case and its circumstances.

Shawn Armbrust, executive director of the Mid-Atlantic Innocence Project (MAIP), was instrumental in recruiting lawyers for the Fuller appellants, as well as in shepherding the case into and through the appellate courts. She and Barry Pollack, now with the DC law firm Kramer Levin Robbins Russell, represented Chris Turner throughout the proceedings.

Other lawyers who gave their time and who played significant roles in the long appellate process include John S. Williams and Rob Cary of Williams & Connolly (for Clifton

Yarborough), Jenifer Wicks (for Charles Turner), Michael Antalics of O'Melveny & Myers (for Russell Overton), Donald P. Salzman of Skadden, Arps, Slate, Meagher & Flom (for Kelvin Smith), Veronice Holt (for Levy Rouse), and Lauckland Nicholas (for Timothy Catlett). Also special thanks to Fran D'Antuono for her work on behalf of Clifton Yarborough.

Several investigators helped me find witnesses and documents: Sean Willetts of MAIP, Faheemah Davillier, Seana Drucker, and the incomparable Rachel Primo, my investigator during most of my time at the Public Defender Service.

During this long journey I received much-needed advice and encouragement from Lucia Ballantine, Jonathan Butler, Tucker Carrington, Mac Chapin, Jason DeParle, Pete Dybdahl, Robert Ludke Jr., Pam Novotny, Helen Prejean, and Dick Tofel. Bill Keller at the Marshall Project published two early excerpts from the book; his support gave me a great lift during a difficult period.

Several friends read earlier drafts of the manuscript and gave me useful suggestions: Mary Bava, Charlie Erdrich, Tom Gammon, Jeff Gass, Jim Mulhern, Bill O'Brien, Rich Pino and Jason Zolle. Thank you all.

Robin Rue led me to the amazing Dana Isaacson. Dana's careful editing and recommendations on format and structure improved my work greatly. My friend and ex-colleague Alec Karakatsanis introduced me to The New Press, and here's the result. Julia Masnick provided excellent, helpful advice through the contract negotiation process.

My editor at The New Press, zakia henderson-brown, believed in me and my idea when I despaired of finding a publisher. She, along with assistant editor Ishan Desai-Geller and managing editor Emily Albarillo, spent a great deal of time helping me make this a much better book. I will always be grateful.

I learned so much from the story of Chris Turner and his comrades in suffering: Timothy Catlett, Russell Overton, Levy Rouse, Kelvin Smith, Charles Turner, the late Steven Webb, and Clifton

Yarborough. I thank them—and salute them—for their courage and their candor.

To my children and their partners—Chloe and Daniel Peterman, Pete Dybdahl and Angela Martin, and Jeremy and Kelley Steen—thank you for the loyal support and for pretending to believe I would ever finish this book. Also, thanks to my grandchildren, Nick, Anna, Sydney Grace, Sam, Samantha, and Harper, for the joy you bring every day. I've named them all in the hope they might want to read this book someday.

Last, and most, deep gratitude to my wife, Trish, companion of my days and nights. Her abiding love and laughter sustain me.

NOTES

Throughout the book, unless otherwise noted, statements in quotation marks are from trial or interview transcripts or notes, police records and reports, or the notes or recollections of someone who was present to hear them.

The facts about Chris Turner's life, and much of the information about his co-defendants, comes from dozens of interviews and conversations the author has had with Chris since we first met at the Atwater (CA) Federal Correctional Institution on May 2, 2010.

The following abbreviations are used extensively:

TT: Trial transcript of the Fuller murder case, October 16, 1985, to December 18, 1985, and sentencing hearings, January 14, 1986, to February 18, 1986. Total number of pages is 8,738.

NTH: New trial hearing transcript of the Fuller case, April 23, 2012, to May 15, 2012. The pages are numbered consecutively, and total 3,092.

GJ: Grand jury testimony related to the Fuller murder case.

MPD: Washington, DC, Metropolitan Police Department documents and reports.

Introduction

1. An inscription on the walls of the U.S. Department of Justice headquarters; cited in *Brady v. Maryland*, 373 U.S. 83, 87 (1963).

2. Samuel R. Gross, Maurice J. Possley, Kaitlin Jackson Roll, and Klara Huber Stephens, *Government Misconduct and Convicting the Innocent, The Role of Prosecutors, Police and Other Law Enforcement* (report, National Registry of Exonerations, September 1, 2020).

1: Love, Death, and the Birth of *Brady*

1. The facts about John Brady in this chapter are from Richard Hammer's biography *Between Life and Death* (New York: MacMillan, 1969), which covers Brady's life up to 1968.

2. Hammer, 94.

3. Hammer, 97.

4. "Police Charge Two with Slaying of Severn Man," *Evening Capital* (Annapolis, MD), July 3, 1958.

5. Hammer, *Between Life and Death*, 114–15.

6. Hammer, 111–12.

7. Hammer, 127.

8. Brady v. State, 174 A.2d 167, 169 (Md. 1961).

9. *Brady*, 174 A.2d at 169.

10. Hammer, *Between Life and Death*, 278.

11. Paul Shechtman, "How a Man Named Brady Made History 50 Years Ago," *New York Law Journal* (May 13, 2013).

12. Brady v. Maryland, 373 U.S. 83, 87 (1963).

13. William C. Plouffe Jr., "William O. Douglas," in *The Social History of Crime and Punishment in America: An Encyclopedia*, ed. Wilbur R. Miller (Thousand Oaks, CA: SAGE, 2012), Volume 1, 488.

14. Arthur M. Schlesinger Jr., "The Supreme Court: 1947," *Fortune* (January 1947), 201.

15. William O. Douglas, *The Court Years: 1939 to 1975* (New York: Random House, 1980), 8.

16. William O. Douglas, "Foreword," *55 Yale Law Journal* (August 1946), 867.

17. Stephanos Bibas, "*Brady v. Maryland*: From Adversarial Gamesmanship Toward the Search for Innocence," in *Criminal Procedure Stories*, ed. Carol S. Steiker (New York: Foundation Press, 2006), 129.

18. Hammer, *Between Life and Death*, 295.

19. Heather F. Williams, "Letter from the Defender," *Federal Defender Newsletter*, Eastern District of California, March 2017, 11.

2: The Woman in the Alley

1. William Freeman, MPD witness statement, October 1, 1984; William Freeman, testimony, TT November 1, 1985, 33.

2. Edward D. Sargent, "Desolate NE Intersection Gave Name to the 8th and H Street Crew," *Washington Post*, December 13, 1984, A38.

3. Carrie Anderson, testimony, GJ May 6, 1985, 60; Christopher Turner, testimony, TT November 27, 1985, 48.

4. MPD witness statements of David Fuller, Jr., David Fuller III, and Barbara Wade, October 2, 1984.

5. Lyle V. Harris, " 'Her Bills Are Paid,' Husband Says," *Washington Post*, October 6, 1984, C1.

6. Mary Overton, interview by author, November 24, 2010.

7. Hattie Raspberry, interview by Faheemah Davillier, November 4, 2010.

8. Overton, interview.

9. Maggie Pendergrast, interview by Faheemah Davillier, March 10, 2008.

10. Freeman, MPD witness statement.

11. MPD Event Report, October 1, 1984.

12. MPD Report of Investigation, October 2, 1984.

13. Patrick McGinnis, interviews by Bill Miller, May 10, 1996, and October 21, 1996.

14. Ruben Sanchez, interviews by Patrice Gaines and Bill Miller, December 5, 1996, and January 3, 1997.

15. MPD Evidence Report, October 1, 1984.

16. Michael Bray, testimony, TT November 18, 1985, 30–32.

17. James Robinson, MPD witness statement, October 1, 1984.

18. Freeman, MPD witness statement.

19. McGinnis, interview, May 10, 1996.

20. McGinnis, interview, October 21, 1996.

21. MPD Report of Investigation, October 2, 1984.

22. McGinnis, interview, October 21, 1996.

23. For more information on go-go, see Natalie Hopkinson, *Go-Go Live: The Musical Life and Death of a Chocolate City* (Durham, NC: Duke University Press, 2012).

24. Lyrics credited to Chuck Brown and the Soul Searchers.

25. Autopsy Report for Catherine Fuller, Office of the Chief Medical Examiner for Washington, DC, October 2, 1984.

26. Toxicology Report for Catherine Fuller, Office of the Chief Medical Examiner for Washington, DC, October 17, 1984.

27. Michael Bray, interview by Patrice Gaines, October 31, 2000.

28. Barbara Wade, MPD witness statement, October 2, 1984.

29. MPD Report of Investigation, October 2, 1984.

30. Levy Rouse, MPD witness statement, October 3, 1984.

31. Jacqueline Watts, MPD witness statement, October 3, 1984.

32. Ronald Murphy, MPD witness statement, October 3, 1984.

33. MPD Report of Investigation, October 3, 1984.

34. Ruben Sanchez, notes, October 2, 1984; Sanchez, interview, January 3, 1997.

35. McGinnis claimed (in an undated interview with the *Washington Post*, likely 1996) that "people did not want to cooperate because so many of their children [were] involved."

36. Sanchez, interview, December 5, 1996; McGinnis, interview, October 21, 1996.

37. Daniel S. Medwed, *Prosecution Complex: America's Race to Convict and Its Impact on the Innocent* (New York: New York University Press, 2012), 22–23.

3: Setting *Brady*'s Borders

1. Bruce Allen Murphy, *Wild Bill, the Legend and Life of William O. Douglas* (New York: Random House, 2003), 329–30.

2. The case facts are from the published court opinion *Giglio v. United States*, 405 U.S. 150 (1972).

3. The case facts and arguments are from the published court opinions ending in *United States v. Agurs*, 427 U.S. 97 (1976).

4. United States v. Agurs, 510 F.2d. 1249, 1253 (DC Cir. 1975).

5. *Agurs*, 427 U.S. at 107.

6. *Agurs*, 427 U.S. at 115.

7. The case facts and arguments are from the published court opinion *United States v. Bagley*, 473 U.S. 667 (1985).

8. Bagley v. Lumpkin, 719 F.2d 1462 (9th Cir. 1983).

9. *Bagley*, 473 U.S. at 667.

10. *Bagley*, 473 U.S. at 675.

11. *Bagley*, 473 U.S. at 709.

12. *Bagley*, 473 U.S. at 685.

4: Prisoners of Their Hunch

1. MPD Report of Investigation, October 5, 1984.

2. Cliff Yarborough, interview by author, May 30, 2010, at Tucson Federal Correctional Institution.

3. Michael O'Connell, PhD, testimony, NTH April 24, 2012, 289.

4. Patrick McGinnis, testimony, NTH May 10, 2012, 2487–88; cf. McGinnis, testimony, NTH May 11, 2012, 2598-99.

5. Cliff Yarborough, MPD Suspect Statement, October 4, 1984.

6. Yarborough, interview.

7. McGinnis, testimony, NTH May 10, 2012, 2597; NTH May 11, 2012, 2639.

8. DC Superior Court Affidavit in Support of an Arrest Warrant for Alphonso Lamar Harris, October 4, 1984.

9. MPD Report of Investigation, October 5, 1984.

10. MPD Report of Investigation, October 5, 1984.

11. MPD Prosecution Report, October 5, 1984.

12. Corinne Schultz, interview by author, October 7, 2009.

13. Kim Eisler, "Need a GOOD Lawyer?," *Washingtonian*, April 1, 2002.

14. Lyle V. Harris, " 'Her Bills Are Paid,' Husband Says," *Washington Post*, October 6, 1984, C1.

15. MPD Report of Investigation, October 9, 1984.

16. Timothy Catlett, MPD witness statement, October 9, 1984.

17. Charles Turner, MPD witness statement, October 10, 1984.

18. John Ward Anderson, "Suspect in Winter's Mugging," *Washington Post*, October 26, 1984.

19. Many of his legal documents and most news reports spell James's last name McMillan, with only a single *i*. But James himself said the proper spelling was McMillian, so that form is used here.

20. Mary Phelps-Hickman, affidavit, sworn January 11, 2011.

21. DC Superior Court Report on Case 1984 CDC 003685.

22. Ammie Davis, MPD witness statement, October 26, 1984.

23. Frank Loney, interview by Faheemah Davillier, June 11, 2008, Carlisle, PA.

24. Patrick McGinnis, interview by Bill Miller, October 21, 1996.

25. Ruben Sanchez, interview by Patrice Gaines and Bill Miller, December 5, 1996.

26. Mary Overton, interview by author, November 24, 2010.

27. Sanchez's claim was further undercut by the fact that none of the people who testified against the defendants at trial ever claimed to have been threatened or intimidated by any of them.

28. Jeffrey Behm, statement, TT November 15, 1985, 217.

29. Scott Turow, *Ultimate Punishment: A Lawyer's Reflections on Dealing with the Death Penalty* (New York: Farrar, Straus and Giroux, 2003), 34.

30. Donald Gossage, interview by Patrice Gaines and Bill Miller, November 21, 1996.

31. Levy Rouse, interview by author, November 2, 2021.

32. Mary Jordan and Alfred E. Lewis, "Police Arrest 5 in Gang Killing of NE Mother," *Washington Post*, December 10, 1984, B1.

33. Bill Allegar, "Four More Arrested in D.C. Sex Murder," *Washington Times*, December 10, 1984, 6B.

34. Gossage, interview.

35. Jerry Goren, notes, undated (likely 1985), 54.

36. Calvin Alston, testimony, NTH April 25, 2012, 528.

37. Sanchez, interview, December 5, 1996.

38. Calvin Alston, interview by Patrice Gaines and Bill Miller, February 12, 1996, at Ashland (KY) Federal Correctional Institution.

39. Calvin Alston, testimony, NTH April 25, 2012, 535–36.

40. Samuel R. Gross, Kristen Jacoby, Daniel J. Matheson, and Nicholas Montgomery, "Exonerations in the United States Through 2003," *Journal of Criminal Law and Criminology* 95 (Winter 2005), 545–46.

41. Maclen Stanley, "Stop Lying to Juveniles During Police Interrogations," *Psychology Today*, posted January 28, 2022. The Central Park Five are now known as the Exonerated Five.

42. McGinnis, interview, October 21, 1996; McGinnis, notes, November 29, 1984.

43. Calvin Alston, interview by Patrice Gaines, August 23, 2000, at Ashland (KY) Federal Correctional Institution.

44. Calvin Alston, video statement transcript, November 29, 1984, 4ff.

45. Alston, video statement transcript, 31.

46. Ruben Sanchez, testimony, NTH May 8, 2012, 2105–07; McGinnis, testimony, NTH May 10, 2012, 2496–2500.

47. Alston, testimony, NTH 551ff.

48. Charles Turner, MPD Suspect Statement, December 5, 1984.

49. Cliff Yarborough, testimony, NTH April 23, 2012, 111.

50. McGinnis, testimony, NTH May 10, 2012, 2509–10.

51. Sanchez, testimony, NTH 2120.

52. Yarborough, testimony, NTH 123–37.

53. Cliff Yarborough, video statement transcript, December 9, 1984.

54. "8th and H," *The Confession Tapes*, directed by Kelly Loudenberg, Netflix, streamed September 8, 2017.

55. Calvin Alston, letter to Judge Reggie Walton, 1985.

56. Calvin Alston, letter to Mrs. Page and family, 1985.

57. His real name was Harry J. Bennett III, but his friends and acquaintances all called him Derrick, so that name is used here.

58. DC Superior Court Affidavit in Support of an Arrest Warrant for Harry Bennette [*sic*] aka Derrick, sworn December 29, 1984.

59. MPD Prosecution Report, February 6, 1985.

60. Derrick Bennett, video statement transcript, September 6, 1985.

61. Bennett, video statement transcript, 60–61.

62. DC Superior Court Order, February 7, 1985.

63. MPD Prosecution Report, April 5, 1985.

64. Derrick Bennett, interview by Patrice Gaines, September 5, 1996.

65. Bennett, interview.

66. Derrick Bennett, testimony, GJ April 12, 1985, 51.

67. Bennett, testimony, 51.

68. Steven Webb, interview by Patrice Gaines and Bill Miller, October 30, 1996, at U.S. Penitentiary Terre Haute (IN).

69. Webb, interview.

70. DC Superior Court Affidavit in Support of an Arrest Warrant for Lisa Ruffin, sworn October 5, 1985.

71. Debra Birnbaum, "The People v. O.J. Simpson Recap: Shuffling the Race Card," *Variety*, March 1, 2016.

72. Jerry Goren, interview by Patrice Gaines and Bill Miller, August 26, 1997, 16.

73. Pretrial hearing, TT October 16, 1985, 10–11.

74. Pretrial hearing, TT October 16, 1985, 11.

75. Goren, interview, 6.

76. Jerry Goren, testimony, NTH May 3, 2012, 1638–39.

77. Goren, testimony, NTH 1772–73.

78. Ronald Murphy, MPD Witness Statement, October 3, 1984; Goren testimony, NTH 1670.

79. William Freeman, MPD Witness Statement, October 1, 1984; Goren notes, 34.

80. Goren, testimony, NTH 1668, 1676.

81. Goren, testimony, NTH 1659–60. Goren also testified he believed he'd talked to McMillian once, though he had no recollection of any interview. There is no record of any such meeting, and in his undated notes he wrote, "We never talked to James McMillian." Goren notes, 46.

5: The Battle for *Brady*'s Heart

1. Most of the facts about Larry Youngblood's life and the legal arguments come from the published court opinions in the case, ending with *Arizona v. Youngblood*, 488 U.S. 51 (1988). Other sources relied on are Marc Bookman, "Does an Innocent Man Have the Right to Be Exonerated?," *Atlantic*, December, 2014, and Norman C. Bey, "Old Blood, Bad Blood, and Youngblood: Due Process, Lost Evidence, and the Limits of Bad Faith," *Washington University Law Review* 86, no. 2 (2008), 241.

2. State v. Youngblood, 734 P.2d 592 (Ariz. Ct. App. 1986).

3. People v. Nation, 26 Cal. 3d 169, 176 (Cal., 1980).

4. Bey, "Old Blood," 252–53.

5. *Youngblood*, 488 U.S. at 51.

6. *Youngblood*, 488 U.S. at 59.

7. *Youngblood*, 488 U.S. at 61.

8. U.S. v. Bryant, 439 F.2d 642, 651 (U.S. App. D.C. 1971).

9. People v. Hitch, 12 Cal.3d 641, 650 (Cal. 1974).

10. State v. Youngblood, 790 P.2d 759 (Ariz. Ct. App. 1989).

11. State v. Youngblood, 844 P.2d 1152 (Ariz. 1993).

12. Barbara Whitaker, "DNA Frees Inmate Years After Justices Rejected His Plea," *New York Times*, August 11, 2000.

13. Matthew H. Lembke, "The Role of Police Culpability in *Leon* and *Youngblood*," Notes, *Virginia Law Review* 76, no. 6 (September 1990), 1213, 1240–41.

14. Sarah M. Bernstein, "Fourteenth Amendment—Police Failure to Preserve Evidence and Erosion of the Due Process Right to a Fair Trial," *Journal of Criminal Law and Criminology* (Winter 1990), 1256, 1276–77.

15. Daniel R. Dinger, "Should Lost Evidence Mean a Lost Chance to Prosecute?: State Rejections of the United States Supreme Court Decision in *Arizona v. Youngblood*," Notes, *American Journal of Criminal Law* Austin 27, no. 3 (Summer 2000), 329, 364–67.

16. Bey, "Old Blood," 287.

17. The facts of Tommy David Strickler's case and the legal arguments come from the published court opinions in the case, ending with *Strickler v. Greene*, 527 U.S. 63 (1999).

18. Mark Morrison, "Jury Gives Second Killer of JMU Student Life Sentences," *Roanoke Times*, March 28, 1991, A1.

19. Tom Campbell, "Judge Nullifies Death Sentence," *Richmond Times-Dispatch*, October 17, 1997, B6.

20. Strickler v. Pruett, Nos. 97-29, 97-30, 1998 WL 340420 (4th Cir. June 17, 1998), unpublished opinion.

21. *Strickler*, 527 U.S. at 263.

22. *Strickler*, 527 U.S. at 289.

23. *Strickler*, 527 U.S. at 296.

24. *Strickler*, 527 U.S. at 307.

25. News sources, "Student's Murderer Executed," *Washington Post*, July 22, 1999.

26. United States v. Bagley, 473 U.S. 667, 701 (1985).

27. United States v. Agurs, 427 U.S. 97, 108 (1976).

28. Zanders v. United States, 999 A2d 149, 164 (D.C. 2010).

29. Oral argument in Smith v. Cain, No. 10-8145, November 8, 2011, 49.

30. *Strickler*, 527 U.S. at 281.

31. Bidish Sarma, "Will the Supreme Court Reinvigorate the *Brady* Doctrine in Turner and Overton?," *American Constitutional Society* (blog), March 13, 2017.

32. Kathleen Ridolfi, Tiffany Joslyn, and Todd Fries, "Material Indifference: How Courts Are Impeding Fair Disclosure in Criminal Cases," *Santa Clara Law Digital Commons*, Faculty Publications (2014).

33. Ridolfi, Joslyn, and Fries, "Material Indifference."

6: The Biggest Murder Trial in DC History

1. Elsa Walsh, "Judge Scott Calling the Shots," *Washington Post*, December 14, 1985, C1; "DC Superior Court Judge Robert M. Scott Dies at 70," Obituary, *Washington Post*, September 17, 1992, D5.

2. Regina v. Saunders & Archer, 2 Plowd. 473 (1573), 75 Eng. Rep. 706 (1576). Opposition to the felony murder rule has been growing in recent years, in large part because it allows someone to be convicted of murder without any intent to kill. The rule has been abolished in Great Britain and Canada and weakened in

California and some other states. A 2022 study found that "[f]elony murder laws have particularly adverse impacts on people of color, young people, and women." Nazgol Ghandnoosh, Emma Stamen, and Connie Budaci, *Felony Murder, An On-Ramp for Extreme Sentencing* (report, the Sentencing Project and Fair and Just Prosecution, 2022), 2.

    3. TT October 31, 1985, 5ff.

    4. TT October 31, 1985, 26ff.

    5. TT November 11, 1985, 7ff.

    6. Barbara Wade, testimony, TT November 1, 1985, 13ff.

    7. William Freeman, testimony, TT November 1, 1985, 38ff.

    8. TT November 1, 1985, 58ff.

    9. TT November 1, 1985, 59.

    10. TT November 1, 1985, 59–60.

    11. TT November 1, 1985, 60.

    12. Freeman, testimony, 77.

    13. Michael Hedges, "6 Guilty, 2 Cleared of Fuller Murder; Jury Still Out on 2," *Washington Times*, December 17, 1985, A1.

    14. Elsa Walsh, "Witness Describes NE Killing," *Washington Post*, November 6, 1985, B1.

    15. Derrick Bennett, testimony, TT November 5, 1985, 35ff.

    16. Michael Hedges, "3rd Defendant Describes Grisly Murder of Fuller," *Washington Times*, November 8, 1985.

    17. Calvin Alston, testimony, TT November 7, 1985, 59ff.

    18. Saundra Saperstein and Elsa Walsh, "Jury Swayed by Testimony of 14-Year-Old," *Washington Post*, December 19, 1985, A1.

    19. Maurice Thomas, testimony, TT November 13, 1985, 5ff.

    20. Michael Bray, testimony, TT November 18, 1985, 22ff.

    21. LaTonya Smith, testimony, TT November 27, 1985, 121ff.

    22. Denise Riddick, testimony, TT November 27, 1985, 177ff.

    23. Christopher Turner, testimony, TT November 27, 1985, 5ff.

    24. Turner, testimony, 86–91.

    25. Elsa Walsh, "1 Defendant in Fuller Slaying Says He Was at Friend's House," *Washington Post*, November 28, 1985, B19.

    26. Katrina Ward, testimony, TT December 2, 1985, 482ff.

    27. Elsa Walsh, "Defendant Linked to Fuller Death," *Washington Post*, December 3, 1985, C1.

28. TT December 4, 1985, 44ff.

29. TT December 4, 1985, 83.

30. TT December 6, 1985, 399.

31. TT December 4, 1985, 137.

32. TT December 6, 1985, 430.

33. TT December 6, 1985, 366ff.

34. TT December 6, 1985, 425ff.

35. TT December 6, 1985, 502.

36. TT December 16, 1985, 623.

37. Courtland Milloy, "Bring Back the Death Penalty," *Washington Post*, December 17, 1985, D3.

38. Fuller trial jury note, December 16, 1985.

39. TT December 18, 1985, 655ff.

40. Patricia Press, "Black on Black: The Catherine Fuller Murder" (unpublished typed manuscript), undated (likely 1988–89), 393.

41. Elsa Walsh, "2 More Convicted in Fuller Murder," *Washington Post*, December 19, 1985, A1.

42. Saperstein and Walsh, "Jury Swayed by Testimony of 14-Year-Old."

43. Willie McCain, interview by Patrice Gaines, undated (likely 1997).

44. Edward D. Sargent, "Convicted Man: 'I Feel Like Dying,'" *Washington Post*, December 19, 1985, A38.

45. TT January 14, 1986, 8ff.

46. Russell Overton and Charles Turner, statements, TT February 4, 1986, 3–5.

47. Christopher Turner, statement, TT February 4, 1986, 14ff.

48. TT February 11, 1986, 4ff.

49. TT February 19, 1986, 63.

50. Cliff Yarborough, statement, TT February 19, 1986, 72.

51. Elsa Walsh, "11th Man Is Guilty in Fuller Case; Final Defendant Admits Slaying Role," *Washington Post*, April 11, 1986, D3.

52. Catlett v. U.S., 545 A.2d 1202 (D.C. 1988).

7: An Epidemic of Violations

1. The facts about Kenneth R. Olsen and his case are taken from the published court opinions *United States v. Olsen*, 704 F.3d 1172 (9th Cir. 2013) and *United States v. Olsen*, 737 F.3d 625, (9th Cir. 2013).

2. *Olsen*, 704 F.3d at 1178–79.

3. *Olsen*, 737 F.3d at 625.

4. *Olsen*, 737 F.3d at 626.

5. *Olsen*, 737 F.3d at 633.

6. United States v. Bagley, 473 U.S. 667, 702 (Marshall, J., dissenting).

7. Clark Neily, *Are a Disproportionate Number of Federal Judges Former Government Advocates?* (Cato Institute Study, updated May 27, 2021; originally published September 28, 2019).

8. Colleen Long, "Biden Seeking Professional Diversity in His Judicial Picks," *Associated Press*, February 10, 2022.

9. " 'Troublemaker' Kozinski Unafraid to Advocate for Change," *Bloomberg News*, December 4, 2015.

10. Hon. Alex Kozinski, "Criminal Law 2.0," *Georgetown Law Journal Annual Review of Criminal Procedure* 44 (2015), xxxvi.

11. Frost v. Gilbert, 818 F.3d 469, 476 (9th Cir. 2016).

12. *Frost*, 818 F.3d at 486.

13. Frost v. Gilbert, 835 F.3d 883, 886 (9th Cir. 2016).

14. Judge Alex Kozinski, interview by Lesley Stahl, *60 Minutes*, April 23, 2017.

15. Dan Berman and Laura Jarrett, "Judge Alex Kozinski, Accused of Sexual Misconduct, Resigns," CNN, December 18, 2017.

16. Troy Closson, "24 Years Later, Freed over Prosecutors' Missteps," *New York Times*, March 6, 2021, A1.

17. Jonah E. Bromwich, "A Group Publicized Prosecutorial Misconduct. The City Isn't Pleased," *New York Times*, November 11, 2021, A14; George Joseph, "Prosecutors Wrongfully Convicted Three Men Who Spent 24 Years Behind Bars. Will They Be Disbarred?" *Gothamist*, May 6, 2021.

18. Civil Rights Corps et al. v. Pestana et al., 21 Civ. 09128 (VM) (S.D.N.Y. June 13, 2022).

19. The facts of Alan Gell's case are taken from *State v. Gell*, North Carolina Supreme Court, No. 469A98, February 4, 2000; Alexandra Gross, "Alan Gell," *The National Registry of Exonerations*, updated July 8, 2019; Joseph Neff, "Who Killed Allen Ray Jenkins?, Chapter 1," *Death Penalty Information Center*, December 8, 2002.

20. Neff, "Who Killed Allen Ray Jenkins?, Chapter 1."

21. Mike Klinkosum and Brad Bannon, "Advocating for Those Left Behind: The Need for Discovery Reform in Non-Capital Post-Conviction Cases," *Trial Briefs*, February 2004, 8–9.

22. Richard Rosen, interview by author, July 26, 2021.

23. See N.C. Gen. Stat. §515A, Art. 48.

24. The Innocence Project, innocenceproject.org/cases/michael-morton/.

25. "Improving Discovery in Criminal Cases in Texas: How Best Practices Contribute to Greater Justice" (report, Texas Appleseed, 2013).

26. "Towards More Transparent Justice: The Michael Morton Act's First Year" (report, Texas Appleseed, 2015).

27. Pamela Colloff, "Jail Time May Be the Least of Ken Anderson's Problems," *Texas Monthly*, November 14, 2013.

28. "Report: Guilty Pleas on the Rise, Criminal Trials on the Decline," Innocence Project, August 7, 2018. For more information on this issue, see "The Trial Penalty: The Sixth Amendment Right to Trial on the Verge of Extinction and How to Save It" (report, National Association of Criminal Defense Lawyers, 2018); Jed S. Rakoff, *Why the Innocent Plead Guilty and the Guilty Go Free* (New York: Farrar, Straus and Giroux, 2021).

29. The case facts are from the published court opinion *United States v. Ruiz*, 536 U.S. 622 (2002).

30. *Ruiz*, 536 U.S. at 634 (Thomas, J., concurring).

31. Brady v. Maryland, 373 U.S. 83, 87 (1963).

32. *Ruiz*, 536 U.S. at 630.

33. "Why Do Innocent People Plead Guilty to Crimes They Didn't Commit?," Innocence Project, guiltypleaproblem.org.

34. "Discovery Reform Legislative Victories," National Association of Criminal Defense Lawyers, April 25, 2019.

35. "Supreme Court of Virginia Has Established a Special Committee on Criminal Discovery Rules," *Virginia State Bar News*, November 25, 2013.

36. Frank Green, "Justices Reject Recommendations on Pretrial Discovery in Criminal Cases," *Richmond Times-Dispatch*, November 26, 2015.

37. Elana Schor, "Alaska Senator Stevens Found Guilty of Accepting Gifts from Oil Executive," *Guardian*, October 27, 2008.

38. Terry Frieden, "Sen. Ted Stevens' Conviction Set Aside," CNN, April 7, 2009.

39. Rob Cary, "Recalling the Injustice Done to Sen. Ted Stevens/ Commentary," *Rollcall*, October 28, 2014.

40. "Justice Should Be Blind, Not Blindly Ignored," Press release, Office of U.S. Senator Lisa Murkowski, March 15, 2012.

41. Statement of the Honorable Lisa Murkowski, *Congressional Record*, June 6, 2012, 5–8.

42. S. 2197, A bill to require the attorney for the Government to disclose favorable information to the defendant in criminal prosecutions brought by the United States, introduced March 15, 2012.

43. Murkowski, "Justice Should Be Blind, Not Blindly Ignored."

44. Prepared Statement of Hon. James M. Cole, Deputy Attorney General, to the Senate Committee on the Judiciary, presented June 6, 2012.

45. Robert Gay Guthrie, Letter from the National Association of Assistant United States Attorneys to the Senate Committee on the Judiciary, June 4, 2012.

46. Avis Buchanan, "Fairer Trials and Better Justice in D.C.," *Washington Post*, October 28, 2011, A1.

47. Jenia I. Turner and Allison D. Redlich, "Two Models of Pre-Plea Discovery in Criminal Cases: An Empirical Comparison," *Washington and Lee Law Review* 73, no. 1 (Winter 2016), 285, 286.

48. David Kocieniewski, "So Many Crimes, and Reasons to Not Cooperate, *New York Times*, December 30, 2007. The quotations from Hester Agudosi and Charles Ogletree are also from this article.

49. Cole, statement; Guthrie, letter.

50. *Olsen*, 737 F.3d at 630–631 (Kozinski, J., dissenting).

51. Brief of Amici Curiae Texas Public Policy Foundation, Freedomworks, Cause of Action Institute, and American Legislative Exchange Council in Support of Petitioners and Urging Reversal, Supreme Court filing in *Turner v. U.S.* and *Overton v. U.S.*, Nos. 15–1503 and 15–1504, February, 2017, 5.

52. Kathleen Ridolfi, Tiffany Joslyn, and Todd Fries, "Material Indifference: How Courts Are Impeding Fair Disclosure in Criminal Cases," *Santa Clara Law Digital Commons*, Faculty Publications (2014), 54.

53. Bennett L. Gershman, "Reflections on *Brady v. Maryland*," *South Texas Law Review* 47 (2006), 685, 691.

54. Brian Gregory, "*Brady* Is the Problem: Wrongful Convictions and the Case for 'Open-File' Criminal Discovery," *University of San Francisco Law Review* 46 (Winter 2012), 819, 821.

55. Tom Jackman, "More Than Half of All Wrongful Criminal Convictions Are Caused by Government Misconduct, Study Finds," *Washington Post*, September 16, 2020.

8: The Long Way Home

1. Courtland Milloy, "Bring Back the Death Penalty," *Washington Post*, December 17, 1985, D3.

2. Mark Mathabane, *Kaffir Boy* (New York: Macmillan, 1986).

3. Mary Overton, interview by Patrice Gaines, August 3, 1999.

4. Patrice Gaines, "A Case of Conviction: A Reporter's Hunch Leads Her on a Six-Year Journey into the Hidden Heart of One of Washington's Most Infamous Murders," *Washington Post*, May 6, 2001, F1.

5. Patrice Gaines, *Laughing in the Dark* (New York: Crown, 1994). The details of Ms. Gaines's life come from this autobiography.

6. Gaines, "A Case of Conviction."

7. Derrick Bennett, telephone interview by Patrice Gaines, November 1995.

8. Calvin Alston, interview by Patrice Gaines and Bill Miller, February 12, 1996.

9. Katrina Ward, interview by Patrice Gaines, February 15, 1996.

10. Maurice Thomas, interview by Patrice Gaines and Bill Miller, January 21, 1996.

11. Ward, interview.

12. Donald Gossage, interview by Patrice Gaines and Bill Miller, November 21, 1996.

13. Gaines, "A Case of Conviction."

14. Ruben Sanchez, interview by Patrice Gaines, December 5, 1996.

15. Jerry Goren, interview by Patrice Gaines and Bill Miller, August 26, 1997, 29.

16. Prisoner order, U.S. Marshals Service, December 24, 1993.

17. Patrice Gaines, interview by author, 2011.

18. 28 CFR § 2.80, "Guidelines for D.C. Code Offenders."

19. See, for example, Paul Willcocks, "The Prisoner's Dilemma: Falsely Confess, or Stay Behind Bars," *Tyee*, January 7, 2019; Daniel S. Medwed, "The Innocent Prisoners Dilemma: Consequences of Failing to Admit Guilt at Parole Hearings," *Iowa Law Review* 93 (March 2008), 491–557.

20. Derrick Bennett, affidavit, sworn February 13, 2009.

21. Calvin Alston, affidavit, sworn March 7, 2008.

22. *U.S. v. Christopher Turner*, "Motion to Vacate Conviction or in the Alternative for a New Trial and Memorandum and Points of Authorities in Support Thereof," DC Superior Court filing, January 6, 2010.

23. *U.S. v. Christopher Turner*, "Amended Motion to Vacate Conviction," DC Superior Court filing, April 6, 2010.

24. See, for example, *Harrison v. U.S.*, 7 F.2d. 259, 262 (2d. Cir. 1925), where the legendary Judge Learned Hand noted that recantations are "for obvious reasons looked upon with the utmost suspicion."

25. Burnett v. Coronado Oil & Gas Co., 285 U.S. 393, 406 (1932) (Brandeis, J., dissenting).

26. DC Superior Court ruling of Judge Frederick H. Weisberg, *Catlett v. U.S.*, filed August 6, 2012, 16–17.

27. Cliff Yarborough, testimony, NTH April 23, 2012, 96.

28. Calvin Alston, testimony, NTH April 25, 2012, 609.

29. Derrick Bennett, testimony, NTH April 25, 2012, 714–17.

30. Richard Callery, testimony, NTH April 26, 2012, 757.

31. Larry McCann, testimony, NTH April 30, 2012, 1074ff.

32. Jerry Goren, testimony, NTH May 3, 2012, 1645–46.

33. Goren, testimony, 1739–43.

34. NTH May 14, 2012, 2784ff.

35. Catlett v. U.S., 545 A.2d 1202, 1206 n.2 (D.C. 1988).

36. NTH May 14, 2012, 3014.

37. See, for example, NTH May 14, 2012, 2828–29, 2837.

38. Goren, interview, 28.

39. DC Superior Court ruling of Judge Weisberg.

40. Weisberg ruling, at 18.

41. Weisberg ruling, at 24.

42. Turner v. U.S., 116 A.3d 894 (D.C. 2015).

43. Associate Judge Anna Blackburne-Rigsby, oral argument in *Turner v. U.S.*, April 29, 2014.

44. *Turner*, 116 A.3d at 901.

45. *Turner*, 116, A.3d at 926.

46. Petition for a Writ of Certiorari, *Yarborough v. U.S.*, filed June 10, 2016, 10–13.

47. Marilyn Edwards Blount, interview by MPD Detective James Trainum, undated (likely October 1992).

48. Faheemah Davillier, interview by author, 2012.

49. After MAIP took over the case, they sent the remaining items of evidence from the crime scene to a DNA lab for testing, but got no results. Several key pieces of evidence, notably Fuller's coin purse, had been lost or destroyed, so they could not be tested.

50. The facts of this incident are taken from various police and court documents in DC Superior Court case F-10635-92, *U.S. v. James F. McMillian*.

51. Transcript of oral argument, U.S. Supreme Court, *Turner v. U.S.* and *Overton v. U.S.*, March 29, 2017, 18.

52. Transcript of oral argument, at 20–21.

53. Transcript of oral argument, at 4ff.

54. Transcript of oral argument, at 47–48.

55. Charles S. Turner et al. v. U.S., 137 S.Ct. 1885 (2017).

56. *Turner*, 137 S.Ct. at 1898 (Kagan, J., dissenting).

9: The Failure and the Hope

1. Transcript of oral argument, U.S. Supreme Court, *Turner v. U.S.* and *Overton v. U.S.*, March 29, 2017, 47.

2. *Turner*, 137 S.Ct. 1893.

3. Oliver Laughland, Sabrina Saddiqui, and Lauren Gambino, "Inauguration Protests: More Than 200 Demonstrators Arrested in Washington," *Guardian*, January 20, 2017.

4. Jessica Brand and Ethan Brown, "US Attorney's Office That Prosecuted Inauguration Day Protesters Has History of Misconduct Findings," *Appeal*, July 30, 2018.

5. Brand and Brown, "History of Misconduct Findings."

6. Justin Dillon, "Video Dimmed the Government Star: The Latest Debacle in the Government's Inauguration Protest Cases," abovethelaw.com, June 1, 2018.

7. Brand and Brown, "History of Misconduct Findings."

8. Dillon, "Video Dimmed the Government Star."

9. Sam Adler-Bell, "With Last Charges Against J20 Protesters Dropped, Defendants Seek Accountability for Prosecutors," *Intercept*, July 13, 2018.

10. Adler-Bell, "With Last Charges."

11. Keith L. Alexander, "Second Inauguration Day Trial Ends with No Conviction of Four Defendants," *Washington Post*, June 7, 2018.

12. Brief for amicus curiae Cato Institute in Support of Petitioners, U.S. Supreme Court filing in *Turner v. U.S.* and *Overton v. U.S.*, Nos. 15-1503 and 15-1504, February 3, 2017.

13. Steve Reilly and Mark Nichols, "Hundreds of Police Officers Have Been Labeled Liars. Some Still Help Send People to Prison. Across the USA, Prosecutors Aren't Tracking Officer Misconduct, Skirting Supreme Court *'Brady'* Rules and Sometimes Leading to Wrongful Convictions," *USA Today*, October 17, 2019.

14. Samuel R. Gross, Maurice J. Possley, Kaitlin Jackson Roll, and Klara Huber Stephens, *Government Misconduct and Convicting the Innocent, The Role of Prosecutors, Police and Other Law Enforcement* (report, National Registry of Exonerations, September 1, 2020).

15. Doug Ramseur, interview by author, August 13, 2021.

16. Rachel Weiner and Laura Vozzella, "Criminal Discovery Reforms Delayed in Virginia; Police Body Cameras Blamed," *Washington Post*, January 29, 2019.

17. Ramseur, interview.

18. New York State Bar Association, *Report of the Task Force on Criminal Discovery*, January 30, 2015.

19. Insha Rahman, *New York, New York: Highlights of the 2019 Bail Reform Law* (report, Vera Institute of Justice, July 2019).

20. Seth Barron and Ralf Mangual, "Big Risks in Discovery Reform: NY Law Tips the Balance Way Too Far in Favor of Defendants," *New York Daily News*, June 3, 2019.

21. Rebecca Rosenberg, Carl Campanile, and Tina Moore, "Why New York Criminals Are Celebrating the New Year," *New York Post*, December 31, 2019.

22. Rosenberg, Campanile, and Moore, "Why New York Criminals Are Celebrating."

23. Nick Pinto, "The Backlash, Police, Prosecutors, and Republicans Are Looking to Undo a Criminal Justice Reform in New York," *Intercept*, February 23, 2020.

24. Jesse McKinley, "Billionaire Is Spending Millions to Defeat New York Democrats," *New York Times*, October 17, 2020.

25. "Building a Safer New York," Safe Together NY, Inc., safertogetherny.com.

26. Dana Rubinstein and Chelsia Rose Marcius, "Republican Tide Swept Away Democrats and Remade Nassau County Politics," *New York Times*, November 9, 2021.

27. *Implementation of 2020 Discovery Law Changes: Update* (report, New York State Division of Criminal Justice Services, December, 2021), 3.

28. Staff report, "Siena Poll: 2019 Bail Reform Law Has Been Bad for New York," *Troy Record*, March 28, 2022.

29. *Post* editorial board, "State's New Discovery Law Is Upending Prosecutions as Dismissals Soar," *New York Post*, March 23, 2022.

30. Nick Pinto, "The Case Against Bail Reform Was Always a Tabloid Mirage," *New York*, April 11, 2022.

31. Krystal Rodriguez, *Discovery Reform in New York* (report, New York Center for Court Innovation, June 2020).

32. Angelo Petrigh, interviews by author, September 16, 2021, and April 10, 2022.

33. Petrigh, interview, April 10, 2022.

34. Richard Rosen, interview by author, July 26, 2021.

35. Jenia I. Turner and Allison D. Redlich, "Two Models of Pre-Plea Discovery in Criminal Cases: An Empirical Comparison," *Washington and Lee Law Review* 73, no. 1 (Winter 2016), 285–408.

36. Victor Li, "50-Year Story of the *Miranda* Warning Has the Twists of a Cop Show," *Journal of the American Bar Association*, August 1, 2016.

37. Barry Scheck, testimony for hearing "From *Miranda* to *Gideon*: A Call for Pretrial Reform," U.S. House of Representatives Committee on the Judiciary, March 26, 2021.

38. Hon. Sheila Jackson Lee (D-TX), Chair of the U.S. House Subcommittee on Crime, Terrorism and Homeland Security, @JacksonLeeTX18, March 26, 2021.

39. It is worth noting that the murder exonerations that sparked discovery reforms in North Carolina and Texas both involved white men—James Alan Gell and Michael Morton. Morton's case, in particular, was unusual. He'd been a supermarket manager, a successful middle-class businessman, before being wrongly convicted.

40. United States v. Bagley, 473 U.S. 667, 693-94 (1985) (Marshall, J., dissenting).

Epilogue

1. Leslie Jamison highlights this issue, and several related questions, in an excellent essay about the case of the West Memphis Three, "Lost Boys," in *The Empathy Exams* (Minneapolis, MN: Graywolf Press, 2014), 182–83.

2. The government considered Cliff Yarborough's video statement a confession, since he (unknowingly) made himself an aider and abettor. But he believed it was only a witness statement, which he quickly disavowed as false. He refused to speak to the police any further, consistently denied any part in the crime, and offered an alibi defense at trial. For more information, see "8th and H," *The Confession Tapes*, directed by Kelly Loudenberg, Netflix, streamed September 8, 2017.

3. Ken Otterbourg, "Vincent Simmons," National Registry of Exonerations, February 22, 2022.

4. "New Evidence Casts Doubt on Black Man's Attempted Rape Conviction," cbsnews.com, February 9, 2022.

5. Dylan Segelbaum, "Kevin Dowling, Sentenced to Death in Infamous 1997 Spring Grove Murder, Awarded New Trial," *York Daily Record*, February 28, 2022.

6. Maurice Possley, "Reynaldo Munoz," National Registry of Exonerations, March 9, 2022; Eric Ferkenhoff, " 'I Feel Free': Chicago Teen Framed for 1985 Murder Becomes 3,000th Person Exonerated in U.S.," *USA Today*, March 9, 2022.

7. George Joseph, "A Wrongful-Conviction Hearing Puts a Heralded Brooklyn Prosecutor on the Stand," *City*, February 24, 2022; Jeffrey Winter, "Man Claiming His Innocence in '98 Slaying Says Prosecutor Withheld Evidence About Key Witness," CNN, February 27, 2022.

8. Amanda Holpuch, "Court Declares Man Wrongfully Imprisoned for 45 Years," *New York Times*, March 11, 2022.

9. Ashley Nellis, *No End in Sight, America's Enduring Reliance on Life Imprisonment* (report, Sentencing Project, February 17, 2021). Life sentences include those serving life without parole, life with the possibility of parole, and virtual life (50+ years).

10. "DNA and Fair Trials," interview by Tim O'Brien, *Religion & Ethics Newsweekly*, PBS television broadcast, June 9, 2006.

11. "DNA and Fair Trials," O'Brien interview.

12. "DNA and Fair Trials," O'Brien interview.

INDEX

materiality standard and the *Brady* rule,
42–43, 45–52, 113–16, 117–22, 149,
212; *Agurs* and definition of material
evidence, 45–48, 50–52, 116, 117;
Bagley and definition of material
evidence, 48–52, 113, 117, 227;
Brennan and, 48, 52; and discovery
reforms, 166; Marshall and, 48, 51–52,
113, 116, 149; prosecutors' decisions
conflating disclosure obligations
and materiality, 118–22; "reasonable
probability" of a different outcome,
51, 113, 114–15, 119, 196; Stevens and,
47, 51, 113–114, 119; *Strickler* and,
113–16, 120
Mathabane, Mark, 174
McCann, Larry, 190–91
McGinnis, Patrick: Fuller murder
investigation, 27–30, 34–39, 53–57,
59–60, 63–76, 79–80, 84, 89–90,
178–79, 189, 191, 230–31; Fuller
murder trial, 126, 127–28
McGowan, Nancy Boblit, 3–4, 7, 9, 11
McMillian, James: eyewitness
identification at Fuller crime scene,
91–92, 125, 127–28, 186, 188, 191,
195, 197, 200, 229; history of criminal
assaults in 8th and H neighborhood,
60–61, 91–92, 201–3; probable
scenario for Fuller's murder, 198–203;
and Supreme Court arguments on
Fuller case, 204–6
McNamara, Scott, 104
Medwed, Daniel S., 40
Melnikoff, Arnold, 145–48
Mena, Ivan, 233
Merhige, Robert, Jr., 112
Merkerson, Gerald, 91–92, 191, 195, 199,
200, 201–2
Miami News, 176
Mid-Atlantic Innocence Project (MAIP),
180, 184–87, 197, 201, 230
Miller, Bill, 178
Milloy, Courtland, 141
Milwaukee Railroad, 48–49
Miranda rule, 14, 57, 64, 68, 70, 79–80,
223–24

Miranda v. Arizona, 14
Mitchell, Donald, 48–50
Morin, Robert, 209–10
Morris, Crystal, 156–58
Morton, Christine, 159–60
Morton, Michael, 159–61, 259n39
Morton Act (Texas), 160, 224–25
Munoz, Reynaldo "Scooby," 233
Murkowski, Lisa, 165–70, 224
Murphy, Ronald "Touché," 35–36
Myers, Jennifer, 232–33

National Association of Assistant U.S.
Attorneys, 167
National Association of Criminal
Defense Lawyers (NACDL), 121–22,
166, 170–71
National Basketball Players Association,
58
National District Attorney's Association,
169
National Registry of Exonerations, 71,
163, 211–12, 233
New York Daily News, 215
New York Post, 215–16, 217
New York State: bail reform, 217;
Blindfold Law on evidence sharing,
214; discovery reform, 214–18, 225;
juvenile interrogation law, 72; law
professors' grievances filed against
Queens prosecutors, 154–55
New York Times, 105, 168–69
Nifong, Michael, 159
Ninth Circuit Court of Appeals: *Frost v.
Gilbert*, 152–54; Kozinski opinions,
145–54; *U.S. v. Bagley*, 50; *U.S.
v. Olsen*, 145–49, 151–52; *U.S. v.
Ruiz* and *Brady's* pre-plea disclosure
requirements, 161
North Carolina's discovery reform:
death penalty cases, 158–59; open-
file discovery, 158–59, 161, 163, 168,
219–23, 225, 226; pre-plea disclosure
requirement, 161, 163; prosecutors'
views of, 220, 221–22, 223; sanctions
for noncompliance, 159
North Carolina Supreme Court, 219

ABOUT THE AUTHOR

Thomas L. Dybdahl, who has degrees in theology, journalism, and law, is a former staff attorney at the Public Defender Service for the District of Columbia, where he worked in both the trial and appellate divisions, and tried twenty-five homicide cases. He lives in Boulder, Colorado.

PUBLISHING IN THE
PUBLIC INTEREST

Thank you for reading this book published by The New Press. The New Press is a nonprofit, public interest publisher. New Press books and authors play a crucial role in sparking conversations about the key political and social issues of our day.

We hope you enjoyed this book and that you will stay in touch with The New Press. Here are a few ways to stay up to date with our books, events, and the issues we cover:

- Sign up at www.thenewpress.com/subscribe to receive updates on New Press authors and issues and to be notified about local events
- www.facebook.com/newpressbooks
- www.twitter.com/thenewpress
- www.instagram.com/thenewpress

Please consider buying New Press books for yourself; for friends and family; or to donate to schools, libraries, community centers, prison libraries, and other organizations involved with the issues our authors write about.

The New Press is a 501(c)(3) nonprofit organization. You can also support our work with a tax-deductible gift by visiting www .thenewpress.com/donate.